Between
the Sign
& the Gaze

ALSO BY HERMAN RAPAPORT

Heidegger and Derrida: Reflections on Time and Language

Milton and the Postmodern

Between the Sign & the Gaze

HERMAN RAPAPORT

Cornell University Press

Ithaca and London

First published 1994 by Cornell University Press.

International Standard Book Number 0-8014-2898-X (cloth)
International Standard Book Number 0-8014-8133-3 (paper)
Library of Congress Catalog Card Number 93-25324

Printed in the United States of America

Librarians: Library of Congress cataloging information appears on the last page of the book.

⊗ The paper in this book meets the minimum requirements of the American National Standard for Information Sciences—Permanence of Paper for Printed Library Materials, ANSI Z39.48–1984.

FOR SUSANNE

Contents

Acknowledgments

I thank the following publishers for permission to reprint my work: University of Indiana Press, "Staging: *Mont Blanc*," *Displacement*, ed. Mark Krupnick (1984); Johns Hopkins University Press, "*Jane Eyre* and the *Mot Tabou*," *Modern Language Notes*, ed. Richard Macksey, 95, no. 5 (1979), and "Can You Say Hello?–Laurie Anderson's *United States*," *Theatre Journal* (October 1986); University of Georgia Press, "*Effi Briest* and *La Chose freudienne*," *Criticism and Lacan: Essays and Dialogue on Language, Structure, and the Unconscious*, ed. Patrick Hogan and Lalita Pandit, © 1990 by the University of Georgia Press, (1990); *Enclitic*, "The Disarticulated Image: Gazing in Wonderland," *Enclitic*, ed. Tom Conley, 6, no. 2 (1982); University of Oklahoma Press, "Geoffrey Hartman and the Spell of Sounds," revised from original publication, *Rhetoric and Form: Deconstruction at Yale*, ed. Robert Con Davis and Ronald Schleifer, © 1985 by the University of Oklahoma Press; and University of Iowa Press, "Forecastings of Apocalypse," *Philosophy as Literature/Literature as Philosophy*, ed. Donald Marshall (1987). I thank my editors, past and present, and close friends in the profession who have been sources of encouragement over the years.

H. R.

Between
the Sign
& the Gaze

Introduction

Between the Sign and the Gaze may be read as a sustained reflection
on how fantasmic constructions traverse both theoretical and applied
analyses that take us from detailed considerations of psychoanalysis
to those of literary study and closely related fields. Some of the applied
readings are based on psychoanalytic points of view; others conform
more to the methods of philosophical analysis. All attend in various
degrees to the governing problematic of the French psychoanalytical
concept of the fantasm, which is reinscribed within a number of very
different contexts and handled in ways that conform to the open end-
edness of how the term has been theorized and applied. In the twelfth
century, *fantasme* originally referred to the experience of an illusion.
Only in the early nineteenth century did it receive a medical definition,
which the *Larousse Grand Dictionnaire Universel du XIXe Siècle* sum-
marizes as a defect of vision in which one thinks one sees objects that
are, in fact, not there. By the middle of the century, however, the term
became psychologized and used as a synonym for "hallucination." And
by the end of the century, writers such as Huysmans were more generally referring to "les fantasmes de l'imagination" (dreams, reveries,
fantasies) as occurrences of everyday life. It is this more casual use of
the term *fantasme* which the early French psychoanalysts appropriated.
Curiously, although the psychoanalytical notion of the *fantasme* was
associated with Freud's term *Phantasie*, *fantasme* is actually quite
unique to the French psychoanalytic movement, and does not exactly

fit Freud's term. Jean Laplanche and J.-B. Pontalis in their well-known dictionary, *The Language of Psycho-Analysis,* are quick to point out that "the term *fantasme* was revived by psycho-analysis, with the result that it has more philosophical overtones than its German equivalent [*Phantasie*]; nor does it correspond exactly to the German, in that it has a more restricted extension; *fantasme* refers to a specific imaginary production, not to the world of fantasy and imaginative activity in general."[1] In fact, it would have been more accurate to say that the word *fantasme* has corresponded to a wide number of specific imaginary productions, among them, dreams, primal scenes, imaginary objects, complexes, and hallucinations. Therefore, although Laplanche and Pontalis are perfectly correct in suggesting that "fantasm" is a more restrictive term than "fantasy," they overlook how French psychoanalysts have used *fantasme* to cover such a wide number of imaginary phenomena that it paradoxically retains much of the open-endedness of its late nineteenth-century meaning ("les fantasmes de l'imagination"). Consequently, despite very closely argued accounts of the *fantasme* as a specific imaginary production, the concept nevertheless lacks determinate boundaries and often inspires definitions and approaches that cannot be entirely reconciled within even a Freudian context. Thus, contrary to what Laplanche and Pontalis suggest in their lexicon, no singular theory or paradigm of the fantasm is sufficient to account for how the term has been applied.

In Chapter 1, "Theories of the Phantasm," I develop a genealogy of the concept *fantasme* and assemble wide-ranging materials with major emphasis on Freud as well as the French analysts who have played a role in determining the significance of the term. This chapter necessarily includes a lengthy exposition of Lacan and dwells chiefly on materials that are supposedly unpublished, though they are available in Parisian bookstores that specialize in psychoanalytical materials. The sections of Chapter 1 devoted to Freud show that, to a very large extent, notions of fantasy remained problematic throughout the major phases of his career, and that Freud attempted a number of strategies in order to come to terms with them, including the theorization of primal scenes,

1. Jean Laplanche and J.-B. Pontalis, *The Language of Psycho-Analysis,* trans. Donald Nicholson-Smith (New York: Norton, 1973), p. 314.

memory screens, the Oedipus complex, the interpretation of dreams, phylogenetic fantasies, and transformative sentences in which imaginary scenes are said to have their origin. Although the history of all these Freudian notions is well known, Freud's own ultimate inability to determine whether fantasized scenes or the processes of language had the greater explanatory power troubled the ground on which the entire genealogy of the fantasm rests, since it is to Freud that French psychoanalysts continually return. Of course, both the French psychiatric tradition, in which Pierre Janet figures prominently, and French surrealism mediate the reception of Freudian psychoanalysis and, not coincidentally, the conceptual articulation of the fantasm. The influence of both French psychiatry and French surrealism is quite significant in the case of Jacques Lacan's formation as an analyst. It also has effects on the history, generally, of early French psychoanalytical theory, which was quite preoccupied with the visual arts and predisposed to think along the lines of Janet, Henri Claude, and G. G. de Clérambault, despite the declared allegiance to Freud. Of special interest, however, is how analysts such as Marie Bonaparte, Eugénie Sokolnicka, and Angelo Hesnard theorized the fantasm and situated it within Freud's work, where the term does not appear as such. Contrary to Elizabeth Roudinesco, who more or less disparages the work of so many French analysts before World War II, my researches have led me to the conclusion that, in fact, such work was by no means naive and that it is quite fundamental for French psychoanalytic thinking after the war. One develops a much better understanding of analysts such as Jean Laplanche, André Green, Guy Rosolato, Maria Torok, and Julia Kristeva once one is familiar with the conceptual history Roudinesco takes so lightly.

The sections on Jacques Lacan trace the entire sweep of his career and, in large part, pertain to a number of seminars that Anglo-American readers have probably not encountered: the seminars on object relations, formations of the unconscious, desire and its interpretation, identification, anxiety, the act of psychoanalysis, and the logic of the fantasm. These sections are intended to reflect a thorough and integral introduction to Lacan's major phase, the work from the mid 1950s to the late 1960s, and I have purposely attempted not to repeat the more familiar account of Lacanian theory, which has been most powerfully

expressed by Guy Rosolato in *Essais sur le symbolique*. My reading
of the complete seminar transcripts has led me to believe that Rosolato's
account—oft repeated in the work of Anglo-American cinema and
literary critics—privileges a structuralist orientation to sex and signification which has overshadowed many other theoretical developments
and constructions in the complete seminars. It should be kept in mind
that the *Écrits*, which have so often been taken as definitive, largely
address Lacanian theory before its most significant turn around 1961
when Lacan began lectures on identification and problematics central
to the question of the fantasm, which reached their apogee in 1966–
67. Of the *Écrits*, only "Position de l'inconscient," "Du 'trieb' de
Freud," and "La Science et la vérité" really pertain strongly to the
theoretical work done after the fifties, and even there care was taken
to conceal historical development of the theories. Although the most
masterful essays in the *Écrits*, such as "Kant avec Sade" and "Le Séminaire sur 'La Lettre volée,' " suggest a synthetic or synchronic theoretical moment, I believe one needs to subordinate them to the seminar
transcripts, which show a very different and, in my view, much more
interesting theoretical unfolding that the showy demonstration pieces
of the *Écrits* do not strive to disclose.

Of course, I limit my account of Lacan to major developments concerning his understanding and use of the term *fantasme*. Not surprisingly, Lacan treats the fantasm from different perspectives, which
means that even within his own oeuvre the term cannot be reduced to
any single theory, formula, or account. In the seminars on object relations, desire and its interpretation, and anxiety (1956, 1958, 1960),
the definition of the fantasm often refers us to the conceptions of earlier
French Freudians of the prewar period, though not without some major
theoretical advances. In the seminars on the four fundamental concepts
of psychoanalysis and the logic of the fantasm (1964, 1966) such early
understandings of the fantasm appear to be exceeded to the point
of unrecognizability, though one can find moments when the well-
established earlier approaches to the topic are presupposed. In other
words, one has to pay attention to a number of theoretical constructions—some older, some newer—which coexist in a discourse that is
reminiscent of a mosaic resisting synthesis. At the same time, one can
uncover a coherent intellectual development that is both daring and

complex. And last, since in this book I make use of theories about the fantasm (and the fantasmic) advanced by figures such as Nicolas Abraham, Jean Laplanche, Julia Kristeva, Serge Leclaire, Charles Méla, and others, in Chapter 1, I place such work into perspective and show that it would be difficult to work seriously in this field of inquiry without working across a number of different though compatible approaches.

The applied readings that follow the lengthy genealogy of the fantasm are interpretations of a wide number of works that draw on compatible approaches to theorizing the fantasm. Taken as a whole, the applied readings traverse two French psychoanalytical orientations to the fantasm marked by the division of the book's two parts, the one visual (iconic), the other auditory (linguistic). The title, *Between the Sign and the Gaze,* refers to the familiar Freudian problem of deciding whether visual or linguistic constructions are considered more originary, and though from today's vantage point we could collapse the difference in advance as undecidable, the fact remains that the French psychoanalytic literature does not do so. Even Lacan, who is famous for having said that the unconscious is structured like a language, defers to originary scenic fantasms as late as 1975. In the following quotation, Lacan intended to be somewhat ironic, even shocking, considering his teachings, but by it he also pays deliberate homage to the orthodox French Freudian understanding of the fantasm: "I hope not to end my life without having found something or another which I can leave to posterity, something I will have invented ... and, since I am very old, I can't invent a new *fantasme.* That's something which no analysis, however supple, can do. Were it possible, it would do a great service, since neurotics are people who aspire to a perversion which otherwise they will never attain."[2] Not only had Freud already discovered all the originary fantasms of analysis, but according to Lacan the very idea of adding or inventing a new originary scene is itself typical of an impossible desire. The idea that one could invent or think up new fantasms would be an attempt to avoid or outstrip the law of the Other (literally, of the unconscious) and to pretend, as does the perverse subject, that there is what Lacan called "an Other of the Other," which

---

2. Jacques Lacan, "Conférences et Entretiens," in *Scilicet* 6/7 (Paris: Seuil, 1976), p. 17. Unless otherwise specified, the translations are my own.

is to say, a court of appeals higher than a supreme court where the law is, in fact, established once and for all. Fantasms, Lacan is saying, are not negotiable, since they express the demand of an Other before which the subject, in Lacan's words, "fades." It is in this fading or fainting of the subject that the image or scene comes about as something inherently ahead of or before the subject, which is to say, prior to the subject's ability to posit the fantasm as an expression of its own will. Whereas in the dream-work, as explained by Freud, language plays an enormously important role in constructing visual scenes, however much this has been "forgotten" by the dreamer, in Lacan it is the "frame of desire" or staging of the fantasm as a structure dependent on an Other's demand which is of central importance. In other words, for Lacan the stress falls on mise-en-scène rather than on the reconstruction of words said or thought on a previous day by a subject who authors his or her own fantasies by displacement and condensation. It is in this sense that Lacan holds to the Freudian suggestion of originary fantasms or scenes that are invariant—dependent on the staging of an Other's demand in the unconscious—and therefore not dependent on the vicissitudes of language.

Yet despite this orientation, there are many senses in which Lacan and many other French analysts do not simply privilege the image, but try to understand how in the so-called act of psychoanalysis—the intervention of the analyst—one gains insight into the interrelation of word and image, their identification with and separation from one another at the very moment they come into correspondence. In Lacan's work this correspondence sometimes depends on how the unconscious facilitates deformations of language—*linguisterie*—on which the image may itself be propped: for example, *les noms du père* (the names of the father) as *les non dupes errent* (the nondupes wander).[3] Of course, *les non dupes errent* is an extended pun that turns *les noms du père* wrongside out, as if someone had blundered or made a mistake. As such, *les non dupes errent* suggests something "other" that is independent of and prior to the names of the father: the image of the wandering

3. This extended pun is also the title of Jacques Lacan's unpublished *Séminaire XXI: Les Non Dupes errent,* in which some of the discussion focuses on marital love. It is actually in seminars following this one that Lacan gives some very useful hints about what the title was meant to suggest.

nondupe. Even so, this image has to lean on signs, "les noms du père," for support. Not only is the fantasm constructed in terms of the intervocative resonances between *les noms du père* and *les non dupes errent* but with respect to how the image of the wandering or erring nondupe visually represents a blunder or lapse in which the Name-of-the-Father is heard otherwise.

Of course, this blunder can always be taken to be an enlightenment in that it takes distance from all dupery, of which the Name-of-the-Father is often considered the most obvious. This, of course, is why in the well-known romance by Chrétien de Troyes, Perceval's mother will not tell him the name of his father: she doesn't want her son to be duped by the same fate that befell her husband. So she encourages Perceval to take his distance from all dupery, though it will be as such a nondupe—as the one not under the sway or influence of the paternal signifier—that Perceval will wander rather aimlessly if not stupidly until he comes upon Arthur's court. And even then his errancy does not cease. Nor has the specter of the father been successfully suppressed. For Chrétien narrates not only how Perceval blunders into the house of God the Father but how he intuits his own name, the name of his father, at that very moment he is told that, in fact, he was a dupe of the codes of chivalry, which taught him not to ask silly questions or show untoward curiosity. But his knowledge of the name, from where does it come? And to whom does it belong? It is here that the questions posed at the Fisher King's castle begin to resonate like phantoms in the service of the father's name and that the name itself accedes to a fantasmic manifestation that insists that we be duped, swayed, taken in by its eerie paternal presence, which is, at the very least, a call to faith. That Perceval can undergo such "influencing" without stepping away from it as mere nonsense means that he is not following in the footsteps of the hysteric who refuses to be taken in by a metaphysics of paternity. When Dora, who like Perceval has been confronted with certain mysteries in a special room, returns to Freud, it is not for nothing that he mentally excommunicates her. For she is still a nondupe for whom psychoanalysis can have nothing to say. In other words, she is incurable for the very reason that as nondupe she is fated to wander in the absence of listening to the demand of an Other. Perceval, to the contrary, will accede to the grail (in analytical terms, the cure) in so

far as he passes over from *les non dupes errent* to *les noms du père.*
Yet in order to do that he must necessarily come under the sway of
the fantasm that mediates the sign of the father (symbolic recognition
by the Other) and the gaze of the nondupe (the imaginary scopic field
of a supposedly autonomous self).

Although coming under the sway of such a fantasm is more or less
fated in medieval romance tradition, Lacan recognizes that, in fact, we
ought to question it as an illusion—as the fantasm it is. In *Le Séminaire
XXII: R.S.I.,* Lacan points out that the unifying trait of the name—
the Other of the signifier—makes one into a dupe who doesn't err or
wander. "That's not like me," Lacan says, "who can only admit that
I err (or wander). I err (or wander) in those intervals in which I try to
situate the meaning for you of phallic pleasure ... the pleasure which
would interest not the Other of the signifier, but the Other of the body,
the Other of the other sex."[4] To be a dupe of the name, then, would
mean that someone like Perceval might have difficulty in situating the
meaning of phallic pleasure with respect to the Other of the other sex,
something that Chrétien takes into account throughout his version of
the romance. In short, the mirror text, *les noms du père/les non dupes
errent,* is a specular structure in which an Oedipal relation is constituted
wherein the subject is split or traversed by the two phrases and cannot
resolve their asymmetry by either becoming a dupe or nondupe. In
fact, even the Name-of-the-Father is not sufficient to overcome this
crisis of mastery and to that extent reveals its imposture. The name
fails the one who would find the meaning of phallic pleasure; in Chrétien Amfortas is the name of that default.

In the applied readings of Part 1, "Appearances of the Fantasm," I
look at a number of aspects in which the fantasm mediates between
the word and the image, sign and gaze. In Chapter 2, "Staging: *Mont
Blanc,*" I turn to the work of Jean Laplanche and others to examine
how the positing of an image is, in fact, a staging of the fantasm in
which image turns into theater, prop into stage. In Percy Bysshe Shelley's literary writings, the language itself repeatedly points to this kind

4. Jacques Lacan, *Le Séminaire XXII: R.S.I.,* in *Ornicar?* no. 4 (1975): 104.

of shift in which the image stages the subject's desire by means of a certain phantomization, or fading, of the image, such that we can see through it onto something else even as a trace or residual effect of the image remains on the very stage or forum it has opened up. Here, of course, word and image support each other, though as I show they are both enlisted at the behest of an obsessive gaze that is stalled in the undecidability of a materialization and dematerialization of a fantasm that follows from the subject's fascination with the obscene (Mont Blanc). I focus on what Lacan calls the Imaginary and consider the anaclitic relation of mother and child as a precondition for understanding how the representation of a symbol is staged in terms of a fantasm of the archaic mother. Mediating word and image, the fantasm becomes the construction on which the drives of the subject lean.

In Chapter 3, "*Jane Eyre* and the *Mot Tabou*," I consider the interrelation of fantasmic sound shapes and how they come into correspondence with apparitions that are akin to transitional objects, except that they are traumatically invested signifiers of desire—the signifier being that element whose signification is disembodied or left in suspense until that point when through repetition another signifier gives it its meaning (its signified) in relation to the subject. In the case of Charlotte Brontë's *Jane Eyre* this repetition is sounded out in terms of a *mot tabou*. The taboo is not merely one of how words are suppressed, but of how they follow paths of avoidance that nevertheless allow for an uncanny disclosure of the Other. My reading of *Jane Eyre* does not substantiate the familiar egological approach to the novel, in which Jane Eyre is seen as well in control of a self-conscious struggle against social oppression. Rather, my reading privileges unconscious processes from which the subject cannot be disentangled in the way some readers have come to expect.

In Chapter 4, "*Effi Briest* and *La Chose Freudienne*," I explore what Lacan during the 1960s termed alienation, a state that he identified with the psychological production of fantasms. Whereas in the chapter on Shelley I focus on the dissolution of the image for the sake of the staging of desire, in this chapter, on Theodor Fontane's *Effi Briest*, I focus on the reification of the image in response to a negation of jouissance from which Effi Briest is, given her marriage and social position, foreclosed. In *Le Séminaire VII: L'Éthique de la psychanalyse*

Lacan speaks of such reification in terms of *das Ding,* something in the margin of the Real which functions as a support of an aversion. "*Das Ding* is that which I will call the beyond of the signified. It is as a function of this beyond-of-the-signified and of an emotional relationship to it that the subject keeps its distance and is constituted in a kind of relationship characterized by primary affect, prior to any repression."[5] What I intend to show is that the Thing speaks in Theodor Fontane's novel, and that although the Thing is perfectly *chosique,* as Lacan says, it is, despite all appearances, a phantom that happens to have taken to the side of the furniture, which is to say, to the side of what Lacan calls the Real. A particularly interesting feature of the Fontane novel is that language itself has taken to the side of the Thing in order to point to the place where jouissance is forbidden to the woman. It is this Thing—this absence of pleasure—which occupies the zone between word and image, sign and gaze. Whereas in *Jane Eyre* the fantasms are spectral and resonant, in *Effi Briest* they are inert and resistant. In a later chapter on Marguerite Duras's work, I take this resistance up once more in terms of what Lacan in his seminar on the ethics of psychoanalysis called *extimité.*

In Chapter 5, "Disarticulations: Between the Sign and the Gaze," I consider the photographs of the child friends taken by Lewis Carroll in relation to the Alice books. What brings sign and gaze into relation here is the inadequation between what one of Lacan's students, Charles Méla, calls *merveille* and *malheur,* the marvelous and the piteous. These terms may remind one of Aristotle's distinction between hope and fear in tragedy, except that in Carroll the marvelous and the piteous refer us to the lack one associates with the child's castration anxiety when he (the gender is male, in this case) discovers that little girls lack penises. In adulthood, there may be overcompensation by the subject who has not worked this through as a child, in which case the piteous reaction is supplemented: the piteous child is thought to have a surplus of beauty, intelligence, or truth. It is significant that mature or adult women are shunned, since, as mothers, they bear the lack unto others

---

5. Jacques Lacan, *Le Séminaire VII: L'Éthique de la psychanalyse* (Paris: Seuil, 1986), pp. 67–68; *The Seminar of Jacques Lacan, Book VII, The Ethics of Psychoanalysis,* trans. Dennis Porter (New York: Norton, 1992), p. 54.

and, as such, cannot be denegated. Hence the appearance of the Queen of Hearts with her "off with their heads!" Both text and image in Carroll bear the brunt of a fantasm delimited by the rift between the marvelous and the piteous. Which is to say, that the fantasm is precisely what falls "between the sign and the gaze" even as it stages them.

In Chapter 6, "Permission Granted, or Beyond the Fantasm," I round out the first suite of essays, in which the fantasm is always localizable to a particular scene or topos and proves significant for a particular consciousness or subject. In this chapter I balance out the theoretical survey of Chapter 1 by mounting a detailed interpretation of the debate that has been taking place for twenty some years between Derrideans and Lacanians. The fantasm, in this case, refers ultimately to what Lacan called the Name-of-the-Father, which can never be thought of for very long without the construction of fantasmic scenes. The privileged scene Lacan uses is one related to us by the French historian of psychoanalysis, Elizabeth Roudinesco, and concerns relations between Jacques Derrida and his son, Pierre. How Lacan takes license with that scene in order to score some points for the Name-of-the-Father is the primary matter here; however, both Lacan's understanding of the Name and Derrida's implicit critique of it—for example, in "La Pharmacie de Platon" and "La Carte postale"—are attempts to get beyond the fantasm, a getting-beyond that requires each to accuse the other of not transcending it. In the case of both Derrida and Lacan, of course, the theory takes to the side of the sign in order to get beyond the scene or image, though, in both cases, this strategy may be accused of rehabilitating the image of the very family romance it wants to exceed.

In Part 2, "Echoes of the Fantasm," I turn mainly to the auditory or linguistic aspect of the fantasm and consider it as an unlocalized sounding or haunting that goes beyond mere place and, too, individual subjectivity. To that extent, one could read this second group of essays as an attempt to surpass the fantasm as a construction of scenes powerful in terms of their framing and to place it, rather, in relation to the subject. In short, whereas in Part 1 the fantasm takes to the side of the scene, in Part 2 it takes to the side of the word.

In Chapter 7, "Geoffrey Hartman and the Spell of Sounds," I take as one of my points of departure Hartman's idea that voice is not located in the subject but *around* the subject, and I elaborate this idea by examining how the laws of literary genre could be reconfigured in terms of how voice is, according to the work of Julia Kristeva, transauthorial and translinguistic. Hartman identifies this with the "psychoesthetic," by which he means a consideration of genre not merely as a formalized textual structure but also as a dialogical relation with others in which psychology is inherently collective, transauthorial, and translinguistic. I undertake a comparative analysis of psychological defense formations disclosed in "the spell of sounds," fantasmic auditory effects or echoes of a reparative nature which are not restricted to an individual psychology but are given in language—everyday speech as well as literature—and sound, generally, as in the case of natural sounds or musical sounds. By examining short passages from Virginia Woolf's *To the Lighthouse,* Herman Melville's *Moby-Dick,* James Joyce's *Finnegans Wake,* and composer Alban Berg's Violin Concerto, I try to show instances in which the intervocative fantasies of defense, security, and mutual support are in each case threatened by individual fantasies and fears. In these instances, the delocalization of the fantasmic sound shapes forestall the subject's encounter with a localized trauma, some less successfully than others. It is at the intersection of the unlocalized and the localized that genre may itself be modalized.

In Chapter 8, "Tonalities of Apocalypse," I shift from psychoanalysis to philosophy as I turn from the notion of fantasmic sound shape as psychic defense or phatic buffer to what Jacques Derrida in the early 1980s called an apocalyptic tone. Central to this transition is intensification of the disembodiment or disincorporation of tonal affects from what one might ordinarily consider a traumatic or catastrophic source, which, in the context of this chapter, is not just imaginary but something quite real and historical. Of significance in considering tonality is that unlike the sound shape, which in Chapter 7 defends against a personal trauma or hurt, tonality refers us to a collective or social experience of catastrophe that is not representable or understandable despite the many attempts at explanation. In the case of the Holocaust, of course, the originary scene of genocide is precisely what has eluded human comprehension; it falls outside our capacity to explain, symbolize, and document. I begin with remarks on Derrida's *Cinder* and then introduce the work of John Ashbery, Maurice Blanchot, and Emmanuel Levinas in order to think through the notion of tone as something detached from any representable scene or individual subject even as it carries within itself a restoration of an originary fantasm of violence experienced by the daydreamer as victim. As in the previous chapter, an intervocative echoing of the word (the aural fantasm) cannot completely forestall the advent of a scene (the visual fantasm) whose traumatic elements, however well defended, assert themselves as a fantasmic return of the repressed.

In Chapter 9, "Durassian Extimité," I use Lacanian psychoanalytic theory sparingly and focus largely on a passage from Alphonso Lingis's philosophical work *Deathbound Subjectivity*. In this chapter I elaborate Lacan's notion of *la chose freudienne* by reinscribing it in terms of what Lingis, following Emmanuel Levinas, calls the existent, a thereness that is not existentially recoverable. Duras's characters achieve such thereness according to a logic of the *après coup* in which the subject is written out of the very relation to an event which he or she could have established under other circumstances. Of the large number of examples to choose from in Duras—not least, the India Cycle—I focus on two texts, *La Maladie de la mort* and *Savannah Bay*. Significant for me are not only the fantasmic constructions that apply to the female figures but the presence of *lalangue,* a feminine murmur discussed by Lacan in his later seminars. My aim is to take us beyond a psychoanalysis of the unconscious even as we acknowledge a logic of the fantasm that echoes the originary fantasms of Freudian analysis. In other words, here too a fantasm effect is taking place from beyond the very subject who will have to reencounter it as hers. In Duras it is this moment of appropriation or encounter which is both infinitely forestalled even as it is stringently desired.

In Chapter 10, " 'Can You Say Hello?'—Laurie Anderson's *United States*," I take up the spectral evacuation of the subject, its death-bound subjectivity, along with the problematic of tone, and develop this in terms of postmodern space and our relation to it. Tonalities in Laurie Anderson's performance art are themselves experienced as archaic in the psychoanalytical sense, since they are a collage that retroactively posits itself as part of a supposedly authentic American sensibility. And yet, the archaic is entirely synthesized or simulated; it is only known to us as a kind of phantom presence largely manufactured by the media. One of the strange contradictions that Anderson exploits is the ideological stress on asserting one's independent selfhood and the dissolution of that self, its liquefaction in tonalities that ensure only a phantom-like relation to others, particularly in terms of television, telephone, radio, or advertisement. *United States* is so tonally saturated with electronically synthesized voices that Anderson herself never really establishes an autonomous identity. Not only the voices, then, but the performer herself is spectral, a point Anderson underscores visually by using a flashlight to illuminate her own face from below.

One of the governing motifs of *United States* is the correspondence of people with dogs, as if the dog were an ideal role model, since it can be friendly with everyone at a most superficial level. To Jacques Derrida, Jean-Luc Nancy, Sarah Kofman, Luce Irigaray, and others who have recently published in *Who Comes after the Subject?* Laurie Anderson had already provided the answer in the early 1980s: the subject is someone who is safe, that is, someone who won't make demands, who won't oblige others, who won't make anything but the most superficial contact, gratify, and then go away.[6] Who comes after the subject? It is the minimalist individual, the inconspicuous person who doesn't inconvenience anyone, the person who touches bases without requiring anyone to feel obliged, responsible, or guilty, in short, the subject as "good dog." Whereas the previous essays in this second part of the book move away from the primacy of the image to discuss aural fantasms, which are unlocalized if not environmental, the closing chapter on the work of Laurie Anderson takes us back to a world in which signs and images sign for one another, as it were, in the service of what Lacan called the fading of the subject before the fantasm.

6. Eduardo Cadava, Peter Conner, and Jean-Luc Nancy, eds., *Who Comes after the Subject?* (New York: Routledge, 1991).

PART I

APPEARANCES
OF THE
FANTASM

I

Theories of the Fantasm

The Fantasm in France: General Overview

Although the concept of the *fantasme* is often said to originate in the writings of Sigmund Freud, it is specific to French psychoanalysis and functions as a general term for a number of imaginary constructions that Freud discussed throughout his long career. Dreams, delusions, hallucinations, primal scenes, day dreams, imaginary objects, introjected symbols, fantasies, complexes, and phylogenetic imaginary constructions are all expressions of the *fantasme*. Yet if *fantasme* appears to be a word whose definition lacks determinate boundaries, it is, nevertheless, one of the major contributions by French Freudians to the field of psychoanalysis and characterizes an approach that struggles with what was essentially a failure on Freud's part to satisfactorily come to terms with the many imaginary constructions he isolated and analyzed. Jean Laplanche and J.-B. Pontalis, especially, recognize that although Freud approached imaginary constructions from a number of different vantage points, he never developed a systematic theory or technique to define, decipher, or, in pathological cases, cure the traumas associated with such constructions.

We may recall that French psychologists of the early twentieth century, including Pierre Janet, had dismissed Freud's theories as arbitrary, unmethodical, and unprovable. The unconscious, they felt, was an alibi for whatever could not be scientifically explained. Moreover, Freud's

so-called pansexual theory was considered far too extreme in that it
subordinated questions of objective social relations (class, education,
and vocation) to subjective structures (scenes of seduction, Oedipus
and Electra complexes, female phalluses) which belonged solely to the
individual's mental world. Not only had Freud turned away from the
kind of nosological analysis which medical practitioners of the time
felt was basic to any psychological study, but he had split off the subject
of analysis from any coherent overall account of mental functioning—
for example, such as that advanced by Immanuel Kant, Henri Bergson,
or Pierre Janet—in order to study what were, after all, very localized
and very intangible phenomena: sexual wishes, repression, traumas,
imaginary scenes of seduction, and dreams. Instead of conducting me-
ticulous case histories in which everything about a patient would be
examined, Freud paid most of his attention to vignettes of a patient's
mental life—fantasies, dreams, memories—and attempted through
interpretation to reconstruct those distortions within which trauma
was encrypted. He abandoned the synthetic approach of the experi-
mental psychologist interested in integrating an understanding of the
subject within the larger architecture of the life world and worked,
instead, on the microlevel of imaginary constructions in which a her-
meneutics of image and word was still to be developed as part of a
clinical technique. Problematic in Freud, then, is how he isolated and
developed rather complex models of fantasy—for example, dreams and
delusions—which when considered together were not especially recon-
cilable or systematizable. This, of course, is the legacy that French
psychoanalytical theory has been struggling to revise.

It is no surprise that French psychoanalysts have taken a number of
approaches to theorizing the fantasm, and it should prove useful to list
some of these from the outset. Early French Freudians such as Eugénie
Sokolnicka and Marie Bonaparte, for example, looked at various imaginary constructions in terms of ontogeny and phylogeny and considered the *fantasme* as a construction that typifies a patient's sexual
orientation. One could say that for such analysts the *fantasme* had
thematic and structural significance in so far as it established the foundation for a pattern of behavior. Marie Bonaparte's own early self-
analysis, "L'Identification d'une fille à sa mère morte" (1928), focuses
on an hallucination of a large swan which Bonaparte experienced at

the age of four, a time when she was clearly obsessed with the death of her mother, which had occurred one month after Marie Bonaparte's birth.[1] The bird, she says, is in a general sense to be considered a phallic symbol, but in her case it represents an iridescent opal or egg that when given to her mother brings misfortune. The *fantasme* that underwrites this hallucination is the Freudian primal scene of the parents engaged in coitus, which the child in this case imagines sadistically. Bonaparte acknowledges that it is "presented by a sort of *mémoire phylogénique*," although, given the fact that she connects her birth with her mother's death, she sees an ontogenetic significance: that the primal scene is being enlisted into an identification with the mother as dead. "Thus the deep drives of the unconscious produce the hallucinatory fantasm [*le fantasme hallucinatoire*]: the swan comes to me, as it had to my mother; thus a child of the father, I am in my turn his wife, his lover, and through him, mother."[2] Actually, there are three fantasms here: the primal scene, the hallucination, and the Oedipus/Electra complex, of which the primal scene is the most fundamental or originary. Marie Bonaparte's *Life and Works of Edgar Allan Poe* is directly connected to the self-analysis insofar as Bonaparte, at age nineteen, was fixating on stories by Poe beloved by her father. The three titles the young Bonaparte privileged, in Baudelaire's translation, were "Double meurtre dans la rue Morgue," "Le Scarabée d'or," and "La Lettre volée."

Self-analysis aside, the kind of literary study undertaken by Bonaparte, which focuses on originary or primal fantasies, is still practiced in France, though with numerous refinements, some of which can be traced to the influence of the Geneva school of criticism. Jean Laplanche, in *Hölderlin et la question du père*, argues that even a psychotic artist "reproduces a preexisting interior universe" in which primary fantasms are situated. Laplanche, in fact, is arguing that Hölderlin was a "borderline" personality, though he doesn't use this terminology. Jean Bellemin-Noël, in *Les Contes et leurs fantasmes*, inquires into how fairy tales appeal to primary fantasms or archaic imaginary construc-

1. Marie Bonaparte, "L'Identification d'une fille à sa mère morte," *Revue Française de Psychanalyse* 2, no. 3 (1928): 541–65.

2. Ibid., p. 548.

tions in children, and how these constructions function with respect to how the text is imagined or worked through by the reader. Vladimir Marinov, in *Figures du crime chez Dostoïevski,* considers primary fantasms of patricide and matricide in Dostoyevsky's novels *Crime and Punishment* and *The Brothers Karamazov.* Marinov demonstrates that the fantasms introduce a complex set of relationships among themselves in which logical contradictions are structured in terms of extreme love and hate.[3]

Julia Kristeva's *Pouvoirs de l'horreur,* though quite removed from Bonaparte's psychoanalysis, is also concerned with a certain comportment to the archaic and the maternal which, in her study, bears on an extremely phobic and sadistic reaction to the primal scene by an onlooker who cannot accept either the father or the mother and is repulsed by them. Obsession (the inability to look away and the compulsion to repeat), phobia (fear of a trauma that has already occurred), and perversion (sadism) characterize a constellation of reactions to the primal scene which Kristeva calls abjection. In her study the incest taboo is treated as an exploded primal scene that leads to violent psychic defense mechanisms that obstruct the capacity to see beyond fragmented imaginary constructions. Yet what is obstructed within is projected without in terms of scenarios of persecution, as in the case of Céline's (and, in general, fascism's) anti-Semitism. In this sense the fantasm is sadistically acted out in the real world on persons who often experience the fantasy of hate as so unreal that they do not fully comprehend the danger it poses. In *Pouvoirs de l'horreur* Kristeva explores the inverse of what she had seen in Renaissance paintings of the Virgin Mother by Bellini, namely, the representation of bliss or jouissance. (In Giovanni Bellini, of course, the painted representation is the fantasm.)[4]

There has been considerable interest, as well, in how the fantasm relates to the drives. In Freud's *Three Essays on the Theory of Sexuality*

3. Jean Laplanche, *Hölderlin et la question du père* (Paris: Presses Universitaires de France, 1969), p. 4. Jean Bellemin-Noël, *Les Contes et leurs fantasmes* (Paris: Presses Universitaires de France, 1983). Vladimir Marinov, *Figures du crime chez Dostoïevski* (Paris: Presses Universitaires de France, 1990). Marinov was a student of Jean Laplanche's, and the book was submitted as a thesis; Julia Kristeva was the head of the jury that evaluated it.

4. Julia Kristeva, *Pouvoirs de l'horreur* (Paris: Seuil, 1980). Kristeva, "Maternité chez Bellini," in *Polylogue* (Paris: Seuil, 1977).

we are told that the instinctual aim (to achieve satisfaction) requires an object and that the choice of such an object is, at some point, made in "the world of ideas." Freud writes, "The sexual life of maturing youth is almost entirely restricted to indulging in fantasies, that is, in ideas that are not destined to be carried into effect."[5] The perversions, of which Freud speaks in these essays, are accompanied, if not determined, by certain fantasies, and early French Freudians such as Angelo Hesnard and Raymond de Saussure were interested in the relationship between such imaginary constructions and the instincts. In *The Language of Psycho-analysis,* Jean Laplanche and J.-B. Pontalis point out that even very early "object-fantasies" cannot be divorced from scenarios of "organized scenes which are capable of dramatization—usually in a visual form." Or, again, "It is not an *object* that the subject imagines and aims at, so to speak, but rather a *sequence* in which the subject has his own part to play and in which permutations of roles and attributions are possible."[6]

Such a theatrical understanding of the fantasm is underscored by Serge Leclaire, who in summarizing Lacan's thinking on the fantasm in the late 1950s, points out that the fantasm is at the heart of the dream and is framed. He points out that the fantasm confronts the subject with a lack that concerns the desire of the subject. Unfortunately, the subject doesn't have the signifier that is key to knowing what it is he or she really wants. The mise-en-scène, therefore, reflects a linking of "signifiers" (words, sentences, scenes, images, actions) which discloses the fantasm's relation or attachment to the body (the erogenous zones). As such, the fantasm reveals how the subject and the object are to be linked in terms of desiring (instinctual) relationships; this linkage concerns a double consciousness of primary and secondary processes. The function of the fantasm is to provide permanence to the structure of the subject's role in consciousness (the ego), a permanence that responds to the evanescence of the subject in the unconscious (the id). Therefore, the fantasm may be considered

5. Sigmund Freud, "Three Essays on the Theory of Sexuality," in *The Standard Edition of the Complete Psychological Works of Sigmund Freud,* ed. James Strachey (London: Hogarth Press and the Institute of Psycho-Analysis, 1974), vol. 7, p. 226.

6. Jean Laplanche and J.-B. Pontalis, *The Language of Psycho-analysis,* trans. Donald Nicholson-Smith (New York: Norton, 1973), p. 318.

analogous to the surface of the mirror in Lewis Carroll's *Through the Looking Glass*, wherein the little girl sees herself (permanence) even as it represents the other world behind the glass where she undergoes "fading." The fantasm, in other words, reveals the difference between that part of the subject which always finds itself as present and that part of the subject which always loses itself as absent.[7]

The *fantasme* has also been considered in terms of imaginary projection as in paranoid or psychotic behavior. In *Totem and Taboo* Sigmund Freud discusses such projection at length in terms of animism. Corollary to projection is the introjection or symbolization of objects that become important as things the subject desires. Freud's "Mourning and Melancholia" (1915) is, of course, a major text for establishing a theory of introjection. In terms of French psychoanalysis, Lacan's famous case of Aimée is an important example of how projection creates doubles that have persecutionary potential.[8] And in his seminar on Shakespeare's *Hamlet*, Lacan considers those object relations established in "Mourning and Melancholia." He determines that the name Ophelia encrypts the word "phallus" (Ophelio; O Phallos) and that a peculiarity of the play is Hamlet's inability to have relationships other than with the dead. In other words, the play enacts a mourning of the phallus, which, in Ophelia's case, only repeats the mourning for the father. "The position of the phallus is always veiled. It appears only in sudden manifestations [*dans des phanies*], in a flash, by means of its reflection on the level of the object." Lacan's seminar claims that the phallus is fantasmic. Hence, "One cannot strike the phallus, because the phallus, even the real phallus, is a *ghost*."[9] Both projection and introjection can be mediated by the Freudian notion of narcissism, and Lacan has referred to his famous mirror-stage theory in order to show how the gaze plays a significant role in the construction of the projective fantasm. In the seminar on *Hamlet*, Lacan argues that the phantom phallus is an effect of a narcissistic structure.

7. Serge Leclaire, "Fantasme et théorie," *Cahiers Pour L'Analyse*, no. 1 (1966): 59–70.

8. Jacques Lacan, *De la psychose paranoïaque dans ses rapports avec la personnalité* (Paris: Seuil, 1975). Thesis originally published in 1932.

9. Jacques Lacan, *"Hamlet,"* Yale French Studies, no. 55/56 (1977): 50, 48.

In the work of Nicolas Abraham and Maria Torok, introjection and incorporation are considered in terms of how taboo words or phrases are preserved in verbal structures whose purpose is to encrypt or dissimulate them by avoiding any phonetic or semantic resemblance. These "absent words" function not to repress something that happened but to generate scenes or events that must be "avoided and voided retroactively." Words are excluded from the preconscious (and from dreams) in order to be replaced "in the name and capacity of the return of the repressed, by cryptonyms or their visual representation that is required for a general preliminary conclusion to our inquiry."[10] In *L'Écorce et le noyau*, Nicolas Abraham writes, "The phantom is the work in the unconscious by the unavowable secret of an other (incest, crime, bastardization, etc.). Its law is the obligation of a state of not knowing. The manifestation which haunts it is the return of the phantom in bizarre acts and speeches, in the symptoms (phobic, obsessional) etc. The universe of the phantom can objectivize itself, for example, in phantastic narratives. One experiences then a particular affect which Freud has described as a 'strange uneasiness.' "[11]

Another approach to the fantasm has been its identification with defense mechanisms, an idea that goes back to the early writings of Freud and to early French analysts such as Eugénie Sokolnicka. The fantasm blocks out or represses unwanted conflicts even as it is the trait or symptom of great psychological disturbance. To some extent, all the considerations of imaginary constructions we have listed involve defense or dissimulation in the service of distorting and protecting. This raises the question of how the analyst is to regard the fantasm when it appears in the clinical setting. Does it reveal or conceal? Is the fantasm a mode of access to the analysand's psychology or a means of throwing the analyst off track? Renée Diatkine has theorized that, in fact, the fantasm is an obstruction in analysis which needs to be taken out of play.[12] In the late 1970s Roman Jakobson noted his interest

---

10. Nicolas Abraham and Maria Torok, *The Wolf Man's Magic Word: A Cryptonymy* (Minneapolis: University of Minnesota Press, 1986), p. 20.

11. Nicolas Abraham and Maria Torok, *L'Écorce et le noyeau* (Paris: Aubier Flammarion, 1978), p. 391.

12. René Diatkine, "La Signification du fantasme en psychanalyse d'enfants," *Revue Française de Psychanalyse* 15, no. 3 (1951).

in the linguistic "sound shape" as a fantasm that was defensive in a psychoanalytic sense. D. W. Winnicott's notion of the "transitional object" formed the basis for Jakobson's speculations.[13]

Early French Freudians also paid very close attention to Freud's short article "A Child Is Being Beaten" (1919) and agreed with Freud that perhaps the fantasm is less an imaginary scene than it is the modulation of a statement in which the subject's position shifts grammatically from active to passive. Lyotard's commentary in *Discours, Figure* on Freud's article takes up this standard view of the fantasm in ways that capitalize on recent developments in logic and linguistics.[14] Lacan's *Séminaire XIV: Logique du fantasme* also attends to this linguistic or syntactical understanding of the fantasm, though Lacan's aim is to transfer the analysis into the context of topology theory, which, in fact, marks a very important advance.

Finally, Luce Irigaray has defined the *fantasme* as the primordial structuring of the subject that results in the integration of body and discourse. In "Du fantasme et du verbe" she argues that the infinitive verb marks a pure relationship that is focalized from the standpoint of neither the subject nor the object. At the fantasmic stage, as she calls it, the subject resides in the pure signification of this infinitive, this in-finity of language. Irigaray, not unlike the early French Freudians, feels compelled to classify or type various primordial fantasmic states, and she does so according to various "infinitives," among them, *vivre, donner, absorber.* In "Le Practicable de la scène" she argues that the subject is traversed or overshot by language and that scenes of representation always dissolve under the pressure of language's excess. This declaration contradicts Lacan, who took the position in the late 1960s that the fantasmic scene is itself a signifier (and as such part of a signifying chain) and that the opposition of word/image is essentially a false dichotomy that will lead any analysis of the fantasm astray.[15]

French psychoanalysts, then, have taken a number of diverse ap-

13. My sources are a personal interview I had with Jakobson as well as an unpublished lecture that he delivered at University of Michigan in May 1978.

14. Jean-François Lyotard, *Discours, Figure* (Paris: Klincksieck, 1971), pp. 327–54.

15. Luce Irigaray, *Parler n'est jamais neutre* (Paris: Minuit, 1985).

proaches to considering the fantasm: as originary imaginary constructions that are both phylo- and onto-genetic; as a scripted scene
determined by the instincts; as what Lacan calls the *cadre du désir;* as
projective and introjective constructions that posit the fantasm either
in the world outside or within the mind; and as linguistic constructions
that concern cryptonymous operations or grammatical transformations
in which the subject position fades and shifts, or again, is itself invaded
by an infinity of signifiers. Following the linguistic turn of Lacan in
the 1950s, French psychoanalysts have become increasingly aware that
the fantasm problematizes the relationships of word and image and
that it also problematizes questions of origination and ground, functioning therefore as a term that resists essentialization and even closure
while positing what analysts consider the fundamentals of Freudian
analysis. Yet whether one can really have a theory of the primal without
the perils of essentialistic thinking is debatable, though the case has
elegantly been constructed by Ned Lukacher in *Primal Scenes.* What
is clear from the following history, at least, is that given the multiple
approaches to the fantasm, it is difficult to opt for any one theory of
it that could be said to dominate all the others. To that extent, we
need to be prepared to see the history of the fantasm as a loose inter-
weaving of approaches that focus on the significance of certain imaginary constructions that have required in-depth analysis in all schools.

Freud and Fantasy

The history of the fantasm in French Freudianism begins at an early
point in Freud's career, specifically his collaboration with Joseph
Breuer, whose patient Anna O. spoke of experiencing her own private
inner theater. Breuer himself posited the idea of a "double consciousness," the one containing primary thoughts, which are normal, and
the other containing secondary thoughts, which are abnormal. Freud
recollected in "Five Lectures on Psychoanalysis" (1910) that Breuer's
breakthrough came at the moment in which he paid attention not only
to the imagined scenes of Anna O. but to the verbal associations she
made with those scenes. In addition, Freud recognized that the sec-

ondary train of thought was, in Breuer's words, "likened to a dream in view of its wealth of imaginative products and hallucinations, its large gaps of memory and the lack of inhibition and control in its associations."[16] These two insights—that the scenes required the analysis of those words associated with them, and that the secondary train of thought functioned along the lines of a dream—form the kernel of what would become Freud's greatest discoveries.

Already in 1885, while Freud was studying in Paris with J.-M. Charcot, he learned that the paralyses of hysterical patients were "the result of ideas which had contaminated the patient's brain at moments of a special disposition."[17] Freud would later link this insight with the realization that hysterical symptoms are closely related to memories. While studying with Charcot, Freud noticed that, "the core of a hysterical attack, in whatever form it may appear, is a *memory,* the hallucinatory reliving of a scene which is significant for the onset of the illness. It is this event which manifests itself in a perceptible manner in the phase of 'attitudes passionelles'; but it is also present when the attack appears to consist only of motor phenomena. The *content of the memory* is as a rule either a psychical *trauma* which is qualified by its intensity to provoke the outbreak of hysteria in the patient or is an event which, owing to its occurrence at a particular moment, has become a trauma."[18] Like Charcot, Freud recognized that trauma was fundamental to the onset of hysteria, but unlike Charcot he argued that the shock is significant not merely as a physiological blow to the nervous system but also as an imaginary construction or "scene" that is remembered. For later French psychoanalysts this kind of "scene" would become synonymous with the word *fantasme,* a concept that Freud did not posit, since he was less interested in the imaginary visual apparatus of the inner theater of the mind than he was in the words associated with the scenes. In short, whereas French psychology was to emphasize imaginary visual constructions as significant in their own right—the hysterical poses or positions of Charcot are already exemplary of this tendency—Freud was eventually to make a linguistic turn

16. Freud, *Standard Edition,* vol. 2, p. 45.
17. Ibid., vol. 3, p. 12.
18. Ibid., vol. 1, p. 137.

that would result in the analyses of *The Interpretation of Dreams* (1900).

In the case of a certain Frau P.J., aged 27, we have a particularly important instance of a patient whose hysterical symptoms are motivated by the conversion of sexual excitation into anxiety.[19] A trained singer who is newly married to a traveling businessman, she suddenly becomes overwhelmed with nausea while sitting at the piano and blames her condition on the eggs and mushrooms she had eaten for breakfast. She thinks she has been poisoned. The next day the maid tells her that in the same house a woman had gone mad, and from that time Freud's patient is obsessed by the thought that she too will go insane. Freud, who recognizes the functions of defense and displacement, does not stop once he has analyzed the conversion of sexual desire into anxiety in the present, but compels the patient to recollect a scene in which forgotten memories are to be located.

In taking the history of the patient's psychology into account, Freud discovers that while the woman was singing arias by Bizet and Mozart at the piano, she had entered a kind of autohypnotic state in which the lyrics had suggested to her an outpouring of love which manifested itself in what she called "a feeling in the lower part of the body, a convulsive desire to urinate." Freud, suspecting the woman's reluctance to speak frankly, offers a substitute interpretation: "so it had been an *orgasm*."[20] With this remark, the materials of the scene at the piano come to an end. Whereas one might have expected Freud to return to his initial hypothesis and claim credit for having correctly diagnosed the woman's psychological conversion of sexual desire into anxiety, he does something that will become very characteristic of the famous case histories: he begins to investigate yet new recollected materials, in this instance, leading up to what he will call scene two.

Apparently, the woman, who was trained to sing in the theater, could remember four years previous to her scene at the piano that she had had a similar attack. Disgusted by the physical intimacy of a cast of singers with which she was working, she recalls being sexually ap-

19. Ibid., p. 216. See also *The Complete Letters of Sigmund Freud to Wilhelm Fliess, 1887–1904*, ed. Jeffrey Moussaieff Masson (Cambridge: Harvard University Press, 1985), "Draft J (1895)," pp. 155–58.
20. Freud, *Standard Edition*, vol. 1, p. 217.

proached by a tenor who had put his hand on her breast, which was partially exposed by a summer dress. Earlier she had admitted to Freud that she had often felt to be in a nervous state because she had not lost her virginity, but in her description of "scene two" she shows only disgust for the tenor's sexual advances. Not surprisingly, Freud senses the contradiction implies the kind of ambivalence that suggests she may have been, in some sense, powerfully attracted to the tenor. Not only has there been an orgasm; there has been a moment of earlier sexual contact which foreshadows it. Also, we have now witnessed two scenes with two leading men. In fact, these scenes are so similar structurally that one would have to admit not only that the scene at the piano was a repetition of the scene four years earlier with the singer but that the scene in question, while concerning the absent husband, is really a displacement for the woman's desire for the male singer, if not her wish to have become part of that world and its sexual behavior.

Curiously, Freud does not elaborate on the relation of these scenes, but ends the draft by saying, "Interrupted by the patient's flight." In this early truncated case history the scenes not only structurally repeat each other according to the deductive hypothesis with which Freud begins, but do so in a way that indicates the trauma is not some sort of psychic accident that shocks the nerves and results in the production of mere delusions (Charcot's thesis), but is itself manifest as the structural relation of two scenes. In other words, the trauma is not an external shock that one day hits the patient out of nowhere, but appears as the effect of a structural relationship between scenes whose souvenirs have become inaccessible to the patient even as they express themselves very concretely as obsessions, delusions, paranoiac fantasies, or hysterical bodily symptoms. Although the trauma may have its roots in the conversion of sexual feeling into anxiety at a physiological level, for Freud the trauma, as such, does not manifest itself until it becomes articulated as the symbolic structure that dictates the formation of scenes.

This early theoretical discovery will become central for French analysts such as Jean Laplanche, who in *Life and Death in Psychoanalysis* argues that the structural relationship between such imagined scenes is connected to the principle of repetition associated with the drives and that the scenography of the patient needs to be considered in terms of a structural relationship traversed by a temporality in which the sexual development of the patient crosses over various developmental stages. Speaking of another case history containing two imaginary scenes experienced by a young woman, Laplanche comments:

> It may be said that, in a sense, the trauma is situated entirely in the play of 'deceit' producing a kind of seesaw effect between the two events. Neither of the two events in itself is traumatic; neither is a rush of excitation. The first one? It triggers nothing: neither excitation or reaction, nor symbolization or psychical elaboration; we saw why; the child, at the time she is the object of an adult assault, would not yet possess the ideas necessary to comprehend it. In that case, we may legitimately ask what the psychical status of the memory of the first scene is during the temporal interval separating it from the second one. It would seem that for Freud it persists neither in a conscious state, nor, properly speaking, in a repressed state; it remains there, waiting in a kind of limbo, in a corner of the 'preconscious'; the crucial point is that it is not linked to the rest of psychical life. We are thus confronted with the formation of what is called in the *Studies on Hysteria* a 'separate psychical grouping.'
>
> If the first event is not traumatic, the second is, if possible, even less so. What is involved here is a nonsexual event, a banal scene out of daily life: going into a shop in which there are two assistants, perhaps convulsed with laughter. And yet it is that second scene which releases the excitation by awakening the memory of the first one: that memory acts from then on like a veritable 'internal alien entity,' henceforth attacking the subject from within, provoking within her sexual excitation.[21]

What interests Laplanche is that psychical trauma comes not from without, but, by way of a scene held in abeyance, is triggered from within. "For the reminiscences are there like an internal object constantly attacking the ego." This internal object is itself nothing less than the *fantasme*, a point curiously elided in the English translation by Jeffrey Mehlman in which the general Freudian term, fantasy, re-

21. Jean Laplanche, *Vie et mort en psychanalyse* (Paris: Flammarion, 1970), p. 69. Trans. Jeffrey Mehlman, under the title *Life and Death in Psychoanalysis* (Baltimore: Johns Hopkins University Press, 1976), pp. 41–42.

places the specifically French term, *le fantasme:* "The reminiscence—
or the fantasy [*le fantasme*]—in the example of Emma is the internal-
ization of the first 'scene.' " Not fantasy, in general then, but the internalized *fantasme* or first "scene" is what attacks the ego, given that
the *fantasme* is the internal imaginary object in the shell of the ego
[*l'écorce du moi*]. "Thus preserved from all attrition by the process of
repression, the fantasy [*le fantasme*] becomes a permanent source of
free excitation."[22] Here again the elision of the correct term in the
translation is problematic because *fantasme* introduces such an important modification of the early Freud, namely that in French psychoanalysis there is a history of thinking in terms of originary fantasms
that have the status of "permanent sources" in the psyche. Note Laplanche: "In this detour through the introjected, fantasied scene [*la
scène fantasmatique*], we rediscover the notion of the *source* of the
drive [*pulsion*] that we commented on in the preceding chapter from
another point of view, based on the 'biological' considerations present
in the *Three Essays on the Theory of Sexuality.* Everything comes from
without in Freudian theory, it might be maintained, but at the same
time every effect—in its efficacy—comes from within, from an isolated
and encysted interior [*intérieur isolé et enkysté*]."[23] Here it is not just
fantasy that is encysted but the *fantasme,* and Laplanche adds that
problematic from the perspective of sexuality is that it comes too soon
in terms of interhuman relations—as something imported from the
world of adults—and comes too late from the point of view of supplying
one with the affective and ideational elements necessary to comprehend
the sexual scene if it occurs before puberty. How the *fantasme* is encysted and kept in abeyance as well as later triggered depends entirely
on the temporality of the *ordre vital* or sexual drive. Laplanche's text
revises Freud's early writings by trying to integrate a number of concerns: the drives, the structural relation between scenes, the introjection
of a scene that is held in abeyance, *Nachträglichkeit* (retroaction),
temporal asymmetries, and, of course, the originary nature of the
fantasme.

On May 2, 1897, Freud wrote to Fliess:

22. Laplanche, *Life and Death in Psychoanalysis*, p. 42. Cf. *Vie et mort en psychanalyse*, p. 70.
23. Laplanche, *Life and Death in Psychoanalysis*, pp. 42–43.

I have gained a sure inkling of the structure of hysteria. Everything goes back to the reproduction of scenes. Some can be obtained directly, others always by way of fantasies set up in front of them. The fantasies stem from things that have been *heard* but understood *subsequently,* and all their material is of course genuine. They are protective structures, sublimations of the facts, embellishments of them, and at the same time serve for self-relief. Their accidental origin is perhaps from masturbation fantasies. A second important piece of insight tells me that the psychic structures which, in hysteria, are affected by repression are not in reality memories—since no one indulges in memory activity without a motive—but *impulses* that derive from primal scenes. I realize now that all three neuroses (hysteria, obsessional neurosis, and paranoia) exhibit the same elements (along with the same etiology)—namely, memory fragments, *impulses* (derived from memories), and *protective fictions;* but the breakthrough into consciousness, the formation of compromises (that is, of symptoms), occurs in them at different points. In hysteria, it is the memories; in obsessional neurosis, the perverse impulses; in paranoia, the protective fictions (fantasies) which penetrate into normal life amid distortions because of compromise.[24]

Freud, then, had himself already made a connection between fantasized scenes and the drives, noting that beneath the fantasies are repressed impulses and not encysted scenes, an insight that becomes important for later studies such as *Three Essays on the Theory of Sexuality* (1905), "Instincts and Their Vicissitudes" (1915), and *Beyond the Pleasure Principle* (1920). Yet at this early date, the impulses are themselves motivated by and derived from "primal scenes" or what Laplanche and Pontalis, in their seminal essay "Fantasme originaire, fantasmes des origines, origine du fantasme," called originary fantasms.[25] Such fantasies stem from language that has been heard even as they are formed in relation to sexual excitation (masturbation) as well as from impulses that derive from primal scenes that according to Freud's letters, relate to seduction by the father.

24. Freud, *Complete Letters,* p. 239.
25. Jean Laplanche and J.-B. Pontalis, "Fantasme originaire, fantasmes des origines, origine du fantasme," *Les Temps Modernes* 19, no. 215 (1964). Trans., under the title "Fantasy and the Origins of Sexuality," *The International Journal of Psycho-Analysis* 49, part 1 (1968).

Freud explicitly connects fantasized scenes with actual scenes of seduction, as in the letter to Fliess of December 6, 1896, in which a
woman recalls her father in the "throes of sexual excitement, licking
the feet of a wet nurse." All hysteria, Freud says, "results from *perversion* on the part of the seducer." Anticipating Lacan, Freud insists
that the hysteric's symptoms are, in fact, "aimed at *another person*—
but mostly at the prehistoric, unforgettable other person who is never
equaled by anyone later," or, in Lacan's terms, the "great Other."[26]
This great Other is never anyone less than the Father. Although Freud
would soon turn away from this theory, he rehabilitated it in *Totem
and Taboo* (1912), in which the prehistoric and perverse Father or
Other prominently reappears, and he also reconsidered it in "From the
History of an Infantile Neurosis" (1914), also known as the Wolf-Man
case.

Although on September 21, 1897, Freud tells Fliess he has abandoned
the "seduction theory"—that hysteria follows from actual scenes of
seduction by a perverse father which are experienced or witnessed by
a young child—he reinstates it shortly afterward with some major
modifications by theorizing the Oedipus complex as a perverse wish
on the part of the child (the subject), not a perverse act on the part of
the father (the Other). October 15, 1897: "I have found, in my own
case too, [the phenomenon of] being in love with my mother and jealous
of my father, and I now consider it a universal event in early childhood,
even if not so early as in children who have been made hysterical. . . .
If this is so, we can understand the gripping power of *Oedipus Rex*."[27]
Early French Freudians such as Eugénie Sokolnicka and Marie Bonaparte took as axiomatic that the Oedipus complex is a universally
shared originary fantasm, a view that many contemporary French
Freudians, such as Vladimir Marinov, still accept.

This is quite interesting when one considers that Freud's rejection

26. Freud, *Complete Letters,* pp. 213, 212.

27. Ibid., p. 272. Shakespeare's *Hamlet* is mentioned almost immediately following.
"His conscience is his unconscious sense of guilt. And is not his sexual alienation in
his conversation with Ophelia typically hysterical? And his rejection of the instinct that
seeks to beget children? And, finally, his transferral of the deed from his own father to
Ophelia's? And does he not in the end, in the same marvellous way as my hysterical
patients, bring down punishment on himself by suffering the same fate as his father of
being poisoned by the same rival?" (p. 273).

of the seduction theory also carries with it an abandonment of previous theories concerning fantasized scenes. Freud argues "that there are no indications of reality in the unconscious, so that one cannot distinguish between truth and fiction that has been cathected with affect." And, "In the most deep-reaching psychosis the unconscious memory does not break through, so that the secret of childhood experiences is not disclosed even in the most confused delirium."[28] This departs quite radically from previous understandings of fantasy in that it suggests the scenic constructions do not lead to some primary or originary tableau whose elements have become fragmented, displaced, and then rearticulated as so many deceptive foils. In fact, there isn't any primal or primary scene at all in any empirical sense, but only a reconstruction of a scene whose originary nature is illusory. Only later experiences, Freud says, really give impetus to fantasies, and these are only recollected *as if* they were authentic memories of something that happened long ago in childhood. In this, of course, Freud broaches his well-known theory of the memory screen, in which a fairly recent imaginary construction is recalled, say, in an adult, as if it were a recollected event that had actually happened in early childhood. The notion of fantasy as screen has often been considered a *fantasme* by certain French analysts, for example, Julien Rouart in "Souvenirs et fantasmes, de la remémoration aux constructions."[29]

With these aspects of fantasy in mind, Freud began work on *The Interpretation of Dreams*. In letters to Fliess in May 1897, some five months before he discarded the seduction theory, Freud has already come to the conclusion that dreams are wish-fulfillments. In fact, it is most likely that the remarks about fantasies in the unconscious made to Fliess in the letter on breaking with seduction theory are motivated largely by the perception that one ought to be treating imaginary constructions in analysis as dreams rather than originary scenes of seduction. In short, it is not the father's desire that is reflected in these fantasies, but the patient's, obscured, as in a dream, by repression and displacement. This insight, of course, lays the groundwork for the

28. Ibid., pp. 264, 265.
29. Julien Rouart, "Souvenirs et fantasmes, de la remémoration aux constructions," *Revue Française de Psychanalyse* 35, no. 2–3 (1971).

Oedipus construction. Moreover, it is only a short distance from here to the famous description of dreams in *The Interpretation* as regulated by the interrelation of representation, condensation, displacement, and secondary revision. In retrospect, then, *The Interpretation of Dreams* provided not only a set of rules that reflect the logic of the patient's dream-work, but an integration of mental registers, the conscious, pre-conscious, and unconscious, which Freud had been considering in the letters to Fliess in terms close to those outlined in the *Project for a Scientific Psychology* (1895). In short, *The Interpretation of Dreams* provided Freud with a synthetic theory that pointed a way out of the labyrinth of hysteria with all its deceptive scenes, traumas, symptoms, events, and illusory origins.

Lacan's semiotic reading of *The Interpretation of Dreams* only rad-icalizes what is inherently significant about Freud's turn toward dreams and away from the hysteric's fantasies: "Freud goes on to stipulate what I have said from the start, that it [the dream] must be understood quite literally. This derives from the agency in the dream of that same literal (or phonematic) structure in which the signifier is articulated and analyzed in discourse. So the unnatural images of the boat on the roof, or the man with a comma for a head, which are specifically mentioned by Freud, are dream-images that are to be taken only for their value as signifiers, that is to say, in so far as they allow us to spell out the 'proverb' presented by the rebus of the dream."[30] For Lacan the "linguistic structure" is itself the "significance of the dream," the medium of linguistic signification is the message. The dream, according to Lacan in "The Agency of the Letter in the Unconscious," is like a game of charades; it lacks the "taxematic material" for making logical articulations such as causality, contradiction, or hypothesis. Like cha-rades, the dream is really "a form of writing rather than of mime," an odd observation when one considers that charades looks a lot like mime. "The rest of the dream-elaboration is designated as secondary by Freud, the nature of which indicates its value: they are fantasies [*fantasmes*] or daydreams [*Tagträume*] to use the term Freud prefers in order to emphasize their function of wish-fulfillment (*Wunscher-füllung*). Given the fact that these fantasies [*fantasmes*] may remain

30. Jacques Lacan, *Écrits*, trans. Alan Sheridan (New York: Norton, 1977), p. 159.

unconscious, their distinctive feature is in this case their signification."[31] Again, although a translator has rendered the word *fantasme* in such a way that no English reader can detect its specificity as a term peculiar to French psychoanalysis, it should be noted that in "The Agency of the Letter in the Unconscious" Lacan has purposefully degraded the *fantasme* from an originary to a secondary role of importance and has reduced it to being merely another "signifier." Lacan compares the role of the *fantasmes* to that of very offputting colors that characterize stenciled images, grotesque in themselves as figures. As if to anticipate Andy Warhol, Lacan points forward to the stenciled or silk-screened Marilyn Monroes in which the color and not the form makes the image hallucinatory.

It would be hard to prove that Freud ever suggested anything of this kind. But Lacan's revisionist radicalization of Freud's *Interpretation of Dreams* shows what Lacan might have called the direction of the cure Freud undertook in order to extricate himself from the impasses of fantasy. Whereas Lacan, in many respects, holds the *Interpretation* as Freud's most advanced theoretical position vis-à-vis a linguistic and semiotic turn that French intellectuals were making in the 1950s, Freud himself tried on a number of occasions to rehabilitate much of the theory on fantasy done prior to 1900.

He attempted to improve on the scenic analyses of the early case histories by integrating them with the various means of interpreting dreams, hence the famous texts on Dora and the Wolf-Man. "Delusions and Dreams in Jensen's *Gradiva*" (1907) is theoretically motivated to demonstrate how a novel that privileges scenes can only be analyzed using the hermeneutical principles disclosed by the study of dreams, whereas in the "Leonardo da Vinci and a Memory of His Childhood" (1910) one finds analyses that stress visual representations, namely the paintings and fantasies of da Vinci. We recall that in this study Freud considers a "vulture fantasy," which is attached to a recollection of the passion with which Leonardo's mother kissed him as a small boy, and Freud wonders whether the enigmatic smile of the Mona Lisa is not, in some sense, itself reminiscent of the mouth of Leonardo's mother? This "smile of bliss and rapture," which Leonardo may have

31. Ibid., p. 161.

identified with his mother, was both attractive and repulsive to him, because, on the one hand, it marked his erotic relation to her, yet on the other, it marked the "dominance of an inhibition which forbade him ever again to desire such caresses from the lips of women." And yet "he became a painter, and therefore he strove to reproduce the smile with his brush, giving it to all his pictures." In the painted figures of these works it is possible, Freud surmises, that "Leonardo has denied the unhappiness of his erotic life."[32]

This study is highly influential for Julia Kristeva's analyses of Renaissance painting, in particular her essay "Motherhood According to Bellini," in which the unrepresentable memory of birth(ing) is fantasmatically rendered. Speaking from the gender of woman, Kristeva writes, "Such an excursion to the limits of primal regression can be fantasmically experienced as the reunion of a woman-mother with the body of *her* mother. The body of her mother is always the same Master-Mother of instinctual drive." Indeed, it is this Master-Mother that Giovanni Bellini painted, though "the very existence of aesthetic practice makes clear that the Mother as subject is a delusion, just as the negation of the so-called poetic dimension of language leads one to believe in the existence of the Mother, and consequently, of transcendence."[33] Like da Vinci, Bellini was, in Kristeva's view, the "servant of the maternal phallus," who rendered it in terms of the representation of woman as mother, which is to say, the archaic as jouissance. Just as the smile described by Freud relates to the bliss that da Vinci recalled through various memory screens or fantasies, the mothers painted by Bellini, similarly, carry the affective charge of jouissance, which one can detect on the surface of the mise-en-scène, namely its interplay of strokes and colors.

In *Totem and Taboo*, Freud develops the theory of a phylogenetic primal scene which takes its inspiration from Darwin. Here, as in the very early studies, Freud considers a number of scenes in relationship to one another: the primal father of the horde who monopolizes many

32. Freud, *Standard Edition*, vol. 11, pp. 117, 118.

33. Julia Kristeva, "Motherhood According to Bellini," trans. Leon S. Roudiez, in *Desire in Language* (New York: Columbia University Press, 1980), pp. 239, 242.

women at the cost of his many sons, the slaying of the father by the sons, the conversion of the slain father into the totem, reenactment of the murder by means of sacrificial rites, and, much later, the conversion of such primitive religious thinking into monotheism. The trace of the primal murder by the sons is carried on in the collective fantasy structure of religion and the social order we call culture. But its trauma is phylogenetically bestowed on each new generation. The Lacanians, especially, have been influenced by this text, and especially in terms of the notion of the phylogenetic and socially constructed law, which contrasts with the Name-of-the-Father, an ontogenetic and Oedipal construction. André Green has noted that the force of the Lacanian interpretation has been to detach the phylogenetic argument from biologistic assumptions and to play down its relationship with the Oedipus complex.[34] Furthermore, analysts such as Nicolas Abraham have considered the taboo as an instantiation of the *fantasme*. Where the taboo was, the fantasm will be.

In "A Case of Paranoia Running Counter to the Psychoanalytic Theory of the Disease" (1915) Freud introduces the notion of "primal fantasies," which he discusses more fully in the *Introductory Lectures on Psychoanalysis* (1916–17): "As specimens of this class I will enumerate these: observation of parental intercourse, seduction by an adult and threat of being castrated."[35] Such fantasies, Freud says, may "screen" the autoerotic period of childhood development. By this time, Freud has come to the conclusion that these fantasies are symbolizations that have their sources in the instincts: "There can be no doubt that their sources lie in the instincts; but it has still to be explained why the same fantasies with the same content are created on every occasion. I am prepared with an answer which I know will seem daring to you. I believe these *primal fantasies,* as I should like to call them, and no doubt a few others as well, are a phylogenetic endowment. In them the individual reaches beyond his own experience into primaeval ex-

34. André Green, "Après coup, L'archaïque" *Nouvelle Revue de Psychanalyse,* no. 26 (Autumn 1982): 195–215. Green comments that of major importance to Lacan was the demystification of the notion of the "archaic" by means of a linguistic turn whose effect would be to articulate the "unconscious."
35. Freud, *Standard Edition,* vol. 16, p. 369.

perience at points where his own experience has been too rudimen-
tary."[36] In short, such fantasies are said to substitute for what were at
one time real experiences within the human family and are inherited
through the instincts themselves. As in the letters to Fliess, Freud is
still, even at this stage, struggling to reconcile with respect to universal
fantasies the dichotomy of reality and imagination, objective influence
and subjective suggestion. And instead of looking for the original traumas of fantasy in the patient, Freud opts for a solution in which the
origin is inherently deferred to an archaic realm that can be known
only by imaginary retroaction. This arché is not so much the real origin
as it is an arche-trace, what Lacan in his brief seminar on the Names-
of-the-Father calls the trait of the primal father. This remark closely
parallels Jacques Derrida's later analyses of the trace and of differential
deferral in "Freud and the Scene of Writing."[37] In other words, in the
context of French psychoanalysis, Freud's phylogenetic understanding
of fantasy does not lead to a so-called metaphysical reduction, but,
quite the opposite, to an understanding of the imaginary construction
as irreducible to an origin as such.

In " 'A Child Is Being Beaten': A Contribution to the Origin of the
Sexual Perversions" (1919), Freud returned, once more, to a linguistic
approach and suggested that an ambivalence between sadism and masochism motivates the transposition of a proposition in order that the
subject who is acting out an imaginary scene may be alienated or cast
outside of it for the sake of her pleasure. The originary scene of the
pervert is, in fact, a visual rendering of a kernel sentence that expresses
the wish or desire of the subject. The wish itself is disguised by the
grammatical transformation of this kernel sentence and the relocation
of the subject to a position exterior to the imagined tableau. The essay
gave credence to the view, held by French analysts in the 1930s such
as Eduard Pichon, that the unconscious is closely related to questions
concerning linguistics; again, this is crucial for Lacanian analysis.

Finally, in essays such as "The Uncanny" (1919), "Fetishism" (1927),
and "The Medusa's Head" (1920), Freud investigates the primal fan-

36. Ibid., pp. 370–71.
37. Jacques Derrida, "Freud and the Scene of Writing," in *Writing and Difference*,
trans. Alan Bass (Chicago: University of Chicago Press, 1978).

tasy of castration under various different auspices; and in "The Infantile
Genital Organization: An Interpolation into the Theory of Sexuality"
(1923), he returns to the question by inquiring into the primacy of the
phallus. Instead of focusing on the double session of object choice first
made in childhood and repeated in puberty, in this essay Freud stresses
the difference between childhood and adult genital organization. The
difference consists in the fact that for the child "only one genital,
namely, the male one, comes into account."[38] When children notice
the absence of the penis, "they gloss over the contradiction between
observation and preconception by telling themselves that the penis is
still small and will grow bigger presently." In this a fantasy of the
phallus-that-mother-never-had is produced as a defense against castration anxiety. In childhood, then, no antithesis between male and female
exists as such; there is only castrated and not castrated. "It is not until
development has reached its completion at puberty that the sexual
polarity coincides with *male* and *female*." In this essay, as well, Freud
outlines the beginnings for a theory of abjection. "We know, too, to
what a degree depreciation of women, horror of women, and a disposition to homosexuality are derived from the final conviction that
women have no penis. Ferenczi (1923) has recently, with complete
justice, traced back the mythological symbol of horror—the Medusa's
head—to the impression of the female genitals devoid of a penis."[39]

These passages have been extremely relevant for not only a Lacanian
theory of the phallus but for the deconstructive and French feminist
interpretations of the Medusa's head and of the problematic of castration. In the 1970s, both Jacques Derrida in "Spurs" and Hélène
Cixous in "The Laugh of the Medusa" put into question Freud's notion
of castration: Derrida by contextualizing it in terms of Nietzsche and
Heidegger, Cixous by attacking a Lacanian psychoanalysis that obliges
women to deposit their lives "on the banks of lack." The analysts,
according to Cixous, "riveted us between two horrifying myths: between the Medusa [Freud] and the abyss [Lacan]." For Cixous analysis
is still in that infant stage where everything sexual is reduced to the
phallic order, to what she calls phallogocentrism. Speaking of castra-

38. Freud, *Standard Edition*, vol. 19, p. 142.
39. Ibid., pp. 144, 145.

tion, Cixous asks, "But isn't this fear convenient for them? Wouldn't the worst be, isn't the worst, in truth, that women aren't castrated, that they have only to stop listening to the Sirens (for the Sirens were men) for history to change its meaning? You only have to look at the Medusa straight on to see her. And she's not deadly. She's beautiful and she's laughing."[40] Fantasy, then, is gendered and, as such, follows the social and cultural interests of gender privilege. And to that extent, the fantasm is really but a myth, a belief that is uncritically internalized.

Cixous's critique departs radically from even later Freudian readings such as that by Nicole Loraux, who in "Le Fantôme de la sexualité" argues that the figure of Helen in Ancient Greek philosophy and literature is internally a phantom and externally split or cut to express "la sexualité comme rapport à la perte" ["sexuality as a relation to loss"]. According to Loraux, Helen is *la chose sexuelle* only because she is inappropriable as a figure who is always absent in the place of her representation.[41] Whereas Cixous discounts such fantasms in order to demythologize them, Loraux elevates the fantasm in terms of Ancient Greek sources in order to establish its veracity as an imaginary construction in whose repetition a certain psychological truth comes to pass. Unlike Cixous, Loraux does not believe in producing different fantasies through the reorganization of erotogenetic zones to overthrow a gender-biased order, presumably because there are fixed psychological limits beyond which one cannot simply go. That is, for more orthodox Freudians, the limitations or laws of the unconscious are disclosed by phenomena such as the fantasm, and neither the laws nor the fantasms are negotiable as theoretical constructions that can be transformed at will for ideological purposes. Still, it is this desire to appropriate Freudian theory for such revolutionary aims that takes us back to the beginnings of much French Freudian thought in the 1920s by intellectuals such as André Breton, whose interests focused on the cultural rather than the clinical aspects of such psychology.

40. Hélène Cixous, "The Laugh of the Medusa," trans. Keith Cohen and Paula Cohen, in *The Critical Tradition*, ed. David Richter (New York: St. Martin's, 1989), p. 1097.
41. Nicole Loraux, "Le Fantôme de la sexualité," *Nouvelle Revue de Psychanalyse*, no. 29 (Spring 1984): 28.

Janet and Surrealism

During the early 1920s Freud had finally become all the rage with Paris intellectuals who were less interested in clinical issues than they were in the cultural appropriation of Freudian theory. At the same time, France had its own indigenous psychological theories, which had been developed by thinkers such as J.-M. Charcot, Alfred Binet, Théodule Ribot, and Pierre Janet, all of whom also lacked a clinical interest in Freudian theory, though on entirely different grounds. Everyone except for the Surrealists appeared to dismiss Freud's so-called degenerate theory of "pansexuality." For its part, the French psychological establishment prided itself on stressing the logical and the methodological and discounted what they considered Freud's "arbitrary" constructions. Pierre Janet, a trained philosopher who turned to psychology, was perhaps closest to Freud in terms of his researches and discoveries, and like Freud himself, Janet would one day formally recognize the importance of a thesis by the young Jacques Lacan. In *Psychological Automatism,* based on research in the 1880s, Janet turned from hypnosis to automatic writing in order to analyze a young woman who had suffered from apparently unmotivated terrors.[42] The automatic writing revealed a childhood trauma as well as two personalities within the young woman. Janet had used the practice of automatic writing in order to bring the personalities into relation so that the dominant, socially acceptable personality could override its double. Janet discovered that under hypnosis his patient revealed a personality structure that is not only obedient to authority but which also manifests itself spontaneously and regresses toward childhood. Janet found under fur-

42. My account of Janet is indebted to Henri F. Ellenberger, *The Discovery of the Unconscious* (New York: Basic Books, 1970), especially chap. 6, "Pierre Janet and Psychological Analysis," from which I draw rather heavily. My aim, of course, is not to present new information on Janet but to suggest the obvious parallels to Lacanian psychoanalysis, which many researchers—certainly all the major analyses to date—have chosen to overlook. Elizabeth Roudinesco gives a very negative account of Janet in *La Bataille de cent ans: Histoire de la psychanalyse en France I* (Paris: Ramsay, 1982). Her reading, in my view, loses sight of the fact that Lacanian analysis is, despite its debt to Freud, actually grounded in the overall philosophical weltanschauung of classical French psychiatry.

ther investigation that his patient could elicit other personalities as well. Janet's notion of automatism could apply to the whole subject or to partial, subconscious processes (one is reminded of Jacques Lacan's notion of the partial drives).

In his study of catalepsy Janet discovered that automatism continues unabated without stimulus from outside, a point that suggests that there are autonomous psychological processes somewhat akin to what Freud would later call the drives. Janet's notion of "successive existences" suggests that individuals comprise a number of personalities that may or may not know of one another. Some are childhood personalities, others not. Instead of insisting on a unified notion of psychological character, Janet developed a theory of *désagrégations psychologiques* (psychological breakdown) and devoted attention to the processes that subtended them: fixed ideas, obsessions, hallucinations, and paranoid suggestibility. He argued that split parts of the personality are related to automatic processes which could organize themselves around traumatic memories, and he posited the notion that one should think in terms of a "field of consciousness" rather than in terms of a cogito. Like Freud, Janet paid attention to "subconscious" processes and tried to cure his patients of fixed ideas and their many substitutes, the theatrical disguises played out by hysterical patients. The use of automatic writing, automatic talking, and crystal gazing allowed the patient to speak involuntary thoughts while being distracted by the doctor. Janet also wrote about the "rapport" between doctor and patient in terms of a "direction" of the cure. In retrospect, Lacanian analysis has considerable affinity with many of Janet's remarks concerning "influence," though Lacan, of course, disavowed hypnosis and mastery. From 1909 on, Janet attempted to develop a synthetic psychological model that integrated a large number of complex issues, among them automatic processes, sociopersonal relationships, perceptual processes, reflexive actions and beliefs, and rational tendencies. Janet also considered language, which he saw in terms of how the symbol gradually became detached from action and resulted in both "inconsistent language"—a speaking to the other that does not take into account the other's speech—and "inner language," which is open to suggestion. Here belief, feeling, wish, and fear all bear on inner language and its representations. The personality takes its cue from these representations, which it acts out in terms of attitudes and roles. Janet coined the term *surréalisation* to account for false representations in which past events are revised by being repeated and disguised in the present.

Clearly, there is much in Janet's work which foreshadows later French psychoanalytic theorizing and, in particular, Lacan's notion of repetition, his commitment to thinking of psychology as a field of relationships or registers, and to those aspects of language/speech which are "automatically" produced or which circulate according to partial processes independent of individual will. The Surrealists, too, learned from Janet and were especially interested in Janet's "states of absent-mindedness," the notion of "automatic writing," and the *surréalisation* of memory. Most important, artists such as André Breton and Philippe Soupault were fascinated by Janet's perception of hysteria as the inability to perceive the real functionally, and his belief that suggestibility along hysterical lines was in fact natural to everyone and aided by sleep. Furthermore, the Surrealists were interested in Charcot and Janet's notion of hysterical simulation, the disguising of the traumatic content in a theatrical manner that brings the erotic and the visual into relationship. They were also interested in the idea of hysteria as a form of mental disintegration or personality breakup. As Elizabeth M. Legge points out in her work on Max Ernst, the Surrealists were attracted not only to the photographs of Charcot's patients but also to Janet's illustrations of hysteria and his theory of the double personality.[43]

During the early 1920s, when Freud's book-length studies first began to appear in French translation, Breton had both rejected and accepted Freud. In "Interview du Professeur Freud" (1922), Breton treated *la psycho-analyse* as a seasonal fashion and tried to deflate Freud's popularity by reporting that he found Freud's milieu to be "de la sorte la plus vulgaire." Of his first impression chez Freud, Breton wrote, "I found myself in the presence of a little old man without allure who was receiving in the quarter's run-down doctor's office. Ah! he didn't

43. Elizabeth M. Legge, *Max Ernst: The Psychoanalytic Sources* (Ann Arbor: University of Michigan Research Press, 1989), pp. 111–13. Legge points out that Ernst's painting "Enter/Leave" is indebted both to Janet's *Névroses et idées fixes* and to Freud's study of *Gradiva*. This hybridization is paradigmatic, I think, for Lacanian psychoanalysis.

like France very much and remained only indifferent to its creations."
Breton, apparently, had been disappointed with Freud because it was
apparent that Freud had absolutely no interest in what Breton and
others like him were doing in Paris.[44] Nevertheless, Breton did an about-
face in the *First Manifesto of Surrealism* (1924) by identifying himself
with Freudian technique: "Completely occupied as I still was with
Freud at that time, and familiar as I was with his methods of examination which I had had some slight occasion to use on some patients
during the war, I resolved to obtain from myself what we were trying
to obtain from them, namely, a monologue spoken as rapidly as possible without any intervention on the part of the critical faculties, a
monologue consequently unencumbered by the slightest inhibition and
which was, as closely as possible, akin to *spoken thought*."[45] This,
however, is less a description of Freudian technique than it is of Janet's
technique of "automatic speech." Philippe Soupault, with whom Breton
wrote automatic poems, claimed that in fact it was not Freud but Janet
whose influence was most felt. For his part, Soupault had never taken
Freud too seriously and, like Janet himself, believed that everything
Freud wrote was inherently indebted to French psychologists.[46] Certainly, Breton's definition of surrealism as "psychic automatism in its
pure state" owes considerable allegiance to Janet, particularly when
he distinguishes the "actual functioning of thought" from the "control
exercised by reason." When Breton invokes the "omnipotence of
dream" he is certainly invoking not a Freudian idea but one taken from
the clinical experience of Janet, whose patients in suspending rational
thought encountered the automatic omnipotence of fixations, dreams,
hallucinations, and so forth. In so doing, they overestimated or overshot
the real in terms of *sur-réalisme*. As if self-consciously to pervert Janet's
thinking, Breton cheerfully announces that "language has been given
to man so that he may make Surrealist use of it."[47] Janet's "inconsistent
language" is endemic to a Surrealist dialogue, in which lightning-like

44. André Breton, "Interview du Professeur Freud," in "Les Pas perdus," in *Breton: Oeuvres complètes* (Paris: Gallimard, Bibliothèque de la Pléiade, 1989), vol. 1, pp. 255–56. The report of Breton's interview was originally published in *Littérature, nouvelle série*, 1 March 1922, p. 19.
45. Quoted in Legge, p. 23.
46. Ibid., p. 21.
47. André Breton, "Manifesto of Surrealism" (1924), in *André Breton: Manifestos of Surrealism* (Ann Arbor: University of Michigan Press, 1969), p. 32.

replies ignore what is being said by the interlocutor. In speaking of dialogue, Breton suggests that "two thoughts confront one another; while one is being delivered, the other is busy with it." Yet in turning to Janet's notion of sensory deprivation, Breton praises inconsistent speeches in which the sentences in dialogue don't follow, since the protocols of obligations, politeness, and response have been subjected to a "disorder": "Each [speaker] simply pursues his soliloquy without trying to derive any special dialectical pleasure from it and without trying to impose anything whatsoever upon his neighbor."[48] This attention to inconsistent speech, of course, informs much of Lacan's thinking about dialogue wherein the subject cannot fathom the desire of an unconscious interlocutor, the Other. Janet and Breton, not Freud, are the source for this kind of interest.

During the period of the dada movement, Breton and his colleagues were interested not in dreams but in questions of chance, the disruption of habits commonly associated with producing speech and texts, and projective techniques associated with personality. In the early twenties, however, Breton, Desnos, Picabia, and others were publishing accounts of their dreams in *Littérature* with the express idea of producing a kind of writing that would abolish or negate literature as such. Similarly surrealistic images or scenes were not supposed to avail themselves to "realization" but were to remain mysterious, enigmatic, and absurdly disturbing. One either overestimated or underestimated the image, since one's consciousness is incapable of realizing it within a stable sense of proportion vis-à-vis its reference to other images, scenes, and constructions. For both Breton and Max Ernst, the imagined or dreamed scene was never too far removed from language. Breton relates how, just before falling asleep, a phrase "was knocking at the window." "I cannot remember it exactly, but it was something like: 'There is a man cut in two by the window,' " a phrase that is accompanied by the phantom presence of a "man walking cut half way up by a window perpendicular to the axis of his body." Breton explains:

> Beyond the slightest shadow of a doubt, what I saw was the simple reconstruction in space of a man leaning out a window. But this window having shifted with the man, I realized that I was dealing

48. Ibid., pp. 34, 35.

with an image of a fairly rare sort, and all I could think of was to
incorporate it into my material for poetic construction. No sooner
had I granted it this capacity than it was in fact succeeded by a
whole series of phrases, with only brief pauses between them, which
surprised me only slightly less and left me with the impression of
their being so gratuitous that the control I had then exercised upon
myself seemed to me illusory and all I could think of was putting
an end to the interminable quarrel raging within me.[49]

No doubt, Breton effaces the difference between word and image even
as he stresses how the one influences the other according to automatic
processes, which are, in Janet's terms, "subconscious." The man cut
in half is, of course, a phantom double of Breton, a barely submerged
personality that has projected itself forth into hallucination at that
moment the dominant personality has relinquished control over all
those automatic processes which underscore the *désagrégations psychologiques,* of which the surreal is an effect.

In Max Ernst's collage novels of the 1930s, images from the popular
press of the nineteenth century are superimposed and carefully sutured
in order to conflate a number of planes of vision into a mise-en-scène
that allows numerous psychological actions to come into collision. In
Une Semaine de bonté, it is not unusual for all the represented figures
to be addressing an absent Other even while they are being positioned
in such a way that they are, supposedly, in communication with one
another. Although a mise-en-scène suggests an "action" in the Aris-
totelian sense, what one has, in fact, are figures who are radically

49. Ibid., p. 22. Jacques Lacan in *Le Séminaire XI: Les Quatre Concepts fondamentaux de la psychanalyse* also tells a story about being knocked awake: "The other
day, I was awoken from a short nap by knocking at my door just before I actually
awoke. With this impatient knocking I had already formed a dream, a dream that
manifested to me something other than this knocking. And when I awake, it is in so
far as I reconstitute my entire representation around this knocking—this perception—
that I am aware of it. I know that I am there, at what time I went to sleep, and why
I went to sleep. When the knocking occurs, not in my perception, but in my consciousness, it is because my consciousness reconstitutes itself around this representation—
that I know that I am waking up, that I am knocked up." Like Breton, Lacan stresses
what occurs in the gap between perception and consciousness, that is, how the knock
creates a structure in which the subject "fades" before a representation. The translation
is Alan Sheridan's. See Jacques Lacan, *The Four Fundamental Concepts of Psychoanalysis* (New York: Norton, 1978), p. 56.

estranged from any immediate interpersonal context visible to us and placed in a false juxtaposition with one another whose consequences are "imaginary" or "suggested" rather than real. In other words, the scenes are largely an accumulation of abrogated encounters in which we are often deprived of seeing a subject's true counterpart—his or her actual other—and are given, instead, a substitute figure, such as the totem, Loplop. Often, figures are merely taken out of one scene and incongruously thrown into another even though, as Werner Spies maintains, a formal compositional relationship is always respected.[50] Although a congruent overlap or perfect formal matching takes place, there is, nevertheless, the strong sense that the figures take place *in* if not *as* a vacuum and, in so doing, suggest a "lack" or "absence," which Lacan, many years later, would term a "hole in the real." This, of course, is the necessary visual precondition of the fantasm in much Surrealist art—that the image not only resist rational comprehension, but that it manifest itself as a hole or tear in the real that marks the disappearance of that something of which trauma is the aftereffect.

In the 1930s too, Salvador Dali published a number of pieces in *Minotaure* which focused strongly on the role of the fantasm in art. For example, in "Le Surréalisme spectral de l'éternel féminin préraphaélite," Dali notes that the Pre-Raphaelite paintings of women are "the carnal *fantasmes* of childhood's 'false memories,' the gelatinous meat of the most guilty of sentimental dreams."[51] Unlike Cézanne whose representations are said to rest on an abstract Platonic notion of form, the morphology of the Pre-Raphaelites is based on a psychology of abjection, revulsion, and terror. The beauty of the Pre-Raphaelite female form is entirely saturated with a traumatic abhorrence of woman. Whereas Cézanne derives his morphologies from an idealized conception of form, the Pre-Raphaelite morphologies are said by Dali to be rooted in false memories of childhood beneath which considerable sexual conflict takes place. Here the influence of Freud's early work on hysteria as well as his conception of memory screens can be detected, and again one is reminded of Ernst's collages in which

50. Werner Spies, *Max Ernst Collages: The Invention of the Surrealist Universe* (New York: Abrams, 1991).
51. Salvador Dali, "Le Surréalisme spectral de l'éternel féminin préraphaélite," *Minotaure* 2, no. 8 (1936): 47.

the figures may all be exemplary of "false memories," which have been realized in a present that reflects an impossible dissociative field of relationships as if it were a commonplace scene.

Dali, in fact, goes so far as to make a distinction between the *fantôme* and the *spectre*. The phantom, he says, is a simulacrum of volume, narcissistically tactile, architectonically anxious, metaphysical, immobile. The specter is an "exhibitionistic erection," capable of destroying illusory volume; it is visceral, physical, terrifying, visually hysterical, and highly volatile. Examples of the phantom include Freud, de Chirico, and Greta Garbo. Examples of the specter include Picasso, Gala, Harpo Marx, and Marcel Duchamp. The phantomized body (identity) is rearticulated, collated, and restored, whereas the spectral body (difference) is disarticulated, fragmented, or deformed. The phantom is analeptic; the specter is proleptic. Moreover, the phantom and the specter are complementary, and one senses that they combine to make up a fantasm.

Again, owing some debt to Janet, Dali was quite interested in double images, which, for him, underscored a paranoid delusional understanding of reality. In *The Secret Life of Salvador Dali* we learn that as a child Dali chanced on "mimetism" when he discovered to his surprise how well an insect imitated the plant on which it rested. In "Interprétation paranoïaque—Critique de l'image obsédante 'L'Angélus' de Millet" Dali outlines two kinds of confusion, the one passive and automatic, the other systematic, active, and paranoid. In citing Lacan's *De la psychose paranoïaque dans ses rapports avec la personnalité*, Dali argues that it is time for Surrealists to turn away from the mechanistic, automatic processes, which were, in any case, merely simulated in bad faith, and turn to an aggressive systematization of paranoia such as described by Lacan. "The work of Lacan takes into perfect account the objective and 'communicable' hyperacuity of the phenomenon [of paranoia], thanks to which delirium takes its tangible and uncontradictory character, which puts it at the antipodes of even the stereotypes of automatism and the dream." Far from being passive, paranoia "already constitutes in itself a form of interpretation. It is precisely this active element born of a 'systematic presence' which, beyond the general considerations which precede it, intervene as the principle of this contradiction wherein resides for me the poetic drama of surrealism. This contradiction cannot find its dialectical conciliation in anything better than new ideas which see the light of day in paranoia, according to which delirium would surface as *entirely systematized*."[52]

Dali's paranoid-critical method suggests, at the very least, that the automatic processes need to be actively subordinated to a paranoid system in which doubles, or doubling, affects how the real is experienced. In addressing the rocky environments of the paintings of Millet, Dali notices that the stones are not just the dull objects they seem, but paranoid things whose oneiric double is the "desired earth of treasures." The workers in Millet are oppressed by these stones even as the stones madly cry out in their most luminous physical contours the preserved or dispossessed dream of becoming rich. The paintings of Millet, therefore, have a fantasmic presence in that they are about something "other" than what we are seeing, something "other" that is a double of what is literally represented. Given such doubling, both love (beauty) and hate (abjection) come to pass as affective states. All of these perceptions, of course, will eventually influence Lacan, and in Dali's examination of Millet one can already glimpse the anticipation of Lacan's three orders: the Real (the stones as such), the Imaginary (the stones as gems), and the Symbolic (the Other intuited in paranoia).

The Early Lacan

Dali, Janet, and Freud all recognized and praised Jacques Lacan's thesis on paranoia, *De la psychose paranoïaque dans ses rapports avec la personnalité*.[53] Lacan himself said that the thesis only brought him to

52. Salvador Dali, "Interprétation paranoïaque—Critique de l'image obsédante 'L'Angélus' de Millet," *Minotaure* 1, no. 1 (1935): 66.

53. David Macey in *Lacan in Contexts* (London: Verso, 1988) is the source for the information on Janet. Concerning the recognition by Freud, see "Une lettre inédite de Freud à Lacan," ed. Roberto Harari, *Ornicar?* 33 (1985): 150–59. Freud writes, "J'ai plutôt du tendance ... à circonscrire, à découper quelques constellations déterminées que l'instrument analytique peut éclairer et, de fait éclaire" ["I had rather the tendency ... to circumscribe, to separate those few specific constellations which the analytical instrument can and, in fact, does enlighten"] (p. 152). In the letter, Freud speaks about the question of writing in relationship to paranoia and reconsiders the case history of Aimée from a much more "Freudian" point of view. It is curious that this extremely important text has not appeared in English translation.

the threshold of psychoanalysis and, indeed, *De la psychose* owes a greater debt to the classical psychiatry of someone like Janet than to an analyst like Freud, though, it has to be said, the theoretical aim of the study is carefully to integrate Freud in order to question the overall conceptual bedrock on which Janet's orientation to psychology depends. Nevertheless, a good contrast to Lacan's case history of Aimée is Freud's "Case of Paranoia Running Counter to a Psychoanalytic Theory of the Disease," which is about a woman who believes she has been intentionally compromised by a male suitor and photographed so that he can later humiliate her. Whereas Freud does, in fact, draw on the details of her life in order to explain the unconscious motivations for her paranoia, his case history is much more intuitive and far less concerned with detailed accounts of the patient's education, social status, family relationships, and multiple personality disorders. Conversely, absent in Lacan's case of Aimée is mention of the unconscious and its processes; conspicuously present is mention of automatism, personality, psychoaesthenic conduits, social inadaptation, and *attitudes vitales,* all concepts stemming, of course, directly from Janet.

The case history of Aimée concerns a woman who stabs a famous actress on account of a delusion in which hate has been deflected from its proper source onto a substitute figure, who occupies the role of the superego. Meanwhile, the proper source for the hatred—Aimée's sister—had gone unrecognized, as if the delusions had been an attempt to protect the sister from Aimée's intense anger. The delusion, then, concerns a simulacrum that is highly ambivalent in that it repeats the double (the sister) who is hated even as it posits itself as a double that is wished for, an idealized image of Aimée. The delusions, clearly, point out an instability in self-other relationships which is being determined by the projection of a second personality in the world. In other words, like Janet, Lacan has seized on a case in which a dominant personality has given over control to a subconscious personality, which, in this case, has projected itself into the world and has been so alienated from the dominant personality that when Aimée meets her self as self and other (her sister) she believes that she is, in fact, being brought under the influence of a different person. What Lacan discovers, of course, is that Aimée's delusion turns into an acted-out scenario that takes place in the real everyday world. In short, a fantasy becomes actively concretized. This happens, as well, in Freud's "Case of Paranoia," in which a paranoid homosexual woman similarly forgets to recognize the source of her delusion, except that Freud analyzed the case much as he would have analyzed a dream—by looking at the transformation or switching of identities. The persecutor, in this case history, was not, as the woman believed, a man, but actually someone of her own sex. And Freud will suspect that even this woman is a substitute or displacement for the mother. In the case history of Aimée, however, the displacements are hardly as devious in that the persecuting doubles are all standing in for a dyadic relation between Aimée and her sister, those doubles wavering between the two inconclusively. The delusion is, if anything, a kind of fixed idea or stationary mechanism that ensures misrecognition of its source by creating substitutes that the subject mistakes as complete strangers.

De la psychose paranoïaque also differs quite clearly from Freudian analysis in that it is interested in nosological classification. It goes so far as to create a new clinical category, paranoia d'autopunition, a phrase that in itself is reminiscent of Janet in that it suggests not just self-punishment but automatic punishment. Paranoia d'autopunition is but one of the mechanisms that developed out of Aimée's various social relationships—on the microlevel with her mother, her sister, and her husband and on the macrolevel with her job and with her relationship to strangers. The mechanism of automatic self-punishment established an ideal female figure or phantom double; thus the delusion or fantasm associated with it is the result of a certain automatic process inherent in the disintegration of the personality as a subject who can properly adapt to others.

Toward the end of his treatise, however, Lacan turns away from Janet and determines that the delusional double is not so much a split-off personality but a symbol.[54] And he will argue that, in fact, Aimée suffers from libidinal fixations whose symbolism is pathological (phobic, fetishistic). It is this libido that has elaborated objects in the real through projection even as it is responsible for articulating a narcissistic relationship between the ideal ego and ego ideal. In other words, Lacan locates his entire analysis within the Freudian coordinates of symbol-

54. Lacan, De la psychose paranoïaque, p. 253.

ized objects in their relationship to a narcissistic stage of development (the double). The narcissistic stage, Lacan argues, is best known as one in which the first interdictions or taboos appear, where one would be most likely to locate the "mécanismes autopunitifs ou du sur-moi."[55]

No doubt, commentators have correctly noted the resonance between Lacan's early interest in misrecognition, paranoia, and mirror doubling and the mechanism of the mirror stage for which Lacan has become so famous. But what they have often overlooked is how much less this orientation to psychology owes to Freud than we have been led to suspect. It is quite interesting that even during the first generation of French Freudians Lacan can say so little that contradicts Janet and that although his artist friends spoke quite openly about phantoms and specters, Lacan could not, given his clinical language, address the *fantasme*.

The First Generation of French Freudians

The so-called first generation of French Freudians began their psychoanalytic society as late as 1926, some sixteen years after the International Psycho-Analytic Association had been established. The Société Psychanalytique de Paris or SPP began publishing the *Revue Française de Psychanalyse* in 1927 and, contrary to what Elizabeth Roudinesco has opined, brought out a number of highly interesting articles, which, unfortunately, are not very accessible today. The earlier volumes contained translations of Freud's articles, significant overviews of Freudian concepts (e.g., the super-ego, fetishism, the "phantasme"), Freudian interpretations of culture and history (e.g., the fine arts, Napoleon), French analytical case histories, and accounts of seminars, conferences, papers, as well as book reviews.

Already in the first volumes of the *Revue* the term *fantasme* figures prominently in a number of articles, among them Eugénie Sokolnicka's "Quelques problèmes de technique psychoanalytique" of 1929, in which we read about masturbatory fantasies as "imaginative infantile inventions that are repeated from one individual to the next with a

55. Ibid., p. 259.

monotony of subject and content, for example, as fantasms [*fantasmes*] of sexual violence, of observing parental coitus, and of castration." Like the early Freud, Sokolnicka wants to sort out the *fantasme* by discriminating between what has really taken place and what has been merely invented: "Of first consideration are the infantile imaginative inventions that are repeated among different individuals with a great monotony of subject and content, such as fantasms [*fantasmes*] of sexual violation, castration, or observation of the parents during coitus. It is necessary to deny these fantasms in analysis in order to discern what has really taken place and what has merely been invented. One gets out of trouble by attributing *psychological truth* to what is recounted and not objective reality." Like Freud, Sokolnicka maintains that the fantasm is an invariant, phylogenetic fantasy. "Freud notes that the fantasms have a phylogenetic patrimony which he calls primordial [*Urphantasien*]."[56] Following Freud in the *Introductory Lectures,* she argues that because the unconscious is phylogenetically given, the fantasm can be considered a primordial fantasy universal to all subjects, though it is expressed or rendered differently in the imagination of each analysand. Hence the term *fantasme* refers to both what is unconsciously given as Ur-phantasie and what is recollected by the analysand as fantasies or reveries that develop scenes of rape, punishment, coitus, and so on. Sokolnicka's thesis is that the fantasm allows the analysand to replace real objects with imagined ones in order to minimize libidinal conflicts experienced by the ego. This substitutive role of the fantasm becomes problematic, however, when physical symptoms start to displace aspects of the fantasm. To make the symptom disappear, the analyst must resolve ego conflicts through analytical use of the transference.

Central to Sokolnicka's understanding of the fantasm is its ontogenetic connection to the Oedipus complex. As one might expect, ontogeny and phylogeny meet with respect to the production of a fantasized primal scene; however, Sokolnicka also recognizes that the Oedipus complex offers other possibilities for fantasmic constructions. For example, she recognizes that during this stage the subject is en-

56. Eugénie Sokolnicka, "Quelques problèmes de technique psychanalytique," *Revue Française de Psychanalyse* 3, no. 1 (1929): 29.

couraged to identify with the *opposite* sex. In part, the girl does this by imagining she has a penis, the boy by imagining he has none. These fantasies of sexual identification with the other sex form the basis for what Sokolnicka believes are bisexual imaginary relays that can be activated later in life and which always accompany neurotic behavior. This ambivalent sexual identity, then, is thought to come into relation with the "primal scene" as an expression of the subject's incestuous desires. Sokolnicka postulates that when fantasies are substituted for real objects, the archaic anxiety motivating such a displacement is inherently tied to the conflicts structured by incestuous desire and bisexual identification. No doubt, Sokolnicka's understanding of the fantasm refers us to a complex interaction of processes occurring on different levels—as a phylogenetic given mediated by ontogenetic development and, in particular, the Oedipal phase wherein an imaginary "primal scene" comes to pass during a phase of sexual ambivalence. After latency, the fantasm appears as a related imaginary construction with thematic sources to be found in aspects of the primal scene (such as rape, castration, identification with the opposite sex) and accompanied, in neurosis, by the consequent emergence of physical symptoms and homosexual inclinations. Whereas Sokolnicka's interpretations are quite dependent on Freud's writings, there is in them a conceptual centralization of the fantasm that runs quite counter to Freud. Moreover, whereas Freud was very suspicious of fantasy and called attention to what motivated it, Sokolnicka uses the fantasm as a ready-made diagnostic tool for establishing given personality types. Such fantasms have archetypal status, and they enable the analyst to pursue a therapy that concerns tension reduction.

Angelo Hesnard's "Contribution à l'étude des phantasmes érotiques" of 1930 is a major statement that situates and defines a typical understanding of fantasy in French psychoanalysis up to the 1950s. Hesnard, who preferred to bring Freudian analysis within the acceptable tolerances of classical psychiatry in France, defines the *phantasme* as an imaginary construction whose primary function is to sexually excite the subject: "Erotic 'phantasmes' are images of imaginative representations of objects or of concrete situations of which the essential characteristic is for the subject to procure an erotic excitement that is conscious and more or less intentional."[57] Like Sokolnicka and, of course, Freud, Hesnard understands the significance of the *phantasme* in the context of "sexual life." But whereas for Sokolnicka the pathology of such imaginary constructions responds to conflicts between the ego's wishes and the reality principle, for Hesnard erotic *phantasmes* are to be understood in terms of how the instincts are being repressed. Unlike other French analysts, Hesnard made the interesting distinction between the existence of a *phantasme* and a *fantasme*. The *phantasme* is an obsessional deep structure of fantasized relations articulated in the unconscious and motivated by "pulsions de divers nature," whereas the *fantasme* is its expression, a surface structure that has undergone all the processes of transformation common to the dreamwork. For Hesnard, every *fantasme* can be reduced to an image or phrase from a limited repertoire that, as in the work of Sokolnicka, has been mediated by the incestuous conflicts of the Oedipal stage.

Quite influential, of course, are Freud's *Three Essays on the Theory of Sexuality* and "A Child Is Being Beaten," which Hesnard used to develop a typology of sexually perverse fantasms: sadism/masochism, exhibitionism/scopophilia, and fetishism/homosexuality. Hesnard couples these categories into opposites, the one inclining more to the real, the other inclining more to the imaginary. Hence the fantasies of sadists are compared in such a way with those of masochists that Hesnard can claim the sadist's fantasies are less symbolic, more mature, and closer to the real than those of masochists, whose fantasies are believed to be more symbolic, infantile, and highly charged. Homicide, mutilation, cannibalism, and castration would be typical themes of sadistic *fantasmes*. Masochistic *fantasmes* are regressive and dissimulate by way of complex imaginary stagings: the child is not castrated but beaten. In exhibitionism, which Hesnard contrasts to voyeurism, the subject passively stands in the place of the gaze and barely masks an incestuous and incompletely repressed wish to be desired by one of the parents. The exhibitionist is said to be more distanced from the real than the voyeur whose fantasies barely disguise infantile curiosity.

---

57. Angelo Hesnard, "Contribution à l'étude de phantasmes érotiques," *Revue Française de Psychanalyse* 4, no. 3 (1930): 525.

The voyeur, according to Hesnard, is especially fascinated with perverse couplings, of which the motif of Leda and the Swan would be typical. The voyeur is somewhat akin to the sadist insofar as the voyeur is rather close to the real and not very interested in the symbolic. Like the masochist, the exhibitionist shows herself or himself to the parent in order to be both desired and punished. In fetishism fantasies are synecdochic and symbolically touch on the body of the mother. Buttons, corsets, and velours are symbolic supplements that give the fetishist access to what has been interdicted—the mother's vagina. The fetishist, moreover, is narcissistic and sexually ambivalent; the fetishist's fantasies bear on what Sokolnicka and Hesnard recognized as an infantile identification with the opposite sex. In contrast, the homosexual is somewhat closer to the real than the fetishist since the homosexual acts out identification with the other sex without total reliance on symbols. Like the fetishist, the homosexual's fantasy structure is said to be highly narcissistic; however, that narcissism is not entirely dependent on an imaginary structure that elicits a need to stage desire with numerous props. Although all fantasy requires a certain staging of desire, masochism, exhibitionism, and fetishism all require extensive symbolic and imaginary structures of dissimulation which are overtly vulnerable and invite shame. Sadism, voyeurism, and homosexuality are thought to be far less symbolic and much more at home in the real per se. Yet Hesnard cautions that even in these cases pleasure is bought at the price of pain. Moreover, in all cases, such neurotics, as he calls them, have a symbolic psychic system whose sexually perverse theme is, whatever else it may be, an expression of unresolved Oedipal conflict. Hesnard believes that in all such cases fantasies are the result of a subject who is condemned to experience sexuality only with himself or herself and that such a narcissistic state of affairs involves self-punishment by the infantile superego. Like Sokolnicka, Hesnard sees the primal scene as a central concern insofar as this imaginary structure establishes a pattern or logic that copes with the incest taboo without ever satisfactorily resolving it. It is no surprise that the *fantasme* is a construction that will repeat itself in the hopes of resolving a conflict its structure preserves in an unresolved state.

In those papers which do not specifically attempt to define *fantasme* precisely, one discovers a range of synonyms, of which "fantasie" is common. As noted earlier, Marie Bonaparte uses the term *fantasme* to mean a hallucinatory construction in her article "L'Identification d'une fille à sa mère morte" (1928). Another interesting instance that establishes a conception of *fantasme* prior to its redefinitions in the 1950s is the *Revue*'s French translation in 1936 of Freud's "Metapsychology of Dreams." Compare the following versions of a pertinent passage. In the *Revue:* "La formation du fantasme du désir, sa regression vers l'hallucination, sont les parties les plus essentielles de l'élaboration du rêve, mais ne lui appartiennent cependant pas exclusivement."[58] The German original: "Die Bildung der Wunschphantasie und deren Regression zur Halluzination sind die wesentlichsten Stücke der Traumarbeit, doch kommen sie ihm nicht ausschließend zu." And James Strachey's translation: "The formation of the wishful fantasy and its regression to hallucination are the most essential parts of the dreamwork, but they do not belong exclusively to dreams."[59] "Fantasme du désir," of course, has very different connotations from "Wunschphantasie" or its rather literal translation into English, "wishful fantasy," which have none of the erotic overtones of the French. The French translation, like the articles discussed from the early years of the *Revue,* typifies that whatever the differences in defining *fantasme,* it occupies a prominent role in the French psychoanalytic literature as an erotic reflection of a subject's desire.

Discontinued during World War II, the *Revue Française de Psychanalyse,* became quite prominent in the late 1940s and for years thereafter. And in 1951 René Diatkine takes up the question of the *fantasme* once more in "La Signification du fantasme en psychanalyse," in which he makes a number of references to the work of Jacques Lacan without affording any specifics. Like Sokolnicka, Diatkine is interested primarily in the techniques of the analyst and how the fantasm is to be treated. Diatkine, who may be following Lacan, attacks Melanie Klein for failing to understand that the fantasm may very well be an analytic construction that has been, in large part, suggested by the

58. Sigmund Freud, "Métapsychologie," trans. Marie Bonaparte and Anne Berman, *Revue Française de Psychanalyse* 9, no. 1 (1936): 97.
59. Sigmund Freud, "Metapsychologische Ergänzung zur Traumlehre," in *Gesammelte Werke* (London: Imago, 1946), vol. 10, p. 420; Freud, *Standard Edition,* vol. 14, p. 229.

analyst. To what extent, Diatkine wonders, is the primal scene itself an analytic construction that gets in the way of the cure? Clearly, transference should be taken into account, and we should become sensitive to the fact that psychoanalysts of the 1920s and 1930s were naive about how the patient may be using the fantasm in analysis as a defense mechanism. Diatkine draws on the work of Piaget and Lacan to argue that before the child can objectivize his or her image, one can speak only of numerous conflicts that make up an irrational pre-specular perception. Only when the child enters the mirror stage, does it become capable of incorporating or rejecting fantasies; moreover, this moment coincides with an ego and superego development that has the consequence of cutting off primitive (pre-specular) objects and experiences. If the superego itself makes frightening imaginary constructions, at least they are rational and respect the boundaries of the child's imago. This leads Diatkine to make the important point that it is quite likely that the *fantasme* is an imaginary construction whose function, in part, is to cut the archaic or pre-specular and irrational life world of the child off from what has become a specular and, in turn, Oedipalized or socialized system of rational relationships. The *fantasme*, then, would be the limit of resistance beyond which analysis is encouraged not to go. And the child therefore isolates the analytical experience by creating repetitive fantasms whose role is to defend the subject against the archaic. Language, Diatkine says, can be used to bring the primitive and the socialized, the pre-specular and the specular into relationship and ought to function as a unified field of reference that is capable of exposing the fantasm as a sham construction that merely poses for archaic experiences, which it, in fact, suppresses.[60]

In 1971 the *Revue Française de Psychanalyse* published an entire issue on the fantasm with articles on the perversions, memory screens, reparative fantasies, mysticism, symbolic reality, and megalomania. René Major, Michel Fain, René Diatkine, Colette Chiland, Julien Rouart, and Françoise Paramelle were among the contributors. Quite evident in many of the articles is an attempt at compromise, namely to bring into relation the theories of the first-generation members of the SPP with a breakaway Lacanian psychoanalysis, whose influence

60. Diatkine, "La Signification du fantasme."

was as difficult for the members of the SPP to accept as it was for them to reject. Lacan, who didn't publish prominently in the *Revue Française de Psychanalyse*, broke away from the SPP in 1953 to form, with Daniel Lagache, the Société Française de Psychanalyse (SFP), and, later, he was "excommunicated" by that group in 1963 as a result of political intrigue on the part of the International Psycho-Analytic Association with which the SFP wanted a direct affiliation. The politics are significant insofar as by 1963 Lacan had developed a very powerful and radically new conception of the fantasm which was kept at arm's length by those analysts who did not follow Lacan. Yet it cannot be said that containment worked; even the most orthodox contemporary analysts have not been able to ignore Lacan's contributions entirely.

Lacanian Theories of the Fantasm

By the early 1950s, of course, Lacan had left Janet's orientation to psychology far behind. He had, in fact, assimilated the theories of his colleagues of the SPP.[61] In the 1950s he went beyond these ideas and, in *Le Séminaire I: Les Écrits techniques de Freud, 1953–1954,* located fantasmic phenomena in the imaginary register of specular misrecognition in which one sees the self as other.

> In fact, the virtual subject, reflection of the mythical eye, that is to say the other which we are, is there where we first saw our *ego*— outside us, in the human form. This form is outside of us, not in so far as it is so constructed as to captate sexual behavior, but in so far as it is fundamentally linked to the primitive impotence of the human being. The human being only sees his form materialized, whole, the mirage of himself, outside of himself.... What the subject, the one who exists, sees in the mirror is an image, whether sharp or broken up, lacking in consistency, incomplete. This depends on its position in relation to the real image. Too much towards the edge, and you'll see it poorly. Everything depends on the

61. For a history of this appropriation, see Macey, pp. 26–43.

angle of incidence at the mirror. It's only from within the cone that
one can have a clear image.[62]

For Lacan the point was not that the subject sees an image of itself in
the mirror, but that this image is realized to a greater or lesser degree—
meaning that the image is always perceived as larger or smaller than
something that cannot be perfectly realized. Unlike Diatkine, for whom
the image would be the point of analytical focus, Lacan has turned his
attention to the field of vision or orientation wherein the image can be
greater or lesser than a field of vision in which the image might not
even appear, given where the subject is standing. "This represents the
uneasy accommodation of the imaginary in man." Lacan takes this one
step further: "Now let us postulate that the inclination of the plane
mirror is governed by the voice of the other. This doesn't happen at
the level of the mirror-stage, but it happens subsequently through our
overall relation with others—the symbolic relation. From that point
on, you can grasp the extent to which the regulation of the imaginary
depends on something which is located in a transcendent fashion ...
the symbolic connection between human beings."[63] This symbolic connection or position defines the place from which the subject sees itself
in the field of specular relations; it is the symbolic—in fact, language
itself—which "determines the greater or lesser degree of perfection, of
completeness, of approximation, of the imaginary." The ideal ego (primary narcissism) and the ego ideal (secondary narcissism) are brought
into relation as the Imaginary and Symbolic. Thus the ideal ego is
mediated and hence brought into view by the ego ideal. Images of
things, generally, are seen in the mirror, too. And these are related to
our image and invested with libido. "What we call libidinal investment
is what makes an object become desirable, that is to say, how it becomes
confused with this more or less structured image, which, in diverse
ways, we carry with us."[64] No doubt, we can still see many remnants
of the case of Aimée in these descriptions and particularly along the
axes of narcissism and libidinal investment in objects as well as in terms

62. Jacques Lacan, *The Seminar of Jacques Lacan, Book I: Freud's Papers on Technique 1953–1954*, trans. John Forrester (New York: Norton, 1988), p. 140.
    63. Ibid., pp. 140, 141.
    64. Ibid., p. 141.

of what Lacan abstractly calls the symbolic connection between human beings (social relations). The issue here, however, is no longer personality disorders, and the question of paranoia is not, in fact, foundational for driving the apparatus of mirroring. Indeed, the problem here is that the mirror image is not the double of the subject, an incongruity with which the subject must come to terms.

Like Diatkine, Lacan argues that whereas the images are somewhat protean or anamorphic—"How does the primitive mouth get transformed, in the end, into a phallus?"—language provides anchorage at the level of "legal" and "verbal" exchange, or, to put it otherwise, social contracts whose function is to establish definite points of reference. "What is my desire? What is my position in the imaginary structuration? This position is only conceivable in so far as one finds a guide beyond the Imaginary, on the level of the Symbolic plane, of the legal exchange which can only be embodied in the verbal exchange between human beings. This guide governing the subject is the ego-ideal."[65] The role of the analyst, then, is to speak from the perspective of the other who manipulates the specular place where the subject finds himself or herself "to a greater or lesser degree of perfection" in the mirror. Lacan speaks of this manipulation as crucial to the question of the transference in which a certain image remains virtual and fantasmic.

In *Le Séminaire IV: La Relation d'objet, 1956–1957*, Lacan continues an analysis of the English object-relations school which he had developed in his first seminar in terms of Melanie Klein. But in this new seminar Lacan is mainly concerned with the signification of the phallus and its role in obsessional neurosis. The seminar concludes with several sessions devoted to a lengthy and masterful analysis of Little Hans's horse phobia as described by Freud. Crucial to that analysis is the notion of an imaginary phallus, the phallus that mother never had, a topic intended to complement Lacan's earlier investigation in the same seminar of female homosexuality, in which an imaginary phallus of the father is constructed and jealously guarded such that no real penis could ever be thought to rival it. In the case of Little Hans, the imaginary phallus is equated with the phobic object of the horse.

65. Ibid.

The phallus not only stands for the maternal phallus, but with respect
to the child's fear of being bitten by the horse's mouth, it also stands
for a traumatic representation of the mother's vagina. One might expect
this imaginary phallus to be thought of as a *fantasme,* but Lacan uses
the term in a very orthodox manner to refer to the primal scene, which
is, in fact, the *fantasme* wherein the boy takes to the side of the mother.
Addressing the primal scene, Lacan comments that there are many ways
in which fantasms [*ces fantasmes*] of the "little boy's passivity" can
enter in the course of an analysis such that the little boy can be taken
in "a fantasmatic relation with the father in which he is identifying
with the mother." Moreover, Lacan correlates Hans's identification
with the mother as characteristic of a male homosexuality in which a
boy's perspective of the primal scene takes to the side of the mother,
rather than the father, and in so doing phantasizes her position in order
to "offer himself up as a victim in her place" with the result that the
boy's entire childhood is experienced in terms of an "importunity of
sexual insistence on the part of the father." In such a case the boy has
been brought to what is called an "impasse with the mother."

In *Le Séminaire V: Les Formations de l'inconscient, 1957–1958,*
Lacan began developing the various stages of the very complex "Graphs
of Desire," which figure so prominently in the essay "Subversion du
sujet et dialectique du désir" of the *Écrits.* Both Catherine Clément
and Slavoj Žižek have elegantly explained these graphs wherein the
fantasm plays an important role.[66] Essentially, these graphs reconfigure
Freud's notions of the unconscious, the preconscious, and the conscious
by means of a communications model in which the trajectory of the
subject's *parole,* or speech, retroactively cuts across *langue,* the signifying chain. In other words, the subject does not found discourse so
much as it retroactively finds itself within a discourse already vouched
for by an Other. This level of everyday communication in which the
subject finds itself situated is flanked on two sides by what are considered imaginary structures of identification with the other. The first of
these structures is that of specular complementarity—recognizing one-

66. Catherine Clément, *The Lives and Legends of Jacques Lacan* (New York: Columbia University Press, 1983), pp. 176–83; Slavoj Žižek, *The Sublime Object of
Ideology* (London: Verso, 1989), pp. 85–131.

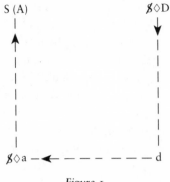

Figure 1.

self in a mirror as an other who is "me." This structure of specular complementarity borders the side of the ego. The second of these structures comprises an identification with an Other which involves a middle term or object that is never entirely stable or adequate. Because of this inadequation the *moi* or me undergoes occultation, what Lacan calls *le fading*. This imaginary structure of inadequation is the fantasm, and it is conspicuously bordering the side of the unconscious. In the graphs of desire of *Le Séminaire V* (which reappear in "Subversion du sujet") the fantasm as dream theatrically stages the communicating circuit of the unconscious wherein the subject's demand for pleasure is mediated by castration. Initially, Lacan had his students memorize the formula, $\$ \diamond a$, according to the following key: the split subject ($\$$) in relation to ($\diamond$) the object of desire (a).

In *Le Séminaire VI: Désir et son intérpretation, 1958–1959,* Lacan simplified matters by means of a diagram (figure 1) in which the circuit of the unconscious—S(A) and $\$ \diamond D$—is shown to traverse the circuit of the fantasm—$\$ \diamond a$ and d. Here $\$ \diamond D$ stands for the relation between the split subject and the demand that the Other makes which renders us powerless (castration). Small d stands for desire. $\$ \diamond a$ represents the fantasm, and S (A) represents the desired jouissance that the Other cannot satisfy. In other words, desire, mediated by the threat of castration, gives rise to the fantasm, which aims at a jouissance that is impossible to achieve. The important point is that the unconscious mediates and hence institutes itself at the level of the fantasm *as if* the fantasm were *langue* and the unconscious *parole*.

Le Séminaire VI can be read as an application of the theoretical model developed in *Le Séminaire V* on formations of the unconscious. It also represents an attempt to extend the insights into object relations of *Le Séminaire IV* to the analysis of obsessional neurosis, which Lacan carries forward with a reading of William Shakespeare's *Hamlet*. It is of interest that in the earlier sessions of the seminar on desire and interpretation Lacan thinks of the *poinçon* or diamond-shaped mark between $ and *a* in terms of phrases such as *en face de* or *en présence de*, whereas in later seminars the *poinçon* is seen in terms of a mathematical relationship ("more than," "less than") or logical operation ("or"). Speaking of the formula for the fantasm, Lacan says it is exactly congruent with what Freud called the dream, "a point of convergence for all the signifiers in which the dream is finally implicated in so far as it announces the unknown itself and isn't recognized except as this *unbekannt*." Lacan says that this is what marks the special nature of the Freudian unconscious, namely "that in the relation of the subject to the signifier there is an essential impasse which I reformulate in terms of there not being any other sign of the subject than the sign of its abolition as subject." In other words, affected by its desire, the subject fades within the dream (or fantasm) before its wish to accede to a pleasure mediated by the Other.

The two major demonstrations of the fantasm in *Le Séminaire VI* are a commentary on a case history by Ella Freeman Sharpe and a commentary on Shakespeare's *Hamlet*. Ella Sharpe's "Analysis of a Single Dream" concerns the symptom of a patient's intermittent coughing, which she relates to a series of sexual fantasies. Having coughed at entering the analyst's door, the patient explained, "It has, however, reminded me of a fantasy I had of being in a room where I ought not to be, and thinking someone might think I was there, and then finding me there I would bark like a dog. That would disguise my presence. The 'someone' would then say, 'Oh, it's only a dog in there.' " Sharpe queried, "A dog?" And the patient continued, "That reminds me of a dog rubbing himself against my leg, really masturbating himself. I'm ashamed to tell you because I did not stop him. I let him go on and someone might have come in." Sharpe adds, "The patient then coughed."[67] After consideration of numerous associations made by the

67. Ella Freeman Sharpe, *Dream Analysis: A Practical Handbook for Psycho-*

patient, Sharpe concludes that the cough relates to an aggressive infantile motive to interrupt the sexuality of the father. In reinterpreting Sharpe's text, Lacan argues that the dog is the Other whose signifier, the bark, has been metaphorically adopted and transformed by the subject into a cough. Whereas the dog is constructed more or less phobically as a disgusting creature by the analysand, it is, as Sharpe points out, the locus of a sexual pleasure to which the subject wants to accede. A very important point for Lacan is that the enigmatic nature of the dog in the analysand's fantasies marks where the subject itself disappears or fades. Not only that, but the dog forces the analysand to ask the question, "What do you want of me?" The symptom of the cough, similarly, raises this question since it is a signifier of the Other, a metaphorical substitute for the dog's bark through which the analysand is hailed or approached. Lacan refines his position by explaining that the dog itself is not the Other but something that signifies in its place. Lacan asks, What does the fantasm mean? And he says, what the subject said right away about the cough: that it's a message even though it is necessary to see that the fantasm really has no meaning and that its eventual efficacy is of a totally irreal character. Hence the subject in barking says simply, "It's a dog." There too it produces itself as other, but that is not the question. Lacan points out that the question is that the subject doesn't ask what the signifier of the Other is in relation to it. For this reason a fantasm is necessary so that an Other is produced, but for the sake of what? a signifier precisely. The barking then is the signifier of that which is not. It isn't a dog, but thanks to the signifier a result is achieved for the fantasm—the signifier is other than what it is.

In the sessions on *Hamlet* Lacan extends the idea, central to the sessions on the Ella Sharpe case, that the function of the fantasm is to express the signifier of the Other before which the analysand fades and is made silent, not having the opportunity to ask what the signifier of the Other means. It should be noted that Sharpe herself wrote several essays that stressed the feminine side of Hamlet—symbolized by Ophelia—and its dependence on the father.[68] Lacan is partial to such a

---

Analysts (New York: Brunner Mazel, 1978), p. 132. The study was originally published in 1937 by the Hogarth Press, London.

68. Ella Freeman Sharpe, *Collected Papers on Psycho-Analysis* (London: Hogarth Press, 1950).

reading, though according to him, central to *Hamlet*'s structure is the extent to which Hamlet's desire is so dependent on the relation with an Other—the S (Ⱥ) of the unconscious—that he is unable to locate what it is that he really wants. This Other is the father, who, as Lacan says, does Hamlet the disservice of revealing the Truth from beyond the grave and, in so doing, prohibits Hamlet from privileging *his* desire. Especially problematic is that whereas the locus of the S (Ⱥ) promises satisfaction, it is, in fact, that locus of Truth where something is lacking, hence the barred A. The subject's error is to assume that in the very place of a revelation by the unconscious, one can find the meaning to one's own desire. And in making this error, Hamlet shows himself to have hysterical and obsessional attributes, since these disorders require subjection to the signifier of an Other, much like the subject whose subjection is marked by the bark of a dog.

Offering an interpretation bound to scandalize Shakespeareans, Lacan suggests that it is not by accident that Ophelia's name has resonances in Ancient Greek with O Phallos, the phallus. This interpretation recalls the discussion in *Le Séminaire IV* of the imaginary female phallus in the analysis of Little Hans, and suggests that Ophelia points to the gap between Hamlet's sexual desire for her and his infantile sexual dependency on his mother. As in Ella Sharpe's analysis of the play, Hamlet takes to the side of the female. Still, Hamlet experiences Ophelia as both fascinating and repellent, since her phallic characteristics are ambiguously associated with both the mother and the father. As in the case of little Hans, the female phallus is strongly associated with the mother, though it has its origin with the father. And this is the real reason, according to Lacan, why Hamlet is so obsessed with Ophelia—she is but a figure that dissimulates the Other (the Father) on whose demand Hamlet is so dependent.

Therefore, even while Ophelia appears as a sexually attractive young woman to Hamlet, as female phallus she screens Hamlet's incestuous desire for his mother. Moreover, as phallus she is also functioning as a dissimulated (or anamorphic) manifestation of the primal father and his demand. That is, Ophelia is both sexual object and agent of sexual demand. Whereas Ophelia cannot experience herself as anything other than what Lacan calls a normal girl, Hamlet experiences her as a fantasm that alienates him from his own desire. This is not surprising, since the fantasm figures the demand of a castrating father. One can summarize by saying that if Hamlet seeks the Truth in an unconscious locus of pleasure where something is lacking—S (Ⱥ)—this comes at the cost of a paternal unconscious demand that cuts him off from achieving his sexual desire—$\emptyset \lozenge D$. Ophelia is the fantasm that supports this unconscious circuit even as she delimits the place where Hamlet's own desire is difficult to retrieve. Lack in the place of S (Ⱥ), castration in the place of $\emptyset \lozenge D$, and alienation in the place of the fantasm (Ophelia as *objet a*) point to breaks or holes, therefore, which mark the relation between the subject and desire. From the standpoint of what is experienced as real, these breaks manifest a "hole-in-the-real" through which the signifiers of the Other stream in.

Identification and Alienation

From 1960 until 1966, when Lacan began his *Séminaire XIV: La Logique du fantasme,* a number of theoretical developments occurred which determined how Lacan would define new approaches to understanding the fantasm. Briefly stated, these developments concern how Lacan rethought questions of identification and alienation. Already in *Le Séminaire VIII: Le Transfert, 1960–1961,* Lacan devoted attention to narcissistic relations and identification by way of the ego ideal. And toward the end of that seminar, Lacan introduced a term from Freud, *ein einziger Zug.* Lacan first dubs it the *trait unique,* though in 1962 he began calling it the *trait unaire.* The "single trait" is James Strachey's authoritative English translation, and the context of the locution refers to what Freud in *Group Psychology and the Analysis of the Ego* viewed as a partial identification in which the ego regresses from object choice to the most primitive emotional tie, which is an identification in which the ego assumes characteristics of the object. If the ego regresses by emulating someone, "the identification is a partial and extremely limited one and only borrows a single trait from the person who is its object."[69] Lacan comments that what is defined by this *einziger Zug* is the punctual character of the original reference to an Other in the

69. Freud, *Standard Edition,* vol. 18, p. 107.

narcissistic relation. Although Freud surely implied narcissism, this differs considerably from what he explicitly says. In Lacan's seminar on the transference, the singular trait is given in the glance of the Other, which functions as a sign the subject can put at his or her disposal, provided the subject coincides with the Other. Narcissistic satisfaction, Lacan says, depends on the subject's ability to relate the ideal ego of primary narcissism to the ego ideal of secondary narcissism by means of the unique and unifying trait of the Other.

In *Le Séminaire IX: L'Identification, 1961–1962,* Lacan contextualizes the unifying trait as something that gives consistency to Descartes's "Cogito, ergo sum." As in the seminar of the previous year, Lacan recognizes two selves who mirror one another, the "I" of "cogito" and the "I" of "sum." Descartes erred, according to Lacan, in thinking that congruence of these two selves is uncontroversial. In fact, Descartes's appeal to God introduces the *trait unique* that guarantees consistency and self-identity. Lacan says that what we find at the limits of the Cartesian experience as such of the disappearing subject is the need for this guarantee, of the most simple structural trait, the unique trait, absolutely depersonalized, not only of all subjective content, but even of all those variations which transcend this unique trait, this trait which is singular. The basis of the one that makes up this trait is not taken as anything other than its unity: as such one cannot say anything else than having this trait for support is common to every signifier before being constituted as trait. Lacan adds that this trait is indistinguishable from a semiological principle of difference. What distinguishes the signifier, he says, is only to be what all the others are not; what implicates the function of unity in the signifier is simply that it is nothing other than difference. There is nothing paradoxical here, since difference ensures consistency and identity to self. Still, one could select other examples, among them, the Name-of-the-Father and the imaginary phallus. Whatever the trait (in a very late seminar Lacan associates it with Hitler's mustache), its function is to support the fantasy of there being only one self-identical *I* that is immune to alienation by iteration. Hence Descartes's "I think, therefore I am" holds true only to the extent that something outside the proposition brings the two *I*'s into congruence or identification. Lacan points out that the unitary trait is, in fact, an arche-trace of a unity that was never originally given but which is only retroactively produced in order to serve as a unifying support.[70] In the following seminar, Lacan considers this unitary trait in terms of an object that brings both fantasy and anxiety into relation, *objet a*.

In *Le Séminaire X: Angoisse, 1962–1963*, Lacan points out that anxiety and the fantasm are to be identified within a mutual relation to an object of desire whose presentation cannot be considered apart from its separability, abstention, and disappearance. In the earlier seminar on transference (*Le Séminaire VIII*), Lacan argued that anxiety maintains a desiring relation with an Other whom the subject fears. Hamlet's anxious relation to the phallus, for example, is mediated by his fear of the father. In *Le Séminaire X*, Lacan associates the fantasm with anxiety and argues that the object of desire is an alienating trait rather than a unifying one. He uses the example of St. Teresa d'Avila to show an instance in which an imaginary object marks the alienation of the desire for a man and "what he represents more or less to the imagination." The *objet a* in this instance is something that has been "elected" by St. Teresa's desire, whether the Other gives permission or not. And pleasure is therefore had at the cost of an erotomania that knows its desire so well that it has, without bothering to ask anyone's permission, elected the imaginary object or fantasm that is to give her pleasure (jouissance). This, of course, differs from the hysteric (Hamlet), whose anxiety results from not knowing his or her desire. St. Teresa's jouissance, when it comes, comes unasked of the Other, and therefore what the famous Bernini statue should connote for us is not simply religious ecstasy, but the rape of God by a woman whose orgasm vouches for her anxiety.

Somewhat later in *Le Séminaire X*, Lacan discusses the castration complex before turning to the Wolf-Man's primal scene as an example of how the fantasm is always traversed by castration. Essential in the disclosure to the Wolf-Man, Lacan says, is the cut that has a function which is scenically rendered by the open window, that is to say, the fantasm itself (or *cadre du désir*) in its most anxiety-laden form. The question is not, Lacan says, of asking where the phallus is, since the

---

70. On the arche-trace, see Jacques Derrida, *De la grammatologie* (Paris: Minuit, 1967).

phallus is there in terms of what Lacan calls the catatonia of the image. The dreamer's primal scene is not simply a setting in which the phallus is viewed among the details, but, already as imaginary construction, is itself an erection that is repeated in the subject as spectator: *l'enfant medusé*. The image, Lacan concludes, is merely the transposition of the subject's state of arrest, the erect penis transformed into a tree whose titular echo will be "a tree covered with wolves." This is, like Bernini's statue of St. Teresa, a scene of *jouissance,* except that in this case, as well, *jouissance* is identified with *angoisse.* The reason for the identification exactly parallels the dynamics of erotomania. "To the extent that orgasm detaches itself from the field of the demand of the other—this is the first apprehension which Freud has of it in coitus interruptus—anxiety appears, if I may say so, in the margin where signification is lost." In other words, the dream of the Wolf-Man is traumatic because, like St. Teresa's ecstasy, it has not bothered to ask either recognition by or permission of the Other. In such fantasms, the image does not satisfactorily support the desire of the subject, since it is the consequence of violence, the subject's refusal to be recognized by the Other, which the subject perceives as the Other's disappearance.

In anticipating *Le Séminaire XIV: La Logique du fantasme,* Lacan turns to *cercles euléreins,* which he illustrates by means of two over-lapping circles. What takes place in the zone where overlap occurs? In the overlap between Subject and Object, for example, the *objet a* is marked. In the overlap of man and woman the phallus as lack is marked. In the overlap of *objet a* and the barred Other, the Subject barred from itself is marked. And in the overlap of the Subject with the phallus, the fantasm is marked. In each of these instances, the zone of overlap is the symptom that characterizes the subject's relationship to the Other in terms of what causes anxiety. It is this symptom which functions much like the *trait unique* or *trait unaire,* of the seminar on identification, except that here, of course, the symptom discloses an alienation of the subject from the fulfillment of its desire. In the fol-lowing seminar Lacan expanded on this understanding of alienation in the overlap of two fields.

Immediately after the seminar on anxiety, Lacan had planned to give a seminar in 1963 on the names of the father, but abrogated it after the first session, since this marked his excommunication from the Société Française de Psychanalyse. He had planned to apply the problematic of anxiety, castration, and the *objet a* to the ontogenetic and phylogenetic conceptualizations of Freud's notion of the primal father. Instead, Lacan delivered *Le Séminaire XI: Les Quatre Concepts fondamentaux de la psychanalyse*, 1964, in which he discusses the unconscious, repetition, transference, and the drives. This seminar has, of course, had immense influence on Anglo-American critics, though it has been studied almost entirely out of context. In it Lacan addresses primary process as taking place in an "other locality," in the rupture between perception and consciousness, and he considers the *objet a* in terms of the gaze. When Lacan considers painting, he is especially interested in how the painted scene marks a locus that outlines the rupture between eye and mind. Although Lacan does not say it here— he does not have to—the painting is itself traversed by a cut (castration, loss, emptiness) that concerns the fantasm. Recalling Freud's study of Leonardo da Vinci, Lacan remarks, "When [Freud] studies Leonardo . . . he tries to find the function that the artist's original fantasy played in his creation."[71] Lacan transforms this elementary insight into his own theoretical terms by saying that the painting is nothing less than a veil behind which there is an "other thing," the "object a." If the *objet a* is the gaze, it is, at the same time, that element in a painting which fascinates or fixes the stare of the viewer. But what lies behind the painting? What fixes our stare? It is the impression that an Other is looking back at us, an evil eye that has a power to separate.

In short, the *objet a* is the locus of a fantasy that exists behind the veil or painted surface that has the force of an evil eye, since it is mediated by the accusatory or damning force of an unconscious Other. The one who stands before the painting, then, is inherently caught in the "field of the Other." And, as Lacan argues, captation by the Other is alienating because the subject can't simply identify or merge as if the two were inherently the same. Rather, the subject and the Other dialectically reveal themselves as inaccessible to each other's knowledge of each other. To be under the evil eye of the Other is for the subject to undergo aphanisia, or fading, whereas for the Other to be under the gaze of the subject means that it too fades, since it can only be

71. Lacan, *Four Fundamental Concepts of Psychoanalysis*, p. 110.

known as unconscious. One of Lacan's conclusions is that every representation requires a subject even if this subject necessarily undergoes
an aphanisia or alienation that undermines its certainty as an observer
of the representation itself. In this subversion of the subject, the representation can no longer be considered merely an object of examination, but becomes a visual construction determined by the psychology
of the gaze or scopic *drive*. Whereas in the previous seminar Lacan
related the *objet a* to anxiety in the Symbolic register, in this seminar
he relates the *objet a* to the "partial drives" in order to establish the
connection between drive, signification, and visual field.

The Logic of the Fantasm

Lacan does not make his most revolutionary turn until near the end
of *Le Séminaire XI,* when he demonstrates how the *cadre du désir*
becomes the border of a logical problem that takes us back to the
overlapping fields of the seminar on anxiety. This turn becomes fateful
for *Le Séminaire XIV: Logique du fantasme,* which, to a large extent,
is an elaboration of it. In the lecture on alienation in *Le Séminaire XI,*
Lacan picks up the familiar relation established in the late 1950s between the preconscious fantasm—$\$ \Diamond a$—and the unconscious demand
of the Other—$\$ \Diamond D$. Now, however, Lacan's main concern is how the
poinçon ("diamond") establishes a disunifying trait located in the demand of the Other which is posed to the subject in the form of a double
bind that exceeds its own stricture.

The function of the diamond, which was always to show the fantasmatic inadequation between the subject and the object of desire, is
now seen in terms of a logical operator, the V-shaped *vel,* the symbol
of the conjunction "or." Lacan points to several modalizations of this
term. It can be exclusive or inclusive. If exclusive—I go *or* stay—I need
to decide. If inclusive—I may either go or stay, it does not matter—I
do not have to decide. But Lacan is not as interested in these alternatives
of difference and identity as he is in yet a third modalization, which
has to do with relating two sets in such a manner that deciding for
one puts the subject in an asymmetrical relation to the other. In the
cases of deciding exclusively or inclusively for A or B, one's relation

to the terms and the relation between the terms remains even. In the third case, the decision forces an occultation of these relations, which Lacan calls alienation.

The privileged example is "Your money or your life!" This is the demand by an Other who sees to it that both choices are bad. If we choose money, we lose both the money and our lives. If we choose for life, we only lose our money. Most important, by joining money and life, the *vel* sees to it that something disappears. "The choice, then, is a matter of knowing whether one wishes to preserve one of the parts, the other disappearing in any case."[72] The choice is not symmetrical. If one chooses the money, one loses both. If one chooses life, one loses the money. Lacan calls this aspect of the Other's demand the lethal factor, and implies, of course, that this lethal factor is castration. If Oedipus incestuously chooses for the mother, he loses both mother and father, and if he chooses for the father, he loses the mother in any case. In both instances there is symbolic castration. In a final twist, Lacan argues that if the losange or diamond of the Other's demand produces alienation, it also produces separation, by which he means the engendering of the subject in the space where the two moments of castration intersect, that is to say, in the space of overlap between the two bad alternatives in which one finds oneself deprived of something. This something, it turns out, is the *objet a* of the fantasm, which is now identified with the "hole in the real" that harkens back the seminar on the object relation wherein Lacan equated privation with the *trou réel*. In the *Hamlet* lectures, of course, it was the alienated and fantasmic signifier of the Other (Ophelia, O Phallos) which occupied this position.

In *Le Séminaire XIV: Logique du fantasme, 1966–1967,* Lacan begins by considering how the splitting of the subject is inherently inscribed into a splitting of the infant's anaclitic object, the maternal breast. Returning to the Eulerian circles of the seminar on anxiety, we are asked to consider two "globes," which Lacan terms desire and reality. Since the seminar begins by addressing primary narcissism, we should not be surprised that Lacan is actually referring us to the mother's two breasts and how for the infant they coincide as if they were

72. Ibid., p. 211.

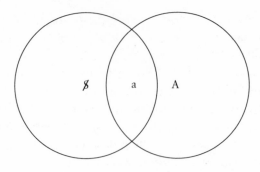

Figure 2.

overlapping circles or, at the very least, surfaces whose outline can be viewed as a Moebius strip. For Lacan, the fact that there are two breasts—one representative of the real, the other of desire—is a physiological reminder to the child that reality and desire are split or, more accurately, alienated, for whenever the child has one breast, it always lacks the other. Yet, as the child knows, the breasts are nevertheless identical; having the one ought to be enough. So, even if the spheres of the real and desire are different, they still coincide or overlap. The imaginary space in which the overlap takes place is called *objet a,* and the two spheres, in turn, are equated with $\cancel{S}$ and A, the barred subject (the subject that cannot entirely know itself) and the great Other, the conscious and the unconscious. *Objet a* conforms to the intermediate zone (the area of *Spaltung*) between them, and the barred subject's relation to that *objet a* is precisely one of underestimation and overestimation, $\cancel{S} \Diamond a$, the algorithm of the fantasm.

In *Séminaire XI,* Lacan identifies this intermediate fantasmic zone as where separation of the subject—its detachment from the mother—takes place. In *Séminaire XIV,* he identifies this area with the preconscious and, in line with orthodox Freudianism, as the place where fantasy occurs. For very small infants, however, the surface of the breasts is still experienced in such a way that the infant cannot distinguish desire from reality and therefore has to experience the mother's body from "beyond the love object"—in terms of an *objet a* that is not to be considered a thing or even a condition, but a trait that signifies or marks a relation. It is this trait that instantiates what Lacan now calls the *logic of the fantasm,* by which he means a logic that grammatically transforms a fantasm into a proposition with a subject and predicate. This logic, however, only follows a prior stage in which the fantasy that occurs in the overlap of the two circles or breasts has its source in the unitary trait (of the mother, between the two breasts) that precedes the infant's coming into its own as a subject. That is, in primary narcissism the mother is not yet capable of being grammatically interpolated as an object by the infant.

However, there will come a time when the child can objectivize and experience the mother's body as divided or unified by those two realms, desire and reality. No doubt, Lacan hasn't departed altogether from Freud's *Three Essays on Sexuality* or from his considerations of the reality principle. But Lacan has drastically redirected us in a way that negotiates what in Freud and Melanie Klein is a rather mysterious and dark theoretical passage, the transition from the pre-Oedipal to the Oedipal stage. Also, Lacan avoids the rather mechanistic accounts of frustration and symbolization which appear in Freud. For Lacan is interested in seeing the mother's body not merely as a binary site in which pleasure and unpleasure are experienced but as a coincidence of reality and desire whose divisibility into two spheres (always already given, by the mother's anatomy) means that a cut or rupture has been introduced. This cut defines the mother's body as a lost unity and, as such, suggests that something exists beyond the love object. It is from the opening introduced here that objects later borrow the function of their cause. Lacan also differs from Freud in postulating an object that is not simply a metaphor or surrogate for what the child wants but cannot have—the oceanic experience of primary narcissism—but a trait or trace of splitting (difference) whose consequence is the awareness of an object that cannot come to appearance as anything in and of itself even if it is conceivable as something that exists beyond the love object and outside the field of the Imaginary.

The *objet a* is therefore capable of being a fantasmic marker of the imaginary relationship that results from having had to recognize and objectivize the object of one's desire in the real world. *Objet a* does not substitute for the mother so much as it *accompanies* the child's recognition of her as a love object. In *objet a* the subject finds its congruity or wholeness with the mother even though *objet a* is alienated from what Lacan sarcastically calls Das-Ein (Heideggerian *Dasein*).

Objet a (or object aleph) is precisely what comes first for each of us insofar as it is the object with which we seek our unalienated and unified relationship to all things. It is, to put matters a bit otherwise, *object aletheia*, that unitary thing which ought to deliver us over to the truth, or which ought to give us what we want. *Objet a,* however, always marks that desire in the place where it manifests itself as "absent object," or, when we perceive it in the possession of others, "the object of the other." Crucial to this way of thinking the *objet a* is that Lacan is addressing not how one self-consciously pursues an obscure object-of-desire but rather how all object relations are based on a pre-reflective or pre-Oedipal moment in which the unitary trait is given, as it were, from birth as an arche-trace outside our field of vision and yet not altogether unknown to us.

Expanding on the seminars on identification and the four fundamental concepts, Lacan considers at length how the logic of the two overlapping circles or breasts can be superimposed on an interpretation of Descartes. This is the point at which the pre-reflective self is mapped onto the reflective self of Cartesian philosophy. Lacan's thoughts on Descartes build on a lecture delivered in the Descartes Amphithéâtre at the Sorbonne in 1957—"L'Instance de la lettre dans l'inconscient ou la raison depuis Freud [The agency of the letter in the unconscious, or reason since Freud]." Already there Lacan switches back and forth from the Latin *Cogito ergo sum* to the French "Je pense, donc je suis." Addressing that proposition, Lacan writes: "Is the place that I occupy as the subject of a signifier concentric or excentric, in relation to the place I occupy as subject of the signified?—that is the question. It is not a question of knowing whether I speak of myself in a way that conforms to what I am, but rather of knowing whether I am the same as that of which I speak. And it is not at all appropriate to use the word 'thought' here." In other words, Lacan sees a rift between two entities or sets, "I think" and "therefore I am," because the "cogito" is not sufficient to function as the cause (the "ergo" or "donc") which links the cogitans (that which thinks) to the cogitatum (the object of thought). Lacan's obvious intent is to revise Descartes's proposition about consciousness by introducing the Freudian unconscious, whose foundational analogue to Descartes is "Wo es war, soll Ich Werden." The following Lacanian permutations result: "I think where I am not, therefore I am where I do not think" and "I am not wherever I am the plaything of my thought: I think of what I am where I do not think to think."[73] These are the propositions Descartes has to repress in order for conscious experience to dominate. But Lacan wants to inquire into such formulations in order to determine whether the place one occupies as subject of the signifier is excentric or concentric with the subject of the signified. In the seminar on the fantasm we learn that this is but a repetition of the anaclitic relation of the infant to the mother, except that in the Cartesian context the subject is constituted within the propositions of logic.

Le Séminaire XIV: Logique du fantasme suggests that we think of the spheres of desire and reality in terms of two logical propositions, Cogito ergo sum and Cogito ergo es. Drawing on the earlier remarks on the two breasts, which the infant cannot have at the same time, Lacan notes that Cogito and sum are in a similar relationship. Ergo is suspect, Lacan now says in this new context, because it presupposes an unproblematic relationship between "thinking" and "being." That is, ergo veils the objet a or trait, which suggests the noncoincidence of the Cogito with all that it presumes to encompass, including the Freudian es. Hinting at Martin Heidegger, who in the pages on Descartes in Nietzsche argues that Descartes's subject-centered rationalism reflects a forgetting of the difference between being and Being, Lacan argues that Descartes intentionally forgets the pathos that marks the gap between thinking and being. Like Heidegger, Lacan questions the "essential cohesion" supplied by the introduction of a self-representing subjectivity that takes itself as the measure for every object that comes into its field of vision, a point that reinforces the early seminars. Heidegger puts this as follows in Nietzsche: "Because the representing person has already come on the scene, along with what has been represented within representation, there lies in every representing the essential possibility that the representing itself take place within the scope of the one representing."[74] Everything is secured by a supposedly unobtrusive "co-representation" of the subject, which facilitates the

73. Lacan, Écrits, p. 166.
74. Martin Heidegger, Nietzsche, vol. 4, trans. David Krell (New York: Harper-Collins, 1991), p. 108.

movement from thinking to being, thoughts to objects. In Lacan, the mirror contrivances of the early seminars and the overlapping circles of the seminar on the fantasm serve to dismantle Cartesian "co-representation."

Lacan also argues that the Cartesian *Cogito* doubts or delegitimizes the Other (God, Being, Spirit) even as it substitutes a structure that it experiences as real, namely a rational or logical structure. This substitution is, in fact, a repression of the Other, a repression in which the occulted Other returns as *Cogito*. This negated Other, however, will leave its mark on Descartes's "Je pense, donc je suis" by insinuating a variant, namely, "Je ne pense pas, je ne suis pas." This "Je" is the Other that haunts Descartes's "Je pense, donc je suis" and is the Other that writes itself *Cogito ergo es* in place of *Cogito ergo sum*. If in Descartes *Cogito* and *sum* belong to sets whose overlap is affirmed (*ergo*), *Cogito* and *es* are sets whose conjunction is not recognized or known about. Lacan's tactic is to modify these relationships by means of the formula S (Ⱥ) in which the conjunction of the *Cogito* with the Other is affirmed at the expense of the conjunction of *Cogito* and *sum*. Hence as the Other comes to pass as a barred (inaccessible) Other, the Subject is exposed as alienated in terms of its dependency on a signifier (the logical proposition, "Je pense, donc je suis"). But since the Other is barred, the subject cannot know the meaning of that signifier or proposition, since this signifier or proposition only makes sense from a Lacanian perspective in relation to the subject's desire, which requires verification by the Other. If we recall Lacan's seminars on *Hamlet*, the analogue to the signifier in Descartes would be Hamlet's "To be or not to be" speech, which also discloses the subject as alienated in terms of his dependency on a signifier whose truth can only be verified by an Other who is excluded in the very articulation of the signifier, "To be or not to be." The logic of the fantasm, then, pertains to what has been logically left out of the proposition or is logically lacking in the signifier: the inscription of an absence of the Other.

At about midpoint in *Le Séminaire XIV: Logique du fantasme*, Lacan asks André Green to summarize and develop some of the ideas that have been presented. Green's remarks are especially interesting in that they address the phylogenetic fantasms (primal scenes, castration, seduction) of Freud's *Introductory Lectures* as "key signifiers." In other words, whereas such originary fantasms have traditionally been considered as scenes, Green presents them as signifiers in whose repetition the occultation between S and A is established even as they are linked by means of overlap. Green, in thinking of the drives, comments that repetition as essence of the pulsional function marks a reprise of a temporality at the level of the subject which he calls impersonal. This, he says, is what belongs to the genetic. In everything that would pass as if in a synchronic moment, we would find a division of the subject which Freud introduces as the temporality of the subject, an other time which is not the same, which Green calls, in accordance with Lacanian terminology, the time of the Other. The fantasm, then, is that repeated signifier in which the temporality of the subject appears as divided, as, once more, the overlapping of two zones whose space of intersection is occulted.

But Green also sees the fantasm as a merging of two different bodies that do and do not coincide. In alluding to paintings by René Magritte, among them "Song of Love," he points to central figures that are half-fish, half-human. He speaks of "l'entre deux corps," which are not one because each construction is not fully "sunk" into the other. The fantasm of the fish-human is not the scene in and of itself but the "signifier," which travels the circuit of the two constructions and, as such, sutures them to the point that we cannot extrapolate one figure from the other even as we cannot think them entirely within the same construction. Magritte's scene cannot be said to take to the side of one thing or another; rather, it is traversed or crossed by a signifier whose circuit menaces the construction. But what is this signifier? Green gives several examples: suture, concatenation, metonymy, and linearity. Although the subject may rely on such signifiers (or figures) for support, these signifiers also introduce nonsense and breakdowns in meaning, what we might call a discourse of the lapse. The fantasm is to be understood as a production within this signifying process. As Lacan will explain later in the seminar, an *objet a* emerges as the effect of a repetition of the signifier which implies some break, which if rectified can resolve or unify an image or signifying construction in such a way that it is no longer disturbing. Readers may find this reminiscent of Freud's letters to Fliess wherein there is talk of the repetition of an absence that analysis would like to complete or fill in for the sake of explaining and resolving an aspect of the trauma which the patient has forgotten. But, in fact, this is not quite what Lacan has in mind. For him *objet a* is constructed by the analysand as the logical effect of a proposition that attempts to exclude it. That is, for Lacan the *objet a* is not to be found in the absence or hole that the analysand has so conveniently prepared for the analyst, but is to be uncovered in the place where the subject resists analysis, in the case of Descartes, in "Je pense, donc je suis." It is in the repetition of this proposition or signifier that the estrangement of the subject from the unconscious is maintained even as the Eulerian overlap between *Cogito ergo sum* and *Cogito ergo es* is effected under the auspices of *objet a*.

In the latter sessions of *Logique du fantasme* Lacan turns to sexual perversions, a turn reminiscent of concerns broached in much earlier seminars, except that here Lacan considers the economy of psychoanalytical relationships in terms of overlapping topologies, in this case, the interpersonal topology of selves and others. It is here that we see the fruition of Lacan's topological turn in *Le Séminaire IX: L'Identification*, which only in *Le Séminaire XIV* manages to reinscribe all materials laid out prior to the 1960s. The fantasm is now seen as the signifier that traverses how the perverse subject comprehends the jouissance of another person. How is the perverse subject "interested" in the other's pleasure? Lacan broaches this topic by arguing that the nonlocalizability of jouissance in the female introduces the problem of there not being a proper place in her body for the experience of the instinctual aims. The perverse subject—who in this case is by definition male—takes to the side of the female in that the zone proper to his jouissance is not locatable; however, unlike the female, the perverse subject has opted to localize pleasure in an "Other" zone than the one "proper" to jouissance. For the perverse subject pleasure does not traverse the entirety of the body, but only concerns a single body part or zone, which has been overvalued (*objet a*). The perverse subject, then, does not try to identify with an Other in terms of a free exchange of pleasure, but valorizes a particular thing (*objet a*) that, for him, represents the truth of his existence as a being who feels pleasure. Lacan formulates this condition as follows: S $(\cancel{A}) \rightleftharpoons \cancel{\$} \lozenge$ a.

The alienated relationship between the subject and the barred Other parallels that of the divided subject in its relationship to the *objet a*.

Consequently, the Symbolic repeats the Imaginary, since in each instance, the "$\cancel{A}$" or "a" represents something other from which the subject is fundamentally alienated and yet on which the subject is entirely dependent for what Lacan calls its Dasein (Das Ein). The fantasm appears in the sigil of the diamond, which represents both the subject's over- and undervaluation of the imaginary object and also its inclusion and exclusion in terms of what the subject experiences as real. The diamond represents the juncture of the unconscious and the conscious, a juncture the subject perceives as the *objet a*, which marks both the unitary trait of the Other and the disunified or alienated condition of the subject in a way that one might call undecidable. Throughout Lacan's analysis one needs to be aware that the primary narcissistic topology of the mother's breasts has merely been repeated as if it were the signifier of dependency on which a perverse construction of pleasure relies. Moreover, the perverse zone of pleasure can be seen as merely a fantasmatic substitution or displacement of the *objet a* which points to the imaginary coincidence of the two breasts as that place where the subject has been alienated.

In *Le Séminaire XV: L'Acte psychanalytique*, 1967–1968, Lacan attempts a total remapping of his theoretical work of the 1960s according to a geometry of interpenetrating equilateral triangles. (See figure 3.) Imagine an equilateral triangle at whose apex is the Symbolic and at whose base on the left is the Imaginary and on the right is the Real. Within that triangle imagine an inverted equilateral triangle whose apex ($\cancel{S}$) bisects the base of the larger triangle. The base of the inverted triangle bisects the left slope of the large triangle at point *objet a* and the the right slope of the large triangle at point "unitary trait." What we find, then, is that the *objet a* mediates the slope of the Symbolic and the Imaginary, the unitary trait mediates the slope of the Symbolic and the Real, and the divided subject mediates the Imaginary and the Real. The *objet a* is the fantasmic link between the unconscious (Symbolic) and preconscious (Imaginary); the unitary trait enables us to identify the Real with the Symbolic (kinship, race, national identity); and the divided subject experiences the Real in terms of Imaginary or narcissistic relations (the gaze, identification, the ego ideal, and so on). Yet the *objet a*, the unitary trait, and the divided subject all lean on an excluded third term in the three orders of Symbolic, Imaginary, and

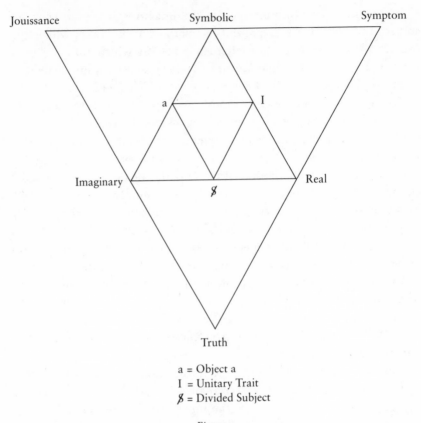

a = Object a
I = Unitary Trait
$ = Divided Subject

Figure 3.

Real. That is, *objet a,* situated between the Symbolic and the Imaginary, is supported by the Real; the unitary trait, situated between the Symbolic and the Real, is supported by the Imaginary; and the barred subject, situated between the Real and the Imaginary, is supported by the Symbolic. Thus the unitary trait and *objet a* are both inscribed in the relationship between the Imaginary and the Real and, to that extent, overlap. In short, for the divided subject, who is always already inscribed in this relationship between the Imaginary and the Real, the unitary trait and *objet a* will appear as one, though in fact this is merely a coincidence: the unitary trait always precedes the object as its arche-trace (its "cause").

Le Séminaire XV: L'Acte psychanalytique also discloses that in retrospect, one should understand *Le Séminaire IX* (on identification) as an explication of the unitary trait mediating the Symbolic and the Real, *Le Séminaire XI* (on the four fundamental concepts) as an explication of the barred or divided subject mediating the Real and the Imaginary, and *Le Séminaire XIV* (on the fantasm) as an explication of how the *objet a* mediates the Imaginary and the Symbolic. In *Le Séminaire XV,* Lacan maps out the trajectory of future seminars by drawing an even larger inverted triangle around the triangle of the Symbolic, the Imaginary, and the Real. The Symbolic mediates pleasure and the symptom; the Imaginary mediates pleasure and truth; and the Real mediates the symptom and truth.

Instead of producing a single account or model of the fantasm, Lacan has actually developed a number of approaches that pertain to various psychoanalytical perspectives: the gaze, the object of desire, imagined scenes, symbolic castration, repetition, perversion, the noncoincidences of reality and desire, *Cogito* and *es,* and the relation of the fantasm to the overall topology of what Lacan would later call R.S.I. (the Real, Symbolic, and Imaginary). As the triangular graphs of *Le Séminaire XV* demonstrate, Lacan embraced a logocentric geometry not foreign to mystics. Indeed, Lacan himself says in *Le Séminaire XXII: R.S.I.* that his tripartite topology is an example of *les noms du père,* which is to say, the holy names of the trinity. To this extent, Lacan purposely made himself vulnerable to attack by critics who would accuse him of metaphysics. Yet Lacan's triadic structures set up a considerable interplay of structural permutations that in and of themselves dismantle rigid formal relations even as they preserve the formal model more or less intact as a logic. At the risk of being reductive, one might well wonder whether these formal structures are not in and of themselves instances of what Lacan calls the logic of the fantasm. In other words, one might well ask whether our relation to these maps or figures does not replicate a certain dependency on the signifier of an Other. Clearly, the mathematical field of topology theory eventually dominated Lacan's thinking in the 1970s, because it allowed for more plasticity than equilateral triangles and offered a much wider range of permutations with which to continue to problematize questions of congruity, adequation, consistency, and identification. Indeed, the knots of topology theory are used in the hopes that they will expose aspects of the elusive *trait unaire,* which during the early 1960s had suggested itself to Lacan as a limit where the oppositional dialectic between identity and difference was exceeded. *Le Séminaire XIV* (on the fantasm), which follows on this insight, is but preliminary to that even more radical inquiry into identification and alienation, namely the theory of the Borromean knot.

Along the way to that exposition, Lacan had, independently of other thinkers, painstakingly established an object relation—the *objet a*—that followed the logic of an arche-trace retroactively posited at the origin of a psychological phenomenon to which it was but the aftereffect. It is in terms of this effect of retroaction that as a concept the *objet a* acceded to a fantasmatic condition of a philosophical or theoretical significance that more than merely anticipated the passages on the trace by Jacques Derrida in *De la grammatologie* (hence Lacan's early enthusiasm for this study). Indeed, it is not implausible to say that *objet a* occupies a status akin to the Derridean notion of *la différance,* since the *objet a* is the effect of a deconstruction of identification and alienation which Lacan had undertaken with reference to symbolic logic and topology theory ever since the delivery of *Le Séminaire IX* in 1961. This important dimension of Lacan's thought is not very well reflected in *Écrits,* which, in general, represents an earlier state of psychoanalytical theorizing focused chiefly on occasional papers and, in the case of the major essays, on the seminars of the late 1950s.

It should also be said that in line with the expanded agenda in *Le Séminaire XV* (on the psychoanalytic act), Lacan would increasingly turn to the question of female sexuality and the inadequation of a relation between the sexes. By the 1970s, he said that, in fact, there is no sexual relation. To a large extent, this statement is an elaboration of the diamond or *poinçon* of the fantasm and demand of the Other in which the problematic of identity and difference has been systematically dismantled, leaving in its wake a nondialectical relation between the unifying trait and alienation, which in *Le Séminaire XX: Encore, 1972–1973,* Lacan tried to reformulate in terms of female sexuality (woman as barred other in the unconscious locus of pleasure), identification across sexual difference (the imaginary phallus), and topology or knot theory (the *trait unaire* of different topologies). In the seminars that followed, Lacan returned to questions of identification outlined over a decade earlier in *Le Séminaire IX* (on identification), which marked such an important turning point for his thought.

The Fantasm according to Laplanche and Pontalis

While Lacan was improvising very complex and ground-breaking theories of the fantasm with detours into set theory, symbolic logic, Renaissance painting, seventeenth-century philosophy, and Heidegger, Jean Laplanche and J.-B. Pontalis, former students of Lacan's in the late 1950s, more or less rejected such a path in favor of a rather orthodox theory that has much more in common with the thought of Eugénie Sokolnicka than with that of Jacques Lacan. Nevertheless, their work has been very influential and represents what one might call a mainstream position within those psychoanalytical circles that are, strictly speaking, outside of Lacan's direct influence. Historically, both Laplanche and Pontalis represent less an attempt to break with the past than a means of bringing the entire history of French psychoanalysis into some theoretical rapport so that insights into psychoanalysis from before World War II might be reconciled with structuralism.

"Fantasme originaire, fantasmes des origines, origine du fantasme" was published by Jean Laplanche and J.-B. Pontalis in *Les Temps Modernes* in 1964. In it they carefully reconstruct the many positions Freud took on the question of fantasy and, in particular, its relationship with sexuality. They notice that the seduction theory "is Freud's first and sole attempt to establish an intrinsic relationship between repression and sexuality" and that Freud "finds the mainspring of this relationship not in any 'content,' but in the temporal characteristics of human sexuality, which make it a privileged battlefield between both too much and too little excitation, both too early and too late occurrence of the event" (p. 5). Laplanche and Pontalis are very sensitive to the asynchronous condition of the subject and pay close attention to how it receives its "sexual existence" from without—from the adult world—before a distinction between a within and without has been achieved. Seduction, therefore, occurs when one is in a "pre-subjectal" state, a state approximating Lacan's anti-Cartesian formulations in *Le Séminaire XIV: Logique du fantasme*. Freud, of course, discarded seduction theory and all the questions concerning the introduction of seduction from without. Instead, he turned to the endogenous question of the sexual drive; however, according to Laplanche and Pontalis, this turn only marked a shift in prioritizing oppositions of subject-object, constitution-event, internal-external, and imaginary-real.

> This would suggest the following paradox: at the very moment when fantasy, the fundamental object of psychoanalysis, is discovered, it is in danger of seeing its true nature obscured by the emphasis on an endogenous reality, sexuality, which is itself supposed to be in conflict with a normative, prohibitory external reality, which imposes on it various disguises. We have indeed the fantasy, in the sense of a product of the imagination, but we have lost the structure. Inversely, with the seduction theory we had, if not the theory, at least an *intuition* of the structure (seduction appearing as an almost universal datum, which in any case transcended both the event and, so to speak, its protagonists). The ability to elaborate the fantasy was, however, if not unknown, at least underestimated.[75]

For Laplanche and Pontalis the dissonance between Freud's theories of endogenous sexuality, which dissimulates representations and obscures structure, and seduction theory, which poses a structure at the same time that it loses sight of the particulars associated with endogenous reality, will require supplementary theories such as that of the Oedipus complex (a variant of seduction theory) and that of primal fantasies, which are inherited memory traces associated with endogenous sexuality. Such theories, the authors argue, are still a prisoner of the opposition between event and constitution, datum and structure. But if that is so, how then are we to overcome this impasse?

Laplanche and Pontalis take a giant step back in history to early Freudian analysts such as Eugénie Sokolnicka and Marie Bonaparte in suggesting that there are "originary fantasies" that lie beyond the history of the subject but nevertheless within it, as well. "A kind of

---

75. Laplanche and Pontalis, "Fantasy and the Origins of Sexuality," p. 7.

language and a symbolic sequence, but loaded with elements of imagination; a structure, but activated by contingent elements. As such it is characterized by certain traits which make it difficult to assimilate to a purely transcendental schema, even if it provides the possibility of experience." The originary fantasies are limited in kind to castration, seduction, and the primal scene of coitus between the parents. "Like myths, they claim to provide a representation of, and a solution to, the major enigmas which confront the child," though, of course, they can signify only retroactively, which is to say, at a time other than when they first emerge. "Fantasies of origins: the primal scene pictures the origin of the individual; fantasies of seduction, the origin and upsurge of sexuality; fantasies of castration, the origin of the difference between the sexes." The content or themes of these originary fantasies, therefore, are iterated as the very structure of their origination, which is nothing less than the structure of difference without which the subject could not come into existence as subject. Although Laplanche and Pontalis are very much aware that this understanding of originary fantasy owes some debt to Lacan's notion of the Symbolic, if not to his idea that the unconscious is structured like a language, they nevertheless distance themselves from this theory by means of historicizing their account within the context of Freud's Standard Edition. Taking a more orthodox Freudian orientation as their guide, they distinguish between daydreams, in which the "scenario is basically in the first person, and the subject's place clear and invariable" (the structure is organized by the secondary process), and "original fantasy," which is "characterized by the absence of subjectivization" even as "the subject is present *in* the scene." Moreover, Laplanche and Pontalis accept much of Susan Isaacs's thesis in her 1948 article, "The Nature and Function of Fantasy," that "fantasy is the direct expression of a drive" and that both drive and fantasy are of a "subjective intentionality" that is inseparable from its object. As Laplanche and Pontalis conclude from Isaacs, "One is therefore obliged to provide every mental operation with an underlying fantasy which can itself be reduced on principle to an instinctual aim." The interest in Isaacs correlates with Laplanche and Pontalis's belief that originary fantasies are to be associated with autoeroticism in the young child, a moment when sexuality moves into the field of fantasy. Autoerotic satisfaction is said to be "the product

of the anarchic activity of partial drives, closely linked with the excitation of specific erogenous zones." It is not part of a "global" pleasure
but of a "fragmented pleasure, an organ pleasure [*Organlust*] and
strictly localized." It is at this juncture that fantasy interrupts, that it
mediates between the source and aim of pleasure even though the object
of pleasure has been lost. In this account, Laplanche and Pontalis rely
on absence and the role that fantasy plays in compensating for this
loss. They insist that if the origin of fantasy is to be found in autoero-
tism, it is not the object of desire, but its setting. "In fantasy the subject
does not pursue the object or its sign: he appears caught up himself in
the sequence of images. He forms no representation of the desired
object, but is himself represented as participating in the scene although,
in the earliest forms of fantasy, he cannot be assigned any fixed place
in it." Here, too, fantasy discloses a logical structure in so far as the
subject appears in a desubjectivized form in "the very syntax of the
sequence in question." Furthermore, to the extent that desire is not
merely a part of the drives but articulated logically into the fantasy
structure, desire is "a favored spot for the most primitive defense
reactions."[76]

Laplanche and Pontalis, then, bring into relationship the theories of
the first generation of French Freudians with a somewhat structuralist
bent that avoids the kind of psychoanalytical overhaul attempted by
Lacan. Laplanche and Pontalis carefully preserve the idea, maintained
by early analysts such as Sokolnicka, of the fantasm as autoerotic and
invariant, though they also show how the fantasm takes place in Freud
as a structural or theoretical weak point that does not satisfactorily
adapt to certain binary logical oppositions. Nevertheless, Laplanche
and Pontalis do make the Lacanian turn of decentering the subject and
point out that the subject appears not in control of the fantasm as if
it were a narrative, but as desubjectivized, which is to say, in the syntax
of "the sequence in question." In this sense, Laplanche and Pontalis
succeed, however modestly, in reorienting a theory of the fantasm
toward some theoretical bearings that break with the older philosophical presuppositions entertained by analysts before World War II.

76. Ibid., pp. 10, 11, 13, 14, 16, 17.

The most interesting analyses of fantasmic constructions by French analysts in recent years have all been influenced by Lacanian analysis. Serge Leclaire, Guy Rosolato, Eugénie Lemoine-Luccioni, André Green, Rosine and Robert Lefort, Michelle Montrelay, Charles Méla, and Contardo Calligaris have all contributed very important work on this subject.[77] One of the obvious questions for some of these analysts has been how to apply Lacan's very difficult and pathbreaking theories to clinical cases. Other analysts, such as Méla and Green, have considered how to apply these theories to literature. This necessitates not only systematizing Lacan's theoretical improvisations, which, in fact, are quite slippery, but also connecting them with clinical or artistic examples. Other researchers, such as Nicolas Abraham, Maria Torok, Pierre Fédida, Masud Khan, Jean Starobinski, and Jacques Derrida, have worked independently, though not without cognizance of Lacan's general direction.[78] Although Abraham worked independently of Lacan, his theory of the phantom is well anticipated by Lacan's *Séminaire VI: Le Désir et son interprétation,* and although Abraham's strategic identification with Kleinian analysis and avoidance of Lacan's elaborations of the 1960s allowed for new explorations into the question of the "crypt," even these dovetailed with much that Lacan wrote. For example, in the Euler circles that so interested Lacan one has the formation of a cryptlike structure in the overlapping of topological regions. Or, again, in Abraham's interest in the Jonah complex one finds a not-so-distant variant of Lacan's conception of Hamlet who overshoots the Other in order to appeal to a Law beyond the Law or Other of the Other, which, according to Lacan, is self-defeating. Derrida's *Glas,* similarly, concerns fantasmic constructions and in so doing raises ques-

---

77. Serge Leclaire, *Psychanalyser* (Paris: Seuil, 1968); Guy Rosolato, *Essais sur le symbolisme* (Paris: Gallimard, 1969); Eugénie Lemoine-Luccioni, *Le Rêve du cosmonaute* (Paris: Seuil, 1980); André Green, *La Folie privée* (Paris: Gallimard, 1990); Rosine Lefort and Robert Lefort, *Les Structures de la psychose* (Paris: Seuil, 1988); Michelle Montrelay, *L'Ombre et le nom* (Paris: Minuit, 1977); Charles Méla, *Blanchefleur et le saint homme ou la semblance des reliques* (Paris: Seuil, 1979); Contardo Calligaris, *Hypothèse sur le fantasme* (Paris: Seuil, 1983).

78. Pierre Fédida, *L'Absence* (Paris: Gallimard, 1978); Masud Khan, *Le Soi cachée* (Paris: Gallimard, 1984); Jean Starobinski, *Montaigne en mouvement* (Paris: Gallimard, 1982); Jacques Derrida, *La Carte postale* (Paris: Flammarion, 1980).

tions concerning castration and circumcision. Although one cannot fault Derrida for not having access to Lacan's seminar on anxiety, it is curious, in retrospect, how much of Derrida's discussion is more than just anticipated by Lacan's lengthy lectures on circumcision among the Ancient Hebrews. What is anxiety? Lacan asked. It is the Heideggerian being toward death, what Derrida radically renames *glas*. In the United States, critics such as Shoshana Felman, Ned Lukacher, Lawrence Rickels, Avital Ronell, and Diane Sadoff have made interesting applications of French theories on the fantasm. The chapters that follow are intended to add to this literature by developing applied analyses that make their own contributions to both specific cultural works and, retroactively, to the theoretical materials themselves.

2

Staging: *Mont Blanc*

Mother of this unfathomable world!
Favor my solemn song, for I have loved
Thee ever, and thee only; I have watched
Thy shadow, and the darkness of thy steps,
And my heart ever gazes on the depth
Of thy deep mysteries.

—Percy Bysshe Shelley, *Alastor*

How can we envisage a teleology of subjectivity which
would have been subjected to the critical examination of a
Freudian archaeology? It would be a progressive construction of the forms of the spirit, after the manner of Hegel's
Phenomenology of Spirit, but one which, to a greater extent
than in Hegel, would unfold on the very terrain of the
regressive analysis of the forms of desire.

—Paul Ricoeur, "The Question of the Subject."

It may have occurred to Percy Bysshe Shelley, who came to Plato in a
skeptical frame of mind,[1] that in the famous allegory of the cave which
Socrates relates (*Republic,* Book VII), the cave itself is a representation
that, like the shadows cast on an interior wall by means of fire and
human shapes (both natural and fabricated), blocks us from seeing the
Real. And yet this very image of the cave is a forum, opening, or stage
by means of which Socrates inspires Glaucon with the knowledge of
the pure forms, of that reality men are bound never to see. Only by
means of the cave image, itself but a prop held up by the men who
walk past the wall, a prop carried here by the philosopher before his

1. Shelley's skepticism with reference to Plato is argued in C. E. Pulos, *The Deep
Truth* (Lincoln: University of Nebraska Press, 1954).

pupil, can Glaucon respond to the eager instructor, "All this I see." So much, then, depends on a stage prop, on the theatricalization of philosophy. Socrates holds up an image, illuminates it by allegorical extension, and on a wall or mental screen a shadow is perceived—the doctrine of pure forms.

Most interesting is how a prop such as the cave image can suddenly turn into a stage, how an image, itself framed, can immediately stage itself as stage and in that way absent itself or disappear from the viewer's consciousness as image, object, or prop. We recall that Socrates begins the allegory by saying to Glaucon, "Picture men dwelling in a sort of subterranean cavern ... " The word "picture" frames, stages, or encloses the image of the cavern, but the cavern will in turn stage or frame other images. What is most peculiar is that Glaucon never calls attention to this bit of Platonic trompe l'oeil, this way of making image into theater, prop into stage.

I started out by asking whether Shelley might not have been aware of this Socratic way of seeing, because, as James Rieger notices in *The Mutiny Within,* when Shelly tries to view an object as it really is, "he either screens the dominant image or takes its measure against a frame in the foreground. Most characteristically, he establishes perspective by looking *through* one thing *towards* another."[2] In a letter to Thomas Peacock dated March 23, 1819, Shelley writes, "I see the radiant Orion through the mighty columns of the temple of Concord."[3] Like the cave image in *The Republic,* the temple functions as an image, but as one that also disappears as it frames or stages an image that appears as if from within, the radiant Orion. Of course, there is nothing remarkable about seeing one thing through another in this way. But when one encounters the following passage from *Alastor,* this mode of seeing may seem less familiar:

> The Oak,
> Expanding its immense and knotty arms,
> Embraces the light beech. The pyramids
> Of the tall cedar overarching, frame

2. James Regier, *The Mutiny Within* (New York: Braziller, 1967), p. 92.
3. Cited in ibid., p. 92.

Most solemn domes within, and far below,
Like clouds suspended in an emerald sky,
The ash and the acacia floating hang
Tremulous and pale ...

In such passages it is clear that images function as frames, and sometimes for images that could be said to be specular doubles. The oak
embraces the beech, but in doing so reminds us that it is a tree framed
by a tree that we are seeing there, a tree at once embedded and embedding, imaged forth and framing. Similarly the "pyramids" are said to
"frame" the "domes within." Then one notices in the comparison
between the clouds suspended or framed in an emerald sky and the
ash and acacia, that it is through the emerald sky that these tree-clouds
are to be envisioned. It is not so much that Shelley depends on the
strict correspondence or analogy between images in order to make
comparisons, something that is rather obvious in the example above,
but that he *stages* his similes by making one image the frame, set, or
screen on or through which another image is viewed. The effect of such
vision is fantasmic, a point Shelley himself recognizes toward the end
of *Alastor,* in an address to the Poet who has died: "Thou canst no
longer know or love the shapes / Of this fantasmal scene ..." (696–
97). Indeed, it is Shelley's staging mechanism, what amounts to a poetic
mode of ocular embedding and dissolution of imagery, that carries us
from the natural to the supernatural, from the canny to the uncanny,
from the image to the phantom of spirit.

Such phantomization is already there in the cavern mentioned by
Socrates, on the wall which is screening the shadows. And one might
argue that the force of Socrates' allegory depends on an image that
knows how to fade into a frame, that the phantomization Glaucon
"sees" in the image of the cave is the consequence of the staging enacted
by the image, a staging that counts on the dissolution or phantomization of an image in order that we can see through it, or, to put it
another way, in order that we can see on the image's faded surface
something else. The image fades, then, and in doing so makes us "forget" this image even as we use it to see something else. What makes
the image fantasmic or powerful in its effect on us is the fact that even

if we can forget it, the image's impression remains. In fact, this impression "houses" or "supports" ("props" is the best term, perhaps) the gaze of the reader, the inquiry of the pupil Glaucon.

We are close to an observation of Geoffrey Hartman's: images serve "to stabilize a fantasm or to frame a fantasy."[4] This is implicit in Sigmund Freud's report of what happened to a small child who had been exposed on repeated occasions to the picture of a wolf, an image that can be seen with or through like a kind of optic glass and thus can frame what will become a traumatic fantasy, a nightmare about six or seven wolves in a tree: "I dreamt that it was night and that I was lying in my bed. (My bed stood with its foot towards the window; in front of the window there was a row of walnut trees. I know it was winter when I had the dream and night-time.) Suddenly the window opened of its own accord, and I was terrified to see that some white wolves were sitting in the big walnut tree in front of the window. There were six or seven of them."[5]

Here the image of the wolf has been phantomized, has faded out, and frames or stages this dream. Although the wolf image has disappeared in its original form, its effect or impression energizes the dream, and it is recollected or repeated six or seven times within the image's little "production," a "production" that is itself seen through a window frame and all because the window can "open of its own accord." Apparently the frame of the wolf image has been metaphorically displaced, figured forth as the window in the dream. Jacques Lacan calls this frame the *cadre du désir* (frame of desire), which, as Catherine Clément notes, is symbolized as the "half-open door, the skylight in the night, the open window."[6] From a Lacanian perspective the fantasm is the frame—that is, the well-known *poinçon* of the $\$ \lozenge$ a algorithm. It is the dissolution of the image into a staging of desire.

If the allegory of the cave allows us to consider what would happen

4. Geoffrey Hartman, *Criticism in the Wilderness* (New Haven: Yale University Press, 1980), p. 36. "I have suggested that the image of Yeats' poem serves to stabilize a phantasm or to frame a fantasy. It is tempting to guess at an equation: the more image, the more fantasy."

5. Sigmund Freud, "History of an Infantile Neurosis," in *The Wolf-Man by the Wolf-Man*, ed. Muriel Gardner (New York: Basic Books, 1971), p. 173.

6. Catherine Clément, *Le Pouvoir des mots* (Paris: Mame, 1973), p. 100.

to a person who could leave the subterranean world, the opening of a window in the Wolf-Man's dream allows the dreamer to open his eyes. It is during analysis that the Wolf-Man recognizes what the open window means, "My eyes suddenly opened," and Freud argues that what the eyes opened on was a memory of something very real, a primal scene of coitus performed *a tergo,* much like wolves. But if the Wolf-Man "sees" his parents making love, he does so only through an image, the fantasmic picture of wolves in a tree. We have noticed that initially the image of a wolf seen in consciousness turns into a stage in sleep, Lacan's "frame of desire." And through this frame we see wolves in a tree. Yet where there was an easy and unpremeditated "dissolve" of the initial wolf image, we discover that there is something more like blockage with the image of the wolves in the tree. Let us say for convenience that what the window in the dream opens on is much like a theatrical backdrop that is extraordinary in one major respect: it is also a theatrical curtain that opens onto another stage behind it, onto an obscene and traumatic spectacle that has already been seen and remembered. Thanks to repression, the moment the window opens of its own accord, like a door in a haunted house, this curtain drops on a most intriguing but frightening spectacle in a bedroom. Yet if the spectacle behind the backdrop is traumatic, so is the image of the protective curtain or backdrop, and thus because of a double bind the dreamer can be said to lose himself in the arras, cannot tell which side of the curtains he is on and cannot differentiate clearly what he has seen behind the curtains from what he sees designed on them. What makes staging pathological in the Wolf-Man's dream is this refusal of an image to be neither fully opaque nor fully transparent, the refusal to fade and the inability to block yet another mise en scène. It is such pathological staging that makes obsession possible.

In the Wolf-Man's dream, then, there is a succession of stagings, and, not only do images frame scenes, but a scene also draws its own curtains, calls for the rematerialization of an image to block (however ineffectively) the dreamer's gaze. Not only fading, then, but blocking or mediation of the image or prop is needed for the kind of theater one encounters in psychoanalysis. This is true as well for philosophy and literature, for there too one posits scenes or acts beyond comprehension that must be staged in order to represent the unrepresentable.

Thus the allegory of the cave attempts to figure forth an Ur-scene of pure forms that the philosopher, not unlike the Wolf-Man, has already "seen" or witnessed. And yet with what curtains or backdrops must the philosopher struggle? Similarly, Shelley's poet in *Alastor* searches for his "vision," which is inaccessible, though representable in terms of a quest in which there occur numerous stagings similar to the kind we encounter in the Wolf-Man's fantasmic experience.

In "Shelley Disfigured," Paul de Man observes that in *The Triumph of Life* the "polarities of waking and sleeping (or remembering or forgetting) are curiously scrambled . . . with those of past and present, of the imagined and the real, of knowing and not knowing." De Man could have been addressing Freud's case history of the Wolf-Man and in particular the dream we have briefly considered. But de Man is reading these lines which Shelley has Rousseau speak:

> So sweet and deep is the oblivious spell;
> And whether life had been before that sleep
> The Heaven which I imagine, or a Hell
>
> Like this harsh world in which I wake to sleep,
> I know not.
>
> (332–35)

"We cannot tell," de Man explains, "the difference between sameness and difference, and this inability to know takes on the form of a pseudo-knowledge which is called forgetting."[7] This is the kind of pseudo-knowledge the Wolf-Man has when he cannot tell which side of the curtain he is on, the kind of knowledge revealed by images that make themselves into undecidable partitions. What is of interest may not be so much the issue of "disfiguration," what de Man calls the loss or fading of a face, the erasure of self-knowledge, but how such a forgetting, manifested in terms of the difficulty of discriminating difference and sameness, gives rise to the kind of staging or framing of desire that we noted in *The Republic*, *Alastor*, and *History of an Infantile Neurosis*. It is in terms of Shelley's fascination with images possessing a

7. Paul de Man, "Shelley Disfigured," in *Deconstruction and Criticism*, ed. Harold Bloom et al. (New York: Seabury, 1979), p. 51.

radical ambivalence concerning the difference of life and death that such a framing or staging not only occurs but does so in an ob-scene, a set or scene that cannot be viewed directly. Moreover, of interest is how the occlusion of an image is invested with a strong regressive tendency that depends on props and stages, a theatrical tendency that, as a matter of fact, has everything to do with what Freud called the *anaclitic,* a leaning of the drive, which will concern itself with a particular mountain in Haute-Savoie.

Perhaps what de Man calls disfiguration has been conceptualized earlier and more theatrically as the "ob-scene" by Philippe Lacoue-Labarthe, who in "La Scène est primitive" writes that "like the female or maternal genitals, death cannot present itself as such, or as Lyotard would say, 'in person.' "[8] Death has to be displaced, shifted, dissimulated, that is to say, forgotten, in order to be represented or viewed, put on stage or "seen" as "scene" and thereby identified or mimicked. Like coitus *a tergo* in the case of the Wolf-Man's history or Medusa's genitals, death is viewed "obscene" or away from its proper and unmediated spectacle. Hyphenating "ob-scene" calls attention to the prefix *ob* (in Latin a preposition meaning in front of, in view of, toward, but also against), which in relation to the "scene" signifies a displacement or removal of a spectacle from the viewer, a distance placed between subject and object. The ob-scene is the scene before the scene or a scene against a scene. To quote Lacoue-Labarthe: "If it is permissible to play on a 'popular' etymology, we might say that death is *ob-scene.* At the very least, Freud is convinced death 'cannot be looked in the face' and that art (like religion) has the privilege of being the beginning of economic representation—that is, of libidinal representation. Death never appears as such, it is in the strict sense *unreprésentable [imprésentable],* or the unrepresentable itself."[9]

Thus any scene representing death merely places itself in front of a scene that properly speaking cannot present itself. To talk about the

8. Philippe Lacoue-Labarthe, "La Scène est primitive," in *Le Sujet de la philosophie* (Paris: Flammarion, 1979), p. 206, and "Theatrum Analyticum," trans. Robert Vollrath and Samuel Weber, in *Glyph* 2 (Baltimore: Johns Hopkins University Press, 1977), p. 135. Lacoue-Labarthe is referring to Lyotard's introduction, "Par delà la représentation," to Anton Ehrenzweig's *Hidden Order of Art* (Paris: Gallimard, 1974).

9. Lacoue-Labarthe, "Theatrum," p. 135.

obscene is to recognize the distance or difference that displaces—in terms of the Freudian sense of staging, dreaming, fantasizing—the mise-en-scène that takes place in front of the primary scene; whatever that may or can be. Such a mise-en-scène is deferred, but is also subject to a disfiguration, to the pseudoknowledge produced by a scene that is but a phantom proxy. Like the backdrop of the wolves sighted by the neurotic child, the mise-en-scène before death is itself subject to phantomization, erasure, or disfiguration, thus allowing itself to open or stage a theatrical production that again only veils that which cannot be represented. Even in the case of the Wolf-Man the curtain opens in this way, sets the stage for the child's gaze by way of recalling a memory of coitus *a tergo,* a primal scene that is viewed as ob-scene in so many senses. The backdrop (or curtain, as I have also called it) is at once opened and closed, presented and removed, known and not known, the same as and different from. It is what Lacoue-Labarthe calls the *theatrum analyticum,* and nowhere is it put to better advantage than in the drama of the romantic period, as Lacoue-Labarthe makes evident in "The Caesura of the Speculative," an essay on Hölderlin's adaptation of *The Antigone.*[10]

Certainly, Shelley's *Prometheus Unbound* is an excellent example of a romantic staging of a death that never manifests itself as anything other than metaphor, vision, tableau, or theater: as a man chained to a precipice who is suffering from having his heart devoured by a vulture, a creature that never gets its pound of flesh no matter how much is taken from the heart of man, as if to insist that death is pure chimera, a limit that displays itself only in terms of delay, deferral, distancing, eternal return, or, to borrow a phrase from Maurice Blanchot that has been much on the mind of Jacques Derrida, an *arrêt de mort,* a death sentence and/or stay of execution.[11] Indeed, much of *Prometheus Unbound* is but the dramatization of this "stay" in which the difference between being put to death and being kept alive is "curiously scrambled." Moreover, this "stay" or refusal, what Blanchot would call a

10. Philippe Lacoue-Labarthe, "The Caesura of the Speculative," in *Glyph* 4 (Baltimore: Johns Hopkins University Press, 1978), pp. 57–85. In French, *Hölderlin: L'Antigone de Sophocle* (Paris: Christian Bourgois, 1978).

11. Maurice Blanchot, *L'Arrêt de mort* (Paris: Gallimard, 1948). The title plays on the double entendre of a sentence or judgment that condemns *and* reprieves.

suspension, is marked all the while by discourse, by the temporality of language. And perhaps Shelley, however indirectly, may be asking in his poetry a question akin to that asked by Blanchot and Derrida: how does one give the sentence of death to language, to the sentence that pronounces sentence itself? What would constitute a "death sentence" in prose, poetry, or drama, for that matter?[12]

No doubt, in *Prometheus Unbound,* the hero is at the *arrêt de mort,* is, like the figures in Blanchot's fiction, suspended in an *écriture du désastre,* but he is also at the *arête de mort,* the ridge or arris of death, while still discoursing, having an *entretien infini,* and right there on the *arête* or peak, that border line (to recall the pertinent essay of Derrida's) or precipice of words.[13] This ridge, we recall, is not just an image, but a kind of stage, a vertical platform on which the drama is played out, on which the hero, Prometheus, is suspended and this "death" represented (repeated) ob-scene. This theatrical rock even speaks as the character Earth in *Prometheus Unbound* and might lead us to consider at length the triumph of Promethean life, were it not that something off-stage or ob-scene, not unlike a faded memory, catches our attention: an "other" *arête, Mont Blanc.*

It is as if *Mont Blanc* anticipates the events of *Prometheus Unbound,* as if desire relays itself back and forth between these two literary sites, each already displaced or displacements, as if one topos is to be seen through another *topos.* In this sense, art is not only chiastic, but also a recurring nightmare about that which cannot appear to us "in person," but only as phantom. This *arête* (ridge, mount, peak, spine, cross-point) may come to be seen as a perpetual shifting, an eternal return to the same as different, an obsession where desire is fixed or pinned down, and precisely there where one has a suspension, not unlike the suspensions in the Wolf-Man's dream. Here the ability to distinguish between identity and difference is lost, for slippage occurs, what de Man in "Shelley Disfigured" calls forgetting, characterized by this sus-

---

12. Jacques Derrida, of course, pursues this question in "Living On: Border Lines," in Bloom et al., eds., *Deconstruction and Criticism.*

13. See Derrida's "Living On: Border Lines" for details on the prolonged play on the words *arête/arrête.* Derrida takes over Blanchot's language in order to examine the supplementary and fantasmic addition of an additional *r,* which has the effect of conflating a noun with a verb.

pension between two sites or scenes (de Man is considering *The Triumph of Life*) at once similar and dissimilar, what I have earlier called a *pathology of staging*. It is a question now of where we are, of a representation that cannot decide a suspended relation and which proposes itself as a repetition (a re-presentation) and therefore as both remembered and not remembered, as present and as lost, visible and invisible. Serge Leclaire in *Démasquer le réel* points out most convincingly that at such points in which the laws of contradiction are suspended, fixated representations make their symptomatic appearances.[14] Suddenly, fantasmic images of power rise up in the thoughts of the patients, and the metapsychological or economic reasons for this are clear: the subject does not want to lose his energy, to break into pieces, but to conserve himself in the monolithic aporia of an axis or crossing point that is endlessly forestalled in the undecidable suspension of an *arrêt de mort* whose herald or emblem is the *arête de mort*. Recall that on the Promethean rock, desire is chained for the purposes of eternal *sparagmos,* repetition, and again, in Blanchot's terms, condemned to speak an infinitely drawn out dialogue, one that is thoroughly fatigued and ends in the full *arrêt,* the sentence that condemns and gives reprieve at the same time, an *arrêt* that, however much it cuts into the sufferer and dismembers him, also keeps him whole and intact, preserves him on the rock eternally.

In *Mont Blanc* the *arrêt/arête* (the suspension and the re-presentation that marks it) figures itself forth most blatantly as a signifier of power, and what is most interesting about this particular representation of the *arrêt* is that it is the major prop or stage on which the discourse of the poem rests, the site or theater for another infinite discourse of subject and object, a dialogue that is very problematic in Shelley, as critics such as Earl Wasserman demonstrate. Wasserman's argument, that for Shelley "the ultimate doctrine of the Intellectual Philosophy is that reality is an undifferentiated unity, neither thought nor thing, and yet both," fits in perfectly with Blanchot's and Derrida's thoughts on an *entretien* that breaks limits, border lines, horizons, that suspends philosophical speculation and throws man into the condition of living out

14. Serge Leclaire, *Démasquer le réel* (Paris: Seuil, 1971), pp. 180–86.

a death sentence.[15] In short, what Shelley believes, according to Wasserman, is that life (thought, discourse, consciousness) and things (matter) cannot be differentiated or confused. Rather, this opposition has to be put out of order.

Wasserman agrees as well that "more precisely, the poem *Mont Blanc* is not lyric but dramatic."[16] And therefore the poem is akin to *Prometheus,* a connection we have already discovered for ourselves. In any case, let us assume for the sake of argument that in *Mont Blanc* the earth speaks, the stage has its say, that the mountain or landscape does not simply support by means of metaphor or allegory a developing consciousness of what amounts to philosophical speculation on sublime sights but serves as a stage that raises or props up the whole problematic of the Promethean suspension between life and death, raises the *arête de mort* as an *arrêt de mort,* as "stays" in a supporting or propping of the impossibility of either life or death. Then it remains for us to investigate how this stage props, or, for our purposes, what the notion of the "prop" signifies for our analysis.

So I will just say one more thing about Shelley's poem: the mountain, a signifier of power and desire, is anaclitic. That is, Mont Blanc is an *étayage,* a supporting or propping up whose function is not unlike the mother's breast as Sigmund Freud and Melanie Klein discuss it in their work on infant sexuality. That is to say, the mountain is not phallic but maternal, like Earth in *Prometheus Unbound,* for it is the Object (Lacan's *objet a*) on which the drives lean. And this is really one of the purposes of my inquiry: to "decide" or "stage" this perhaps silly or frivolous question, put to us by Freudians of an earlier age, as it were, of whether the mount is phallic or maternal; that is, to speak in this gap of gender, in the obscene and on the *arête* where the drives attach themselves and, it must be admitted, save themselves.

Jean Laplanche explains this notion of the leaning of the drive when he writes, "Thus the term *propping* [*étayage*] has been understood ... as a leaning on the *object* [*un appui sur l'objet*], and ultimately a *leaning*

15. Earl Wasserman, *The Subtler Language* (Baltimore: Johns Hopkins University Press, 1959), p. 204.

16. Ibid., p. 208.

on the mother [un appui sur la mère]. . . . The phenomenon Freud describes is a leaning *of the drive [d'appui de la pulsion]*, the fact that emergent sexuality attaches itself to and is propped [*s'étaye*] upon another process which is both similar and profoundly divergent: the sexual is propped upon a nonsexual, vital function or, as Freud formulates it in terms which defy all additional commentary, upon a 'bodily function essential to life.' "[17] Sexuality is ob-scene to the degree that it is a function that imitates another function that is inherently nonsexual. Sexuality leans on the child's experience of sucking the breast for the purposes of nourishment, or, as Freud writes, "Sexual activity attaches itself to functions serving the purposes of self-preservation."[18] But if sexuality leans on a function, it is also propped up by an object, the mother's breast. The sexual drive asserts itself when the breast is removed, when the breast can only serve as a symbolic support, as an image or part-object, when the breast menaces with its absence, its afterimage of the having-been-present. That is to say, the breast makes an appearance, sooner or later, as a representation, and this image is, like Plato's famous cavern, subject to fading or disfiguration. This occurs because the sexual drive defines itself most strongly when the breast reveals itself as the peak of deprivation (*arête de mort*) or the withholding of nourishment, but also as the *arrêt* of deprivation, the pleasures of feeding, the horizon of fulfilled desire, as potentially present even when absent. In this sense the breast is a prop not unlike a stage prop, which serves as a stage set for sexuality, which becomes a theater where the drives can lean, where such drives can play out their scenario using whatever props are at hand. If this sounds odd, recall that a well-known American psychoanalyst, Bertram Lewin, advances precisely this argument when he claims in "Sleep, the Mouth, and the Dream Screen" that the mother's breast is introjected by the infant as a "dream screen" upon which or through which other images present themselves, for particularly after feeding the child sleeps and stages whatever scenes he wishes on the imaginary maternal screen.

17. Jean Laplanche, *Vie et mort en psychanalyse* (Paris: Flammarion, 1970), pp. 30–31. Trans. Jeffrey Mehlman, under the title *Life and Death in Psychoanalysis* (Baltimore: Johns Hopkins University Press, 1976), p. 16.

18. Sigmund Freud, *Three Essays on the Theory of Sexuality* (New York: Harper, 1962), p. 48.

What is significant for Lewin is that adults "regress" at night when they sleep by reenvisioning this screen, by propping or leaning the drives on this fantasmic sheet or curtain, which, as Lewin's patients say, "unfolds" or simply "unrolls." Such an *étayage* is nothing less than a compulsive restaging of a primordial relationship with what Lacan calls the *objet a* (the Mother).[19] And this *objet a,* according to Lacan, comprises the locus of the gaze.

Lacan, not unlike Melanie Klein and Bertram Lewin, argues that the breast is by no means unambiguously cathected; it is not just pleasurable, but menacing or threatening as well. Indeed, the breast is an *arrêt de mort,* as far as the child knows, a sentence pronouncing death (the end of nourishment, peace, bliss, attachment) and a stay or reprieve from being cut off from the pleasures of the mother. And it is this *arrêt de mort* that the obsessional craves, as Serge Leclaire makes explicit when he observes that obsessives like Philo (a patient so dubbed by Leclaire) see themselves as the proper objects for their mother's desire, as "the chosen," but that such an alliance (Eros) is paid for by a heavy mortgage: the interdict of incest, which articulates itself as a death sentence. In the case history of another patient, Jerome, Leclaire writes (note the *arrêt* in the original text):

> ... ce qui frappe le plus Jérôme, c'est la formule que pronounce *le juge lorsqu'il rend son arrêt:* "... est condamné à être pendu par le cou, jusqu'à ce que mort s'ensuive."
>
> "Eh bien, pour moi," ajoute-t-il, "c'est comme si l'on m'avait dit un jour: *Tu vivras jusqu'à ce que mort s'ensuive.*"
>
> ... but most striking to Jerome are *the judge's words when he passes sentence:* "... is condemned to be hanged by the neck until dead."
>
> "Well," Jerome says, "for me it is as though someone had said to me one day, '*You will live until dead.*'"[20]

19. Bertram Lewin, "Sleep, the Mouth, and the Dream Screen," *Psychoanalytic Quarterly* 15 (1946).

20. Serge Leclaire, *Démasquer,* p. 128, and "Jerome, or Death in the Life of the Obsessional," trans. Stuart Schneiderman, in *Returning to Freud,* ed. Stuart Schneiderman (New Haven: Yale University Press, 1980), p. 99. I have altered the typography of the translation to conform with the original text. I have also added italics; only the sentence "You will live until dead" is italicized in Schneiderman's translation.

The obsessional patient articulates yet once more an *arrêt de mort* whose purpose is to evade the difference between life and death, to forestall the deciding of this antinomy. And this forestalling is nothing less than a regressive activity, as we will see shortly. At the axis or arris of the cross between life and death is implanted the neurotic's own tombstone, *arête,* or mound. Am I dead or alive? Jerome cannot answer, exactly, but has half-remembered dreams to show as compensation for what he does not know, faded dreams about mummies, corpses, and tombs. What is problematic, implies Leclaire, is that Jerome has constructed a theater of transference in which he cannot decide whether to play Oedipus or the Sphinx. Given that one figure is invaginated in the other, Jerome necessarily stars in both roles at the same time. As Oedipus, Jerome questions himself from within the figure of the Sphinx; which is to say, each figure becomes a prop for the other. Yet it is in Leclaire's case histories of Philo and Ange Duroc that we learn who this Sphinx really is, namely, a figure for life with mama. It is the mother for whom Philo longs, and she whom the Angel of the Rock wishes to save (for himself) even at the expense of his own sexuality. At the crossroads, then, one encounters an *arrêt de mort* and clings to it for dear life, or should we say, to mother's breast? Clearly we are now far beyond the pleasure principle, though by no means within the vicinity of the death drive. Rather, we are in an eddy, a suspension in which the drives circulate without going anywhere.

And yet, for all that, there is direction in the sense of a regression. Thus it is to *Mont Blanc* that I must return, particularly to the lines introducing part 3.

> Some say that gleams of a remoter world
> Visit the soul in sleep,—that death is slumber,
> And that its shapes the busy thoughts outnumber
> Of those who wake and live.—I look on high;
> Has some unknown omnipotence unfurled
> The veil of life and death? or do I lie
> In dream, and does the mightier world of sleep
> Spread far around and inaccessibly
> Its circles? For the very spirit fails,
> Driven like a homeless cloud from steep to steep

That vanishes among the viewless gales!
Far, far above, piercing the infinite sky,
Mont Blanc appears,—still, snowy, and serene—
                                                (49–61)

The "veil of life and death" is not unlike a screen on which the pleasure
and death drives represent themselves, impossibly, undecidably, lim-
inally. It is that stage or platform (veil or mount) between sleeping and
waking, a kind of mystic writing pad articulated at the preconscious
level, somewhere between looking and dreaming, gazing and recol-
lecting images involuntarily, either in the tranquility of sleep or the
astonishment, so overdetermined, of serene wakefulness, like the Wolf-
Man's casual glance. What else is this mount, this blank mountain, but
the maternal screen on which the child regressively and therefore paradoxically individuates with pleasure, and precisely because the child
recognizes the power of the breast, this transitional object figured forth
in regions not wholly conscious? This *arrêt de mort,* this sentence that
prolongs life and commands death, produces pleasure and pain, relief
and anguish, presence and lack, this prop, so still, snowy, and serene,
is, like woman, veiled. It is a part of woman that needs to be unveiled
by some "unknown omnipotence," the child's desire to "see," to
"stage" his desire, to situate an Eros/Thanatos whose difference will
not simply cleave in two up there on the invisible white heights.

From this perspective, *Mont Blanc* is situated in terms of a *theatrum
analyticum* where the drives are featured as stage props, in terms of
the stage itself, which is its own prop or "set" of props, or, to put it
another way, a base that is its own superstructure, a Hegelian stage of
Aufhebung: ça as SA (*Savoir Absolu*).[21] That is, with Hegel, but also
Shelley, Plato, and Freud in mind, it would be naive to consider Mont
Blanc merely an image, for this mountain is exactly the kind of prop
that frames or stages desire, the phantomizing image that turns into a
forum and frames as well as replicates fantasy. Mont Blanc is the dream
screen, to recall Lewin, which facilitates a passive and regressive return

---

21. Let us just say the floor is tilting, that what is flat becomes suddenly upright:
the horizontal becomes vertical. Thus the mountainous platforms in Shelley, those
gigantic props, which are their own stages, which collapse and erect, are apotropaic.
The frame or stage of desire is driven along certain somatic lines.

to the maternal, a return that is obsessively concerned with an undecidable problem: this breast is not merely a site for past pleasure but
constitutes a crossroads, an *arrêt/arête de mort.*

In *Mont Blanc* the alliance of the maternal with death or threat
reveals itself as "the naked countenance of earth / On which I gaze,"
where the phallic mother presents herself, for there the "glaciers creep
/ Like snakes that watch their prey" (100–101). Perhaps it is all a
defense, this apotropaic leaning of the drive, and from what else, Leclaire might say, but that which the phallic mother veils, the sight which
must, according to Freud in "Medusa's Head," turn the spectator to
stone (to an Ange Duroc): the "Dizzy Ravine"?

> ...and when I gaze on thee
> I seem as in a trance sublime and strange
> To muse on my own separate fantasy,
> My one, my human mind, which passively
> Now renders and receives fast influencings...
>   (34–38)

Before this ravine the mind is rendered passive; it cannot engage the
landscape in any other manner but in finding fantastic substitutions
for it. Thus the mind produces "wild thoughts" which rest

> In the still cave of the witch Poesy,
> Seeking among the shadows that pass by—
> Ghosts of all things that are—some shade of thee,
> Some phantom, some faint image; till the breast
> From which they fled recalls them, thou art there!
>   (44–48)

In the cave the mind seeks some faint image of the ravine, as if the
ravine itself were perpetually ob-scene (as ob-scene as the mount), and
precisely for the reason that this ravine is vaginal, is that part of woman
that has to be retracted, derealized, dissimulated, faded, even as the
mind contemplates from within the security of this trench, this witch
or Sphinx, poesy, this "still cave." As Lacoue-Labarthe puts it, "La
scène est primitive." Moreover, it is but a repetition of what Shelley

calls the "breast" from which the·thoughts fled: the *arête/arrête* de mort. Mont Blanc is what Shelley himself calls "A city of death ... Yet not a city" (106–8). It is some kind of horrible power that cannot be precisely specified, looked at, determined, and yet, for all that, this mountain is the screen on which the poet individuates with pleasure. And because he recognizes the power of this mount as a prop for fantasy, a dwelling place for the imagination, he comes to accept it as the rightful stage, spatially and temporally, to situate his desire, as the *theatrum analyticum* in which even philosophies of the mind can be figured forth.

If more conservative readers of *Mont Blanc* have followed with great care Shelley's theory of mind, particularly its development by stages, it has been my wish to posit an archaeology of the libido on which any such theory is inevitably couched, an archaeology of figural attachments and stagings whose regressive force we have recognized and surveyed without disdain. Indeed, such a return to the primitive is all a matter of saving a text from its own death sentence, of what Derrida calls *sur-vivre* in relation to *The Triumph of Life,* a survival that has everything to do with a coming into one's own that is peculiarly attached to a secure loan, fastened onto a maternal bond that is safely kept in its vault or tomb, off-stage or ob-scene. If the poet as obsessive builds his monoliths at the crossroads, places his *arêtes* on the *arrêt de mort,* it is not only to ward off death by means of an ambivalent forestalling, but to build a monument to mother, to worship the virgin and child, or *le très haut* (the All High), to recall Blanchot once more. It is this debt to the past, always symbolic, that underwrites Shelley's poem and engenders what we call a "passive tropology," something Leclaire's obsessive patients would find quite familiar. Of such passivity Blanchot writes, "Passivity is without measure: it goes beyond being, being at its very limits [*être à bout d'être*]—the passivity of a bygone past that never has been: the disaster understood, deeply felt, not as an event of the past, but as the immemorial past (the All High) [*le très haut*] which comes back while scattering by its own return the present time in which it would be experienced as coming back [*vécu comme revenant*]."[22] Another title, *Le Très-Haut,* re-marks the most extreme

22. Maurice Blanchot, *L'Écriture du désastre* (Paris: Gallimard, 1980), p. 34.

suspension between life and death, is synonymous with *L'Arrêt de mort,* but also refers to a man being propped up by a woman, raised by her, lifted in a *récit* to *la plus haute.* And can there be any doubt that *le très haut* in the passage above taken from *L'Écriture du désastre* is not in some sense already visible in *Mont Blanc* as a coming back of a fantasm in the Haute Savoie, a passive monument that overcomes itself on the high road to self-consciousness in that curious return to an immemorial and haunted past that scatters the very present by which it can only return, that regressive and obsessional urge that it is the poet's fate to live over: *sur-vivre?*

3

Jane Eyre and
the *Mot Tabou*

If one were to pursue a poetics of hauntedness, of a text that disclosed disembodied voices, perhaps the voices of ancestors or departed lovers or of the damned, then one might turn to Charlotte Brontë's *Jane Eyre*, for in that novel one has the opportunity to witness more than a few disembodied outcries, more than a few voices whose subjects are either missing or in some way concealed when the act of enunciation takes place. To name *Jane Eyre* within a poetics of hauntedness is to define Brontë's novel in terms of what Jacques Lacan might describe as a text set in motion by a "hole in the real" which results from loss (death) or repression (privation); it is to talk about a text haunted by voices whose speakers are distanced, displaced, cut off.[1]

Indeed, the first major scene in which the disembodied voice discloses itself dramatically takes place in the "red room," whose Sadean overtones should not be overlooked, even if we do not choose to analyze them here.

> Mr. Reed had been dead nine years: it was in this chamber he
> breathed his last; here he lay in state; hence his coffin was borne
> by the undertaker's men; and, since that day, a sense of dreary
> consecration had guarded it from frequent intrusion.... I began to
> recall what I had heard of dead men, troubled in their graves by

1. Jacques Lacan, "Desire and the Interpretation of Desire in *Hamlet*," *Yale French Studies*, no. 55/56 (1971): 11–52.

the violation of their last wishes, revisiting the earth to punish the
perjured and avenge the oppressed; and I thought Mr. Reed's spirit,
harassed by the wrongs of his sister's child, might quit its abode—
whether in the church vault or in the unknown world of the departed—and rise before me in this chamber. I wiped my tears and
hushed my sobs, fearful lest any sign of violent grief might waken
a preternatural voice to comfort me, or elicit from the gloom some
haloed face, bending over me with strange pity. This idea, consolatory in theory, I felt would be terrible if realized: with all my
might I endeavored to stifle it—I endeavored to be firm.[2]

But a sound fills Jane's ears, "which I deemed the rushing of wings,"
and it prompts from her a terrible scream. Mrs. Reed, who suspects
Jane is merely trying to upset the household with her tantrum, refuses
to release Jane from the red room, the haunted room, no matter what
Jane's anguish. "Mrs. Reed, impatient of my now frantic anguish and
wild sobs, abruptly thrust me back and locked me in, without further
parley. I heard her sweeping away; and soon after she was gone,
I suppose I had a species of fit: unconsciousness closed the scene"
(p. 20).

   A psychoanalytically inclined reader will immediately perceive that
Jane is something of a hysteric. She wishes the ghost to appear in order
that it may avenge her wrong, that it may haunt and punish Mrs. Reed
and her cruel (even sadistic) children, but by making that wish come
true, by fantasizing a ghost, by hearing in her ears a "rush," which we
may link to the hypertension she experiences, she only succeeds in
frightening or traumatizing herself. The fantasy of the ghost is, one
might argue, an essentially pleasurable one to the degree that it gives
Jane sadistic pleasure in thinking it will hurt others and at the same
time masochistic pleasure in knowing that it will hurt ("kill" is the
word Jane uses) her. In this context the punishment is repeated, the
death wish reinforced, at the same time that it is negated, revenged,
mastered. And the ghost, that necessary accomplice, is acting as a
signifier of desire, an imaginary agency facilitating the achievement of
pleasure.

2. Charlotte Brontë, *Jane Eyre* (New York: Signet, 1960), p. 19. Hereafter cited in
the text by page number.

There is transference in this scene as well, since Jane is acting out her desires, embodying them, investing them in the fantasm of a Mr. Reed. We know that Jane is acting out, because she is transferring unconscious wishes and fantasies onto an imaginary person who is able to realize Jane's wishes in terms of the real world of adults. Such transferences in children are common and only become traumatic when the child "forgets" that he or she has imagined a double that now stalks around as if it were real. We might call this the playmate-to-monster transformation.[3]

Theoretically, anything can become a playmate. It is just a matter of what signifier the child chooses to privilege as the locus of her desires. But it is not surprising that children seek imaginary constructions that in some way resemble them, since resemblance "automatically" facilitates transference by very rapidly representing the "me" in the "other." For Jane Eyre the privileged signifier is the departed Mr. Reed, or to be more exact, the "memorial" of Mr. Reed as Jane safeguards it in her imagination. To introject Mr. Reed is to make safe; it is for Jane to create a shelter blessed by the protective spirit, the "good" wish of the departed, charitable man. In short, of the Father. In this there is deadly pleasure, and Jane never hesitates to play with this pleasure. She explains, "I began to recall what I had heard of dead men, troubled in their graves by the violation of their last wishes." Jane's premise is that ultimately everyone's desire must be fulfilled (indeed, this is the working thesis for the novel in general), and that no one may disturb or interfere with a person's last wishes without suffering severe consequences: the return of the dead. Clearly for Jane the dead are far more powerful than the living, since their passion, their will, their desire is so strong that nothing will stand in the way of its fulfillment. In short, to be dead is to be omnipotent, and it is this omnipotence the child craves and gets in the form of transferring her desires (both mastery and revenge) onto the dead. However, once Jane has recalled

3. D. W. Winnicott's concept of the "transitional object" or "transitional phenomenon" becomes of interest, since it could be argued that Mr. Reed's ghost is such an "intermediate zone" or "toy" that objectifies inner experience, manifests it in the so-called real world. Yet in that very manifestation, experience becomes alienated from itself: "forgetting" occurs. See Winnicott's *Playing and Reality* (London: Tavistock, 1971).

what she has heard of the dead, she forgets that the departed Father stands in for her physical and social inadequacy; she forgets that she recalls and hears only because she is, by means of a fantasm, transferring her desire onto an uncanny other.

Of course, once Jane has imagined the return of the dead—a kind of secularized last judgment in which Jane herself is vindicated—she not only "forgets" that the fantasm of Mr. Reed is her production, but also that she wants his consolation. The idea of the ghost bending over Jane with strange pity is consolatory in theory, she tells us, but "terrible" if realized. With all her might she wants to "stifle" her outcry of grief for fear that such an outcry might be a summons, might elicit a response from the ghost, and it is in this sense that she tries to repress what has already returned: the Father, the Law, death. But by now the acting out of the unconscious is well under way, and no amount of stifling will stop it, since the will to power or the desire for omnipotence has found an agency within which to invest itself: the fantasm. So powerful is this agency that it can speak in a "preternatural" voice to the grief-stricken girl.

Guy Rosolato in *La Relation d'inconnu* argues that the voice is the expression of "total power," that it is the human voice that is "linked to a dynamic of the body and its fantasmatics."[4] The voice is omnipotent because it is essentially a spreading out of the body, an expansion of the self whose motive is the acting out of desire. In *Jane Eyre* the ghost is perceived as voice, as the speaking or signification of desire, and it frightens Jane, because this speaking has dismembered or estranged itself from the subject, from the Jane who wants something, who wishes it so strongly that she "forgets" the voice of her own desire when she hears it, when she summons it to speak in an Other of her own making. If Jane's fantasy has attempted to raise the dead from the grave, to restore to the deceased body its wishes and commands by means of transference, it has, at the same time, managed to empty the living subject of its expressive power, its voice, its formulated desire. In this way, fantasy reveals itself as a self-destructive activity, a terrifying act directed against the self and not just against others, as the initial impulse toward fantasy had projected. Clearly to act out one's

4. Guy Rosolato, *La Relation d'inconnu* (Paris: Gallimard, 1978), p. 34.

desire in this way does not merely constitute the self's wish for mastery over others, a wish for power that can even extend to the raising of the dead, but also constitutes one's self-annihilation. To spread out too far, to allow the voice to expand the body to omnipotent proportions is nothing less than a mastery unto death. And Jane Eyre does die, in a sense, for "unconsciousness closed the scene." The terror of the voices, of the return of the dead or repressed, culminates in a loss of consciousness, in the ego's temporary dissolution, in a kind of madness. "The next thing I remember is waking up with a feeling as if I had had a frightful nightmare, and seeing before me a terrible red glare, crossed with black thick bars. I heard voices, too, speaking with a hollow sound, and as if muffled by a rush of wind or water: agitation, uncertainty, an all predominating sense of terror confused my faculties. Ere long, I became aware that some one was handling me" (p. 20). But if Jane Eyre hears a voice, listens to that "rush" of wind and the hollow speaking, so do we, for what we hear is the eerie sound-shape of a name, a sound shape built into the passage just cited.

"Eyre" as in "a frightful nightmare," a "terrible red glare," a "sense of terror," "Ere long," "became aware." This part of *Jane Eyre* is similar, perhaps, to the "coming to" section of *Finnegans Wake* (part 4), in which certain sounds begin chiming through words. This should not surprise us, since at this point in Brontë's novel Jane is still recovering from a coma, is still somewhere between unconsciousness and consciousness. What ought to surprise or at least interest us is that we, too, begin to hear disembodied voices, experience a kind of disorientation that results from hearing an unexpected message, a ghostly sound that haunts certain words whose denotative meanings have no ostensible connection with what we hear: the repetition of Jane Eyre's family name.

Our hearing the name takes us, at this point, to recognizing that what Lacan calls the *automatisme de répétition* grasps "its principle in what we have called *l'instance de la chaine signifiante*."[5] To take this further, we might add that what insists in the signifying chain is nothing less than a letter hidden from sight, repressed. Lacan studies the course of that repeated letter in thematic terms when he looks at

5. Jacques Lacan, *Écrits* (Paris: Seuil, 1966), p. 11.

Poe's story of the purloined letter, whereas our study leads us to analyze the passage of a repressed letter in terms of a sound shape, that is to say, in terms of a recognizable sound that keeps resounding within many different words, that keeps repeating itself, and perhaps for precisely the reason Lacan might give, in order to stay hidden from consciousness.

Nicolas Abraham and Maria Torok, analysts independent of Lacan, have completed extended studies of the trajectory of sound shapes whose force is the constant reference, however negative, to a *mot tabou,* to a hidden letter or concealed script. While Lacan has studied such reference in terms of metaphor and metonymy, Abraham and Torok have suggested that thanks to phonic slippages (sound distortions) there appear "cryptonyms which apparently no longer have any phonetic or semantic relation with the prohibited word."[6] These slippages occur, Abraham and Torok believe, because signifiers can metonymically represent other signifiers without reference to the signified. This means that "ere" can metonymically refer to "Eyre," can isolate itself as part of a name, and that in turn other metonymies can substitute "ere." A series of substitutions or *cryptonyms* is formed in this way. According to Abraham and Torok all of this occurs not on the level of one thing representing another (signified for signified) nor on the level of one word representing another (by this they mean entire morphemes) but on the level of "a lexicological continuity of diverse meanings of the same word, that is to say, *allosemes,* such as those found in a dictionary."[7] For Abraham and Torok it is not so much that words repress but that they follow paths of avoidance, sound themselves out allosemically.

The hazards of such a theory when put into practice are only too clear: one can construct almost anything one wants. Yet a reader of *Jane Eyre* cannot deny that something like what Abraham and Torok describe does occur in Brontë's novel and occurs with no little force. The sound shape of the name *is* repeated. A voice keeps calling out "Eyre" (*ere, air, aware, beware, nightmare, glare, terror,* but also *ere,*

6. Nicolas Abraham and Maria Torok, *Cryptonymie: Le Verbier de l'homme aux loups* (Paris: Aubier-Flammarion, 1976), p. 117.
7. Ibid., p. 118.

ire, Ireland, I, Vampyre, wild) through a rather large verbarium whose entire range exceeds our list. What is certain, however, is that Eyre is sounded in words whose associations often touch on what could be constructed as frightful or traumatic. That is to say, we are to associate her family name with horror, with the kind of scene one has in the red room when Jane fantasizes the return of Mr. Reed. This, of course, is well supported by the observation that Jane's fantasm of the voice in the red room is accompanied by a dissolution of the ego, a loss of consciousness, a dispersion of the "I" (of Jane Eyre) into all that terrifies her, all that she has fantasized but has "forgotten" as the object of her transferred desire.

Thus in one sense we can explain the repetition of the name as a kind of mania that has been turned onto oneself, as merely an extension of the fantasizing process we examined in the red room, or, if one likes, the place of Jane's christening, aligned here with omnipotent wishes and thoughts about death. But we can go further. Abraham and Torok mention that in the discourse of Freud's Wolf-Man there are crypto-nyms, words that hide a *mot tabou*. I am observing, of course, a similar phenomenon in Brontë's novel, which is to say, that the name Eyre similarly conceals a word by means of hiding from us a letter that even when most apparent could escape our grasp. What makes the *verbier* of the Wolf-Man even more relevant to us is that such a *verbier* straddles two languages, a straddling we might have overlooked in *Jane Eyre* and the missing letter itself.

We recall that Jane learns French at Lowood and that it is her position at Thornfield to be the governess of little Adèle, a French child by birth and, it must be said, by speech. Most curious is that the rather extended development of Jane's relation to Adèle is dropped quite suddenly and that Adèle herself is very much phased out of the novel at about the time Jane discovers that Rochester has a mad wife. Someone with an organic approach to literature might well wonder whether or not the inclusion of the Adèle figure, or at least the rather full development of it, is merited. I want to suggest that this novelistic dead end is rather important, because Adèle points to an issue that is repressed in the narrator's discourse: the figure of the mother.

A reader of *Jane Eyre* cannot fail to notice that the mothers in the novel are represented as perverse. For example, Mrs. Reed, Jane's foster mother, is a monster bent on destroying the adopted child. She spoils her own children and so dotes on them that in later life they become self-destructive. Adèle's mother, similarly, is perceived by Rochester and Jane as a rejecting woman. She is, as Rochester has it, a whore and is most happy that Rochester has taken the unwanted child away from her. Bertha Mason, the wife who should give "birth" to Rochester's children, is congenitally insane; she is not even considered a woman, but an animal. To this list we may add Jane's real mother, whose maiden name, incidently, we never discover, a daughter of a rich man who rashly married a curate against all the wishes of her family and friends. Her child, Jane, was simply the mark of her disobedience; her death the payment. Had she married the right man, St. John Rivers suggests to Jane, she would not have been a "bad mother"; she would not have abandoned her child. And finally there is Jane herself, who with little Adèle never rises above being a governess. In her, too, the motherly affections remain somewhat stillborn.

Adèle, in contrast to Jane, is striking, because she does not reject the mother; "maman" is very present either in the child's discourse or in the child's miniature reproductions of Céline Varens's decadence. Showing off her new dress, Adèle comments, "C'est comme cela que maman faisait, n'est-ce pas, monsieur?" (p. 143). Rochester can only comment, "Coquetry runs in her blood." To the adults the French connection is amusing, but only for the time being, and it is decided by both Mr. Rochester and Jane Eyre that what is best for the little girl is a heavy dose of English boarding school, or, to get at the deep structure of the decision, the destruction of the connection between Adèle and Céline, which in still other terms signifies the negation of even the possibility of a "good mother." Yet, if we can again see Jane acting out (this time passively) hatred against the "bad mother," we can also see that little Adèle has silently but profoundly pointed to the *mot tabou* that Jane so carefully dissimulates: the French word *mère*.

So it is with what at first seems a far-fetched cue that I propose the idea that it is not "Jane Eyre" we are hearing, but the words "Jane *Mère*" that sound when we begin looking at the long *verbier* whose sound-shapes include "ere." It is most interesting that this cue is strongly supported by the scene we have already discussed in the red room. For if we go back to that room, we notice that Jane's traumatizing experience is initiated by the action of Mrs. Reed, the bad foster mother of what commentators have identified as a Cinderella story. Is it not possible, one might ask, that this "terrible mother" is the trigger for the fantasm inside the room? Isn't Mrs. Reed the "night-*mère*"? Assuredly one may say she is, for the return of Mr. Reed is desired by the young Jane in order to punish or kill the mother. And that punishment, as we know, is masochistically turned on Jane herself. Sadism turns into masochism. It is precisely here that a confusion takes place, that the foster mother becomes introjected in terms of Jane Eyre's self-identity. What we have in the red room, then, is a conflation of mother and daughter, a desire for union, for connection, a desire that, unfortunately, can only be worked through in sadomasochistic terms. Within such an emotional economy Jane Eyre's family name dissolves, liquefies, slips only in order that it function as a fantasmic cryptogram for a missing letter, the *m* of *mère:* the *mot tabou* behind the locked door.

Startling, too, is the fact that when one pronounces the heroine's first name, "Jane," a half rime can be heard: *haine* (hate). The sound shapes of these words are close enough, especially if Adèle tried to pronounce them with her accent, that one can no longer feel secure that the rime between Eyre and *mère* is entirely coincidental. What Jane Eyre (*haine-mère*) sounds, then, is not simply the name of the real father, but by its sound shapes the naming of the mother; and it is this clandestine naming, this repressed relation towards *m* that produces an even more eerie ghost-like effect than that of the returning Father, an effect we hear whenever "Eyre" is sounded. Moreover, this interpretation fits the *verbier* of terror, of the nightmare that should actually be read "night-*mère*": the monster, Mrs. Reed locking up a helpless maligned girl. "Terror," "Beware," "Glare" not only stick together allosemically, but conceptually uphold this signifying chain. They all relate to the abandoning mother, to the hated mother: of the Bertha who does not produce flesh and blood, but consumes it, as the Vampire. And here the subset "ire," "I," "Ireland," "fire" appears in its attachment to "Vampyre," to another naming of the hated hysterical mother; here "ere" and "ire" meet.

From here on out a reader can trace the numerous instances in which the heroine's name is echoed in "other" words, words whose foreign soundings must never be lost on us. Perhaps one of the most striking of these instances is that of the formal introduction between Jane and Adèle when Brontë tries to make sure we know she is consciously playing with the heroine's name in terms of sound slippages.

> "And Mademoiselle—what is your name?"
> "Eyre—Jane Eyre."
> "Aire? Bah! I cannot say it."
>
> (p. 104)

Thus Adèle concludes, staying clear of the *mot tabou*, it seems, yet suggesting all the same that Eyre is subject to displacement, and that this name is fixed in one of the images of such semantic slippage: air, the image of dispersion, certainly, but also a word strongly connected to sound, as in aria, a sung "air." Moreover, the image of air has negative, even nightmarish overtones in the novel. It is filled with smoke when Jane enters Rochester's chamber shortly after Bertha has attempted to incinerate him in his sleep; it sighs low in the firs as Jane runs after the familiar voice that calls her away from St. John, a sighing that signifies Jane's loneliness, but also Rochester's desolation, his ruin, and the harshness of the countryside, the world Jane must bear.

However important these English associations are in the little introduction scene, they are but secondary to an intralingual association that Adèle is making on a semantic level, and this intralingual association is of extreme importance, for it sounds the *mot tabou*. *Aire,* we recall, means "eyrie" in French, and it is this association of Jane with a "nest" that Adèle so cleverly makes at this point, an association whose deep structure is only too clear: Jane is like a mother. In this sense, Adèle actually speaks the *mot tabou* straight to Jane's face, describes "Eyre's" hidden meaning, though in the process even this is accompanied with a certain repression or evasion. "Bah! I cannot say it." In short, she has to take "it" (*ça?*) back.

Such an association of "eyrie" with motherlines is not simply a fortuitous pun, but is taken up again in a very significant passage. In one of the middle chapters, when Jane reacts to the screams of the mad Bertha, she narrates, "Not the widest winged condor on the Andes could twice in succession, and send out such a yell from the cloud shrouding his *eyrie*. This thing delivering such utterance must rest ere it could repeat the effort" (p. 208). We know by now that Charlotte Brontë consciously plays with the sound shape of the heroine's name (that's clear in the little interchange between Adèle and Jane), and we also know that Jane is associated from time to time with birds. For example, we see Jane reading Bewick's *History of British Birds* near the opening of the book; Rochester compares Jane to birds, and so on. So it should come as no surprise that Jane herself may be represented in the comparison of the condor with Bertha as the great bird, as a solitary creature who lives in a remote place (Thornfield?) shrouded by clouds (mystery). Surely this suggests that Jane is very unlike Bertha, that the author of the terrible cries that Thornfield must be far more awesome than the magnificent bird. Yet the comparison also suggests the opposite, for it suggests the nearest thing to Bertha's cries are the cries of a condor, for Bertha's shrieks are inhuman, ferocious, animal; and these nocturnal cries at Thornfield come from above, from lairs overhead Jane as if they emanated from an eyrie, from a large bird's nest. The ambivalence of the comparison is reinforced by the semantic slip of "Eyrie" whose force is to identify Jane with "eyrie," an identification already made by little Adèle, though far more directly. What is more complicated here is that Jane is not identified simply with a nest, but with a mad wife's nest, with Thornfield itself, removed, as it were, to the Andes. And it is this more complex association that suggests the allosemes Mason = Maison = eyrie/aire = Jane Eyre.

At points such as these, one may well ask the favorite question of the *École Freudienne:* who speaks? And one wonders, of course, whether this who is not the M(Other) who is making herself heard despite the fact that she has been sealed up in a secret room, encrypted in the vault of a family name of the father, the mausoleum, "Eyre"? Furthermore, is not this encrypting of the M(Other) something that bears on what Lacan calls the "hole in the real," or to borrow a term from Marguerite Duras's *Le Ravissement de Lol V. Stein*, the *mot trou?* This is what Lacan describes as "the place for the projection of the missing signifier, which is essential to the structure of the Other. This is the signifier whose absence leaves the Other incapable of responding to your question, the signifier that can be purchased only with your flesh and your blood, the signifier that is essentially the veiled phallus."[8]

In *Jane Eyre* this veiled phallus ought to be identified with the Name-of-the-Father, which cannot be spoken without reference to the *mot trou* as *mot tabou:* the M(Other). That is, the father's name cannot be spoken without reference to its own inadequacy or fundamental impotence. Indeed, the hole in the real will be supplemented with ghosts, fantasms, and disembodied voices, all of which rush in to cure a gap past healing, as if fantasy could redeem what comes only after the Other has been encrypted for good in the *mot trou* of a surname.

As if that were possible. Yet the "subject's" thinking so is what counts. And it is precisely on this point that Abraham and Torok have written that the "subject" in mourning loss has a tendency to kill off the beloved in such a way that its "remains" remain, interred in the *Moi,* kept "safe" in something of a "false" unconscious. It must be kept taboo, and yet the "subject" is obsessed with it, wants to play with that dark corpse encrypted "there," wherever "there" may be. And that obsession expresses itself precisely in those deviant allosemic chains, in the *verbier* of the Wolf-Man, designed to hide and show at once. In *Jane Eyre* it would be the figure of the heroine's mother, that figure without a name, who lies interred "there" in the "false bottom" of Jane's *Moi,* but, too, in the *Moi* of Charlotte Brontë, herself a motherless child, a possible case study of mourning and encrypting.

No doubt Abraham and Torok part company from Lacan in serious ways, among them in denying the distinction between the imaginary (narcissistic) and symbolic (unconscious) registers, a major theoretical discrepancy that need not concern us unduly here, since it is enough to suggest that it is because of a denial or repression or encrypting of the mother figure in *Jane Eyre* that we hear the disembodied or floating signifiers, those fantasmatic voices. Certainly, as in Shakespeare's *Hamlet,* there may be what Lacan might call a "collective madness" in *Jane Eyre* that results from a denial of primary process, of listening to the

---

8. Lacan, "Desire," p. 38.

unconscious, and it is this refusal that brings us to the crossroads of mourning and psychosis in *Jane Eyre,* just as it does in *Hamlet.* Thus it is no wonder that sounds make their ghostly echoes as they swarm from the "hole in the real," the repression of woman, of the unconscious, of the encrypted M(Other). Certainly, to speak of this "hole" more than anticipates the question of a sexuality in *Jane Eyre* bearing on castration. For if we have touched on the *mot trou* that is the place of the mother in Brontë's novel, we have to consider castration in terms of a woman whose desire searches out a man half blind and crippled, a Master who fears women and yet manages to survive them, manages to rule still another *Belle du jour* with his magnificent impotence. But what does it mean for a castrated male sexuality to rule woman's psychology in this way? And how does this bear on the production of the fantasm? These are questions largely foreclosed by feminist readings of *Jane Eyre* inspired by Sandra Gilbert and Susan Gubar's *Madwoman in the Attic,* wherein it is assumed the novel demonstrates female empowerment to overcome paternal oppression with the result that madness is not to be considered a psychological phenomenon but, rather, a political condition resulting from the abuse of male power.[9] Contrary

9. For all its recourse to psychological explication in the case of the doubling of Jane and Bertha (Bertha as Jane's Jungian shadow), Sandra Gilbert and Susan Gubar ensure that the entire analysis is subordinated to the thesis that Jane Eyre is involved in self-conscious liberation and that Charlotte Brontë purposely wrote the novel to critique Victorian society from what we would today call a feminist perspective. Jane Eyre, therefore, fights for independence from patriarchy in the name of Everywoman. "Every-woman in a patriarchal society must meet and overcome: oppression (at Gateshead), starvation (at Lowood), madness (at Thornfield), and coldness (at Marsh End)." Sandra Gilbert and Susan Gubar, *The Madwoman in the Attic* (New Haven: Yale University Press, 1979), p. 339. Also note Rosemarie Bodenheimer's remark, "In fact, Jane Eyre's history may be read as the story of an empowered narrator, which describes her gradual, though partial release from conventional bondages, both social and fictional." Rosemarie Bodenheimer, "Jane Eyre in Search of Her Story," in *Charlotte Brontë's "Jane Eyre,"* ed. Harold Bloom (New York: Chelsea House, 1987), p. 98. Again, see Jean Wyatt, who sees *Jane Eyre* as a pragmatic text that works through female fantasies in order to critique patriarchal authority. Wyatt asks the rhetorical question: "Can a novel release the energy stored in a reader's unconscious fantasies of rage against patriarchal family structures and rechannel it into a desire for social change?" Wyatt's thesis is that Brontë self-consciously "manages" the reader's fantasies in such a way that social change can come about. In other words, there is no primary process at work here, a point with which I don't agree. See Jane Wyatt, "A Patriarch of One's Own: Jane Eyre

to the politics of power paradigm, we have noticed that in fact *Jane Eyre* is an overdetermined text that obeys the psychoanalytical laws of a tear in the real. As such, the novel challenges the credibility of arguments which would suggest that Jane Eyre is not affected by a primary process whose spectral and fantasmic effects are everywhere to be seen and heard. This ghostly condition of the novel is not being managed, controlled, or mastered by anyone, let alone the author, but is the unpredictable effect of cryptonomy, what Abraham and Torok say results from "the radical exclusion of the words of desire."[10]

---

and Romantic Love," in *Critical Essays on Charlotte Brontë*, ed. B. T. Gates (Boston: G. K. Hall, 1990), p. 200.
  10. Abraham and Torok, p. 21.

4

Effi Briest and
La Chose freudienne

Le sujet est parfaitement chosique, et de la pire espèce de
la chose. La chose freudienne précisement.

—Jacques Lacan, *Le Séminaire XIV*

[The subject is entirely thing-like, and in the worst sense
of the thing: The Freudian thing, precisely.]

In the *Écrits* by Jacques Lacan a desk begins to speak and has the
effrontery to ask the following question: "In what way, then, is this
ego that you treat in analysis better than the desk that I am?"[1] It is
precisely this question I wish to address with respect to Theodor Fontane's *Effi Briest,* a work filled with fantasies and fantasms that are
oddly concretized. They are, to put it in the language of toyland, stuffed.
Yet whereas stuffed fantasies in the nursery may function as transitional
objects, so comforting in play as a permeable psychic membrane that
gives the unconscious access to the real, in *Effi Briest* these solid or
thing-like fantasms are both alienating and worrisome. They belong
to a reality that is both ghostly and overly concrete. Implicitly these
fantasms are also asking Lacan's question, "In what way, then, is this
ego that you treat in analysis better than the desk that I am?" It is a
questioning that points to a consideration of Fontane's novel from the
standpoint of a Lacanian relation among the fantasm, the thing, and
the subject.

In this chapter I make three analytical interventions. The first concerns the signification of "things" as they come to appearance as agen-

1. Jacques Lacan, *Écrits* (Paris: Seuil, 1966), p. 425. Trans. Alan Sheridan (New
York: Norton, 1977), p. 135.

cies of law and desire. A sewing table speaks of betrayal; a packet of letters, whose materiality takes precedence over its contents, condemns someone to death; and a child who has been transformed into a parrot speaks in such a way that it crushes her mother's will. The second intervention focuses on the thing as ghost or fantasm, which takes place in the Lacanian notion of the Real. In what way does the speaking thing operate as a ghost in the house? The third intervention considers the phenomenon of a woman's withdrawal. Despite her position in a Prussian world, Effi Briest will bind social relations without quite taking place within them; she will become the "thing" in the Real that lends credence to desiring relations while absenting herself completely as if she were a fantasm. That Effi Briest will sacrifice herself in order for the expired fantasy between her husband and mother to persist is the precondition for her alienation or *parti pris des choses* (a taking to the side of things).

In addition, in this chapter I intend to read some well-known key moments in *Effi Briest* to counter the view that Effi Briest is guilty of adultery. Given that psychological evidence from a Lacanian perspective disagrees with the adultery interpretation, I hope to demonstrate that the assumption of adultery is not uncomplicated. I also intend to draw from Fontane in order to better understand the complex interplay in Lacan between the notion of the fantasm and the Freudian thing. Peculiar to my approach is that instead of trying to read a literary work primarily in terms of the Lacanian orders of the Imaginary or the Symbolic, I am focusing on a work that emphasizes something very analogous to Lacan's conception of the Real. Indeed, *Effi Briest* is most unusual in that it gives us extraordinary insight into some very difficult psychoanalytical problems concerning the appearance of fantasms in the place of the Real.

The Speaking Thing

Effi Briest is a novel in which the unconscious of a social order happens to be reflected in the materiality of the letter. In this sense, the novel is not so far removed from a well-known story by Poe in which something has been purloined. We ought to recall that Effi Briest has married her mother's former lover and suddenly finds herself isolated in a small drab town on the Baltic coast in northern Germany. The wife of an official of the Prussian government, she is largely an outcast, not unlike an object that has no proper place. She befriends Major Crampas, her husband's womanizing friend, and finds him rather sympathetic. Whether or not she behaves indiscreetly with the Major we are never privileged to know, because Fontane does his utmost at various points in the novel not to play the omniscient narrator. Whatever the *Naturkind* does with the Major in the little forested nook behind the cemetery is left unsaid. It is blanked out by the homespun dialogues and the tedium of everyday life. But then letters are found by Effi's husband, and where passion is silent, the furniture begins to speak. It is here *Effi Briest* differs quite markedly from Poe's short story about a missing letter, because although the letter in Poe's story also accedes to thinghood in the Minister's room, blending in so well with the furniture, we are not privileged to experience the dire consequences of the letters being read by a genuinely interested party. In Fontane the question is not a search for what has been missing, but the accidental interception of something that has expired and been forgotten.

Let us turn, then, to the moment the letters are found. Annie, the daughter of Effi and Geert Innstetten, has accidentally fallen on the stairs in the big house in Kessin and injured her head. There is bleeding, and the maids frantically look for a long bandage they believe is locked away in Effi's sewing table. The lock is child's play, the maids assert, and with a chisel they break into the mistress's furniture. If the bandage is not found, at least the contents of the table are spread along a window sill with haste and fury, and only after the linen has been torn up for bandages does Geert notice a packet of letters tied by red string. First the bed sheets are torn, the blood is absorbed by them, and then the letters are noticed. Perhaps it is appropriate that Geert has to ask the maid Johanna where these letters come from. After all, it is the maids who know where things are kept, who are proficient in the language or placement of objects. He is told with virtuous malice that these letters were found in a separate compartment in Effi's sewing table. It is as if this script had been given a safe burial place in the sewing table's interior.

As Geert gazes at the letters he seems to recognize the writing without being able to place it. The narrator dryly comments, "Von deutlichem Erkennen konnte keine Rede sein, aber es kam ihm doch so vor, als habe er die Schriftzüge schon irgendwo gesehen. Ob er nachsehen solle?" ["While it could not be said that he clearly recognized anything, none the less it seemed to him that he had seen the writing before somewhere. Should he look more closely?"].[2] It is as if something were being remembered, as if these letters were already known but forgotten, as if they were being recalled by the unconscious. Gazing at the letters, something from the past seems to be repeated. But what can it be? Looking closer, Geert is concerned less with what the words say than with how they look, for Geert has suddenly recognized the hand of Major Crampas. It is now that the script or signature drowns out the words. "... Und in seinem Kopfe begann sich alles zu drehen" ["... And in his head everything began to spin"].[3] Written in the wrong hand, the feared hand, the materiality of the script suggests the very scene Geert fears: that he has been made a cuckold even while on the most painstaking guard, while having so successfully played the school-master in a dour German school for wives.

We learn that Effi has probably "forgotten" these letters (she says she never loved the Major). In this sense, the sewing table may appear to us in the role of a material unconscious, a place where an awkward slip occurs, which is to say, where desire is unconsciously expressed through the retention of some thing. If from Geert's perspective the "thing" is an occasion for jealously constructing a mise-en-scène in which his wife is being made love to by another, from Effi's perspective the forgetting of the "thing" probably marks a wish for an attachment that, in fact, did not occur. As the site of Effi's slip, the sewing desk mediates imaginary or fantasmic scenes of desire. Whereas the furniture once escaped much notice, it now becomes a suggestive site where fantasmic whisperings and sexual innuendoes can be heard.

Indeed, like any policeman, Geert recognizes that things always speak louder than words, that people's confessions of truth are to be squared against the evidence that one can find in the tangible world of things,

2. Theodor Fontane, *Effi Briest,* in *Fontanes Werk,* vol. 4 (Berlin: Aufbau Verlag, 1977), p. 250. Trans. Douglas Parmee (New York: Penguin, 1967), p. 211. All trans-lations are taken from this volume.

3. Ibid., p. 250; trans., p. 211.

as if things speak the truth, the whole truth, and nothing but the truth. "In what way, then, is this ego that you treat in analysis better than the desk that I am?" This Lacanian question is, now that we look at it again, also the question posed by the law in both psychoanalytical and legal contexts. The "things" speak for themselves, and yet all this speaking comes from a place of distinct silence, that place which Lacan calls the Real. It is a place of materiality in which signification disappears for a time. And yet, given the right conditions, things may become accusatory. On account of what has been chiseled out of the sewing table, Major Crampas is challenged to a duel and shot to death at ten paces. Then Effi is sent packing to Berlin where she is left to rot in a small apartment. In such instances *la chose* comes to appear in a most terrifying manner. In the duel scene there is hardly any dialogue and all we hear is the sound of guns and the thud of the body. After Crampas receives the fatal wound, he summons Innstetten and mutters, "Wollen Sie ... " It is as if a corpse or thing has spoken; the words themselves become thing-like, inert. One can infer the phrase begins an appeal to Innstetten with a double motive. For the scene in which Crampas dies is reminiscent of the nook behind the cemetery. The phrase suggests both an appeal to Effi and to Geert, an appeal that is not consummated in the death scene, suggesting something similar may have been abrogated before with Innstetten's wife. But all we have as evidence is the fragment, "Wollen Sie ... " For Geert the confrontation with Crampas was not motivated out of love for Effi but love for the law. Once his anger is allayed by an appeal to the code of masculine honor, he can live knowing that his name is intact. It is the law of how things must be.

In Berlin we notice *la chose* even more strikingly where we least expect it. Effi has been grudgingly allowed to see her daughter, whose mind has been poisoned by the father. Annie only parrots polite and vacant expressions. Effi cries out in response to this emptiness in a passage strangely, almost uniquely unrepressed for a novel in which passion is so seldom allowed to surface. Alone, Effi says aloud to herself,

"Das hat *er* dem Kinde beigebracht, ein Schulmeister war er immer, Crampas hat ihn so genannt, spöttisch damals, aber er hat recht gehabt. 'O gewiß, wenn ich darf.' Du *brauchst* nicht zu dürfen; ich

will euch nicht mehr, ich haß euch, auch mein eigen Kind. Was
zuviel ist, ist zuviel. Ein Streber war er, weiter nichts.—Ehre, Ehre,
Ehre . . . und dann hat er den armen Kerl totgeschossen, den ich
nicht einmal liebte und den ich vergessen hatte, weil ich ihn nicht
liebte. Dummheit war alles, und nun Blut und Mord. Und ich
schuld. Und nun schickt er mir das Kind, weil er einer Ministerin
nichts abschlagen kann, und ehe er das Kind schickt, richtet er's ab
wie einen Papagei und bringt ihm die Phrase bei 'wenn ich darf.'
Mich ekelt, was ich getan; aber was mich noch mehr ekelt, das ist
eure Tugend. Weg mit euch. Ich muß leben, aber ewig wird es ja
wohl nicht dauern."

Als Roswitha wiederkam, lag Effi am Boden, das Gesicht abge-
wandt, wie leblos.

["He taught the child that; he always was a schoolmaster, Crampas
called him one (he was joking then but he was right). 'Oh yes, if I
may!' You don't need to say that, because I don't want either of
you anymore, I hate you both, even my own daughter. Too much
is too much. He was always thinking of his career and nothing
more. Honor, honor, honor, . . . and then he shot that poor man,
whom I didn't even love, and whom I'd forgotten because I didn't
love him. It was all just stupidity and then blood and murder. And
it's my fault. And now he's sent me my daughter because he can't
refuse a minister's wife anything and before he sent her, he trained
her like a parrot and taught her the phrase 'if I may.' What I've
done disgusts me but what disgusts me even more is how virtuous
they both are. Go away, the pair of you! I have to go on living but
I suppose it can't go on forever."

When Roswitha came back Effi was lying, face downward, apparently lifeless.][4]

The word *leblos* is not accidental. It echoes the inertness of a daughter
who is described as a parrot, passively and automatically saying what
it has been instructed to say. "Dummheit war alles," Effi says. And
"Dummheit" is very much the appearance of the thing. Indeed, this is
not only a question of stupidity but of "Blut und Mord," the corpse
of Crampas. Such things stand for the word "alles": that situation in
which Effi finds herself. And to this condition of thing or corpse Effi

---

4. Ibid., p. 297; trans., p. 249.

will herself accede; at the close of this outburst she too is lying, face downward, apparently lifeless.

This identification between woman and thing is suggested more than visually; for all its passion, Effi's speech marks a withdrawal of feeling even from Crampas of whom she says little else than that she never loved him. Similarly, the repudiation of husband and daughter denies an emotional relation since the speech is never really delivered to them. The speech is said at a time when it does not express feeling directly toward others, as if the speaker had somehow excommunicated them. Here the fact that passionate outburst is timed in such a way that it misses its proper address should concern us, because in the awkward delay of passion affect is being withheld. The speech is inert, as if its speaker had intended it to miss its mark and fall flat.

Bad Timing

The temporality of misfiring repeats other instances of such bad timing. For example, the story of how Luise and Geert fell in love but resisted marriage because of bad timing is absolutely fundamental to the novel. And the marriage of Effi to Geert is nothing less than a way for Luise and Geert to compensate for bad timing by fulfilling their passion through proxy: the handing over of a daughter to her mother's former lover. Like Effi's Berlin soliloquy, the substitution of daughter for mother lacks affect. The episode of discovering the letters is most similar: the maids and the husband have come upon the letters a bit late, about six years late, to be more exact. They were addressed to Effi, who by the time Geert finds them, had more or less forgotten of their existence. But upon being discovered by Geert their focus of address shifts. He reads the letters from the position of someone who has been excluded from a passionate relation that bears directly on him. Yet by the time Geert discovers the packet this passionate relation, whatever it might have been, has expired. It is, to put matters bluntly, irrelevant.

Here, too, something lags and falls due at precisely that moment when its emotional or affective force is at its weakest. But, of course, Geert will try to compensate for the six-year lag by exercising his moral anger long after there is any emotional relationship that can be intelligently addressed. It is for this reason that the Prussian social mores enacted by Geert will strike the reader as so utterly alienated from any genuine emotional response to a specific set of interpersonal relations. Suddenly, Effi emerges from Geert's perspective as merely a "thing" that belongs to a material order of existence, a piece of property that is meant to ensure the smooth economic transition from one generation to the next. Geert's response to his belated interception of the letters, then, is a response to this concretization of woman according to Prussian notions of the law and the family. Not surprisingly, this response is mechanical and radically estranged from affect.

Of course, Geert knows the futility of his actions, the uselessness of exercising a license over an affair that has expired and which, in any case, cannot be recovered or addressed. And yet, despite the fact that he knows the materiality of the letters has led him to fantasize and hence assume the worst, he says to his friend, Wüllersdorf, who wants to know why Geert is so intent on vindicating himself, "Man is nicht bloß ein einzelner Mensch, man gehört einem Ganzen an, und auf das Ganze haben wir beständig Rücksicht zu nehmen, wir sind durchaus abhängig von ihm. Ging' es, in Einsamkeit zu leben, so könnt ich es gehen lassen" ["We're not isolated persons, we belong to a whole society and we have constantly to consider that society, we're completely dependent on it. If it were possible to live in isolation, then I could let it pass"].[5] He can't let "it" pass, he is saying, because the Prussian law-of-the-Father—the social dynamics of the family—forbids him to. Therefore Geert, who knows he has intercepted Effi's letters too late, refuses to acknowledge that these scraps of paper have expired, that whatever they may have meant, they are now irrelevant "things." He appeals to social "law," rather, to reanimate the "thing" as an expression of passion so that he may better determine in what position he finds himself, if not to position his desire, generally. Yet, just as Effi cries out at a time that resists the communication of affect, Geert similarly enacts the law at a moment that sadly ensures the suffocation of passion and the concretization or reification of fantasy.

Fontane, for his part, clarifies that not only Geert Innstetten, but all

5. Ibid., p. 254; trans., p. 215.

the protagonists, live in a social order characterized by bad timing. Moreover, all the protagonists accept the individual's dependency on the whole of society and its social laws, even if each protagonist is aware that the relations of society do not coincide with conscious individual desires. At work in the novel, then, are autonomous social relations that crush the emotional lives of those who uphold them. Moreover, in the very materiality of relations something goes against what characters inwardly feel, though at the same time some "thing" structures these characters in terms of distinct desiring relations that they cannot escape. In Fontane's novel, the contradiction between the logic of things and the logic of feelings results in a curious asynchrony between emotional and material relays. In this world, events happen only when they no longer matter. A man finally marries after he is no longer of a passionate age, letters are found long after they are really relevant, a woman cries out long after there is anyone to hear her, a mother fulfills her dreams in a way that cannot be entirely satisfying, a man is shot to death long after he can either prove or disprove any connection with what he has supposedly done wrong. Given this textual allergy to synchronization, it would appear in *Effi Briest* that the "thing" is positioned in the place where everyone is overdue with the consequence that desire and its affect are withheld. It is in this withdrawal that a fantasm will come to appearance.

Appearance of "the Thing" in Freud

In Sigmund Freud's "Case of Paranoia Running Counter to the Psychoanalytic Theory of the Disease" (1915), a woman of about thirty has contacted a lawyer to protect her from a man who had seduced her. In describing the woman's complaint Freud writes, "She declared that this man had abused her confidence by getting unseen witnesses to photograph them while they were making love, and that by exhibiting these pictures it was now in his power to bring disgrace on her and force her to resign the post she occupied."[6] The lawyer, suspecting

6. Sigmund Freud, "A Case of Paranoia Running Counter to the Psychoanalytic Theory of the Disease," in *The Standard Edition of the Complete Psychological Works*

the accusation extreme, has asked Freud to examine the young woman. Could she be overreacting?

The woman's two interviews with Freud are guarded. The analyst is not sure she has been telling him everything, but she does admit to having been seduced by a young man who worked in her office.

> As he had promised not to expose her to any risk, she had at last consented to visit him in his bachelor rooms in the daytime. There they kissed and embraced as they lay side by side, and he began to admire the charms which were now partly revealed. In the midst of this idyllic scene she was suddenly frightened by a noise, a kind of knock or click. It came from the direction of the writing-desk, which was standing across the window; the space between desk and window was partly taken up by a heavy curtain. She had at once asked her friend what this noise meant, and was told, so she said, that it probably came from the small clock on the writing desk.... As she was leaving the house she had met two men on the staircase, who whispered something to each other when they saw her. One of the strangers was carrying something which was wrapped up and looked like a small box. She was much exercised over this meeting, and on her way home she had already put together the following notions: the box might easily have been a camera, and the man a photographer who had been hidden behind the curtain while she was in the room; the click had been the noise of the shutter; the photograph had been taken as soon as he saw her in a particularly compromising position which he wished to record.[7]

Freud suspects that the young woman is suffering from a paranoid delusion that is motivated by fear of an imaginary onlooker, her mother, with whose sex the young woman identifies. Hence the famous remarks on homosexuality which Freud makes in this particular case history. As Freud puts it, the young woman has come into conflict with a maternal interdiction against having sexual relations with men. And because of this conflict, the young woman experiences a delusion or fantasm in which a knock or click is heard. "I do not believe that the

of Sigmund Freud, ed. James Strachey (London: Hogarth Press and the Institute of Psycho-Analysis, 1974), vol. 14, p. 263.

7. Ibid., p. 264.

clock ever ticked or that there was any noise to be heard at all," Freud says. In fact, "the woman's situation justified a sensation of a knock or beat in her clitoris. And it was this that she subsequently projected as a perception of an external object."[8] In Lacanian terms, the woman has lost her place as an "object of desire" in the Imaginary which knows what the other wants and instead constitutes herself as a Freudian thing somewhere else in the room. Here, in place of a discourse of the object of desire, a "thing" in the Real begins to speak in its place. And this thing might as well be asking Lacan's question: "In what way then is this ego that you treat in analysis better than the desk that I am?" Since, in essence, this is what the things are whispering in the young woman's imagination when she relates her history to Freud— in what way, then, is the ego that you, Freud, are analyzing more knowledgeable than the things that I, the subject, have heard speak to me in the manner of a click? The desk, a clock, possibly something from behind the curtains has been tapping, knocking, ticking. But Freud, who never gets very far beyond the phallic stage, is unconvinced.

For Lacan, however, the identification between the woman's body and the furniture would mark a negation of pleasure that brings to the surface a resistance to jouissance. What the object of desire cannot resist, the thing resists quite well. And yet, as Freud dryly remarks, the young woman is angry at her lover not merely out of a sense of moral propriety but because he hasn't satisfied her. It is a question, once more, of bad timing. Even Freud, who is quite insensitive to the woman's interest in the clock, unintentionally points to the problem: "I do not believe the clock ever ticked." Which is to say, Freud suspects the clitoris has ticked for the clock but that only the clock or some other thing in the vicinity of the desk is capable of representing this tick to the woman with whom it originates. But from a Lacanian perspective one needs to add that Freud has touched on something else besides that which is throbbing. For without there being a clock in the room that works, there is certainly no standard time by means of which pleasure can be achieved. Sexual pleasure, as we know, runs on standard time and the probabilities of there being coincidence. But given bad timing, the woman, for her part, is barred from that satisfaction

8. Ibid., p. 270.

which would enable her to psychologically express herself as desiring object and object of desire—Lacan's *objet a*.[9] Given this depression of the *objet*, the woman appears to take the side of things in a very peculiar manner: she intuits the presence of phantom others in the woodwork. As she leaves the gentleman's room, she notices men on the stairs carrying a small box that reminds her of a view camera. Was this the phantom-like object she hadn't seen but which she suspected clicking in time with desire? Enter the Freudian Thing.

The Chinese Phantom

Not long after Effi arrives in Kessin, she begins to experience a cree-piness that quickly turns into the kind of night terrors which wake people up in the middle of sleep. Effi is suggestible, and on hearing about a Chinese servant buried in the dunes she begins to imagine that he may well have the power to visit her. This fear is reinforced after a night's sleep in Geert's house when she asks why she has been hearing the dancing of slippers above her. The maids point out that the hall above is empty, though it has long curtains which rustle in the wind. But upon inspecting the almost empty room the next day, Effi notices that someone has pasted a little picture of a Chinese man to the back of the chair. Later, Effi wakes in great fright in the middle of sleep and asserts to Johanna, the maid, that "he" has brushed up against her in bed. Geert has been away on government business and on inquiring from the maids upon his wife's well-being is told that she has noticed what they call the "man upstairs." Geert tells the maids to stop talking such nonsense immediately.

Soon after her marriage to Geert, then, Effi notices a fantasmic corpse

9. The *objet a* receives numerous definitions in Lacan's work. See J. D. Nasio, *Les Yeux de Laure: La Concept d'objet a dans la théorie de J. Lacan* (Paris: Aubier, 1987): "The *objet a* is a formal rather than a descriptive category. It has no empirical reference and is in no sense definitively grasped. Rather than a concept, the *objet a* is a logical value without any other consistency than a letter; a letter combinable with other letters." Nasio sees the object as constructed in the transference and identifies it as either the "object of the fantasm" or object of desire and drive, the "erratic object," or object of hallucination, and the "imaginary object" or missing phallus (pp. 82, 91; my translation).

that seems all too real. For her, a bit of local folklore has been converted into a tale of terror. Fontane specifies that this Chinese servant is somehow connected with the marriage of a seaman's niece or grand-daughter—indeed, Nina's origin is mysterious—to a ship's captain. However, at some point in the wedding, held in the room above where Effi sleeps, the bride danced with many sailors, only to disappear like a phantom. The Chinese died a fortnight later though the connection with previous events is unclear. Most curious is how the underdetermination of the story's affect is accompanied by an overdetermined spectral effect for Effi. Why is it that this inert story becomes like a speaking thing accompanied with fantasms?

After Effi tells Geert about having perceived the fantasm, he tries to calm her. "Du siehst, Effi, man kann das furchtbare Wort aussprechen, ohne daß er erscheint" ["You see, Effi, it's possible for you to utter the dreadful word without conjuring him (the Chinese)"]. Effi's response is whether or not her husband can say for certain that the fantasm does not exist, and he responds, "Es ist eine Sache, die man glauben und noch besser nicht glauben kann. Aber angenommen, es gäbe dergleichen, was schadet es? . . . Spuk ist ein Vorzug" ["It's something that one can believe or, better still, refuse to believe. But assuming that such a thing does exist, where's the harm? . . . A ghost is a privilege"].[10] "It" is a thing, in other words, which one can believe in or not, take or leave. Ironically, this reasoning applies as well to the letters in the sewing desk, a point I won't develop here, the point being that the question of belief applies not only to fantasies but to the things the fantasies accompany: the Freudian things in Geert and Effi's world. Like the ghosts, a thing like the picture of the Chinese pasted on the chair is merely "eine Sache." Or, as Lacan would insist, with the Freudian id in mind, "Es ist eine Sache."

Perhaps *Effi Briest* could be called a ghost story haunted by the spectral *Es* as Freudian thing. No one who has read the novel, however, can escape the conclusion that for a Freudo-Lacanian ghost story, Fontane's text lacks the requisite uncanniness, or, if you like, spookiness. For as in the room of the paranoid young woman who wanted to bring love before the law in Freud's case history of 1915, things in

10. *Effi Briest*, p. 85; trans., p. 78.

Effi Briest are going "click" in the wrong places, though here it is the pitter-patter of slippers which Effi begins hearing upstairs and the brushing up of bodies against her which she feels. Here, again, we find a woman situated in a frigid if not frightening place, and we should not be surprised, in this place, to find the concretization of the fantasm. Indeed, one suspects that Geert himself ensures the possibility, since all of Effi's suggestions to change the things of their environment— relocation, redecoration, and so on—are met with an impotent immobility, an insistence that how things are is how one has to live with them. Effi has quickly recognized that Geert is asking her to acclimatize to an aporia where the fantasm inheres, in that aporia of the thing where pleasure is being converted to terror. It is here the all-too-real fantasm of the Chinese corpse, the letters, the sewing table, the body of Crampas, the dehumanization of Annie, and other such "things" will knock about.

In "Language, Psychosis, and the Subject in Lacan," John P. Muller notices that the Real in Lacan has no "gaps or lacks, and this absence of lack (if that can be conceived) is the inverse of what goes on in signification." Muller continues with the following statement: "The real, on the contrary, is a kind of static whole as well as a kind of black hole void of internal relations. To 'live in the real' means then to experience not just 'loss of self' but an unbearable plenitude; the term 'jouissance' catches the ecstatic quality of it but not the horror."[11] My suspicion is that in *Effi Briest* the construction of the fantasm allows the subject access to this "living in the real," this living in which jouissance catches the ecstatic quality and perhaps even enough of the horror to make a traumatic impression. What makes the Real peculiar in this sense, however, is that it is not composed of objects like the purloined letter in Poe which are signifiers of desire, but that it is composed of a setting into which the subject may itself withdraw as if it had suddenly become a thing about which nothing can be properly said, though its fantasmic "effects" can be felt.

11. John P. Muller, "Language, Psychosis, and the Subject in Lacan," in *Interpreting Lacan: Psychiatry in the Humanities,* vol. 6, ed. J. H. Smith and William Kerrigan (New Haven: Yale University Press, 1983), p. 28.

Ça Souffre

With respect to the "Freudian Thing" Lacan has said, "On se prenait seulement à répéter après Freud le mot de sa découverte: ça parle, et là sans doute où l'on s'y attendait le moins, là où ça souffre" ["One only needs to repeat after Freud that expression of his discovery, 'it speaks,' and without doubt there where one would expect it least, there where it hurts"][12] Lacan suggests that the where of "it speaks" is not always displaced but there where one finds it, there where "it hurts," or where one does not feel pleasure.

In *Effi Briest* the Real is a landscape of things that bear pain, a pain that not only Effi experiences but which is shared with Johanna, Frau Kruse, Roswitha, and Innstetten. In this landscape, the things whisper there where it hurts. In this sense, we can take things at the level of symptoms pointing to where there is pain, something that is embodied not so much within the individual mind but more generally in the setting or world of the novel. Indeed, the *ça souffre* is detected not only in the letters Innstetten finds, the wound of the daughter, in the pried-open sewing table, but also in the hen that Frau Kruse obsessively holds as if this black creature were a substitute for a child. Again, the materialization of the *ça souffre* is repeated where the dog Rollo stands by Effi when all others have abandoned her, where the Chinese servant is buried, where the curtains scrape against the floor. But with respect to Effi there is an alienation that goes beyond even the collective listening to what the things say, this shared social materialization, for Effi is so alienated that she does not just listen but herself accedes to the frigid condition of the house's furnishings, that extremely reified expression of the place where *ça souffre*. And if the symptom appears, it does so in the speaking or rustling of things, whether they are fantasmic slippers or bandages that can't be found. Indeed, one recalls the bandages needed for Annie's wound are an excellent example of how the stuff of the house materializes in the place of the *ça souffre* and how oddly this is linked to what binds Effi to the house and the family that exists inside that house. Of course, the question of binding is

12. Lacan, *Écrits*, p. 413; my translation.

crucial, and there are many bindings operative in the novel, as we shall see. All I wish to suggest at this point, however, is that one of the "things" that binds in the household is the appearance of the symptom, the *ça souffre,* as both spectral affect and physical object. In this appearance of the binding as thing, we cannot ignore how the symptom installs itself in the appearance of things that speak the language of the unconscious in the Real.

The Logic of the Fantasm

If Effi Briest is bound to be Real, it is not because she wills it but because she is fated to become the Freudian thing, that thing through which the fantasm makes its approach. That the Freudian thing, for all its solidity, *is* a fantasm we cannot ignore.

In *Le Séminaire XIV* Lacan spends considerable time demonstrating that the fantasm appears where one has logical, structural transformations of language as exemplified by Freud in the well-known essay "A Child Is Being Beaten."[13] That is, like Freud, Lacan maintains that the fantasm is ultimately tied to language per se. In *Effi Briest* many transformative sentences are suggested which would characterize the repositionings of the subject. For example, from Effi's perspective we could read "My mother would make a better wife for my husband than I," or "My husband is the lover of my mother who I really am," or "My husband is really my father whom my mother loves," or "I replace my mother who is the object of my father's desire," or "I am married to the man my father should have really been and whom my mother does not love," and so on. In other words, Effi is positioned as something that can shift. In this sense, the subject experiences a desubjectivization that both Freud and Lacan would have seen as es-

13. Sigmund Freud, "A Child Is Being Beaten," in *Standard Edition,* vol. 17, pp. 179–204. The sentence transformations include "My father is beating the child," "My father is beating the child *whom I hate,*" "I am being beaten by my father," "A child is being beaten." See J.-F. Lyotard for an informative reading of the relationship between language and fantasy with respect to "A Child Is Being Beaten" in *Discours, Figure* (Paris: Klincksieck, 1971), pp. 328–33. At this point in his career, Lyotard drew considerably from Lacanian analysis.

sential for the appearance of fantasmic scenes that the subject sees as if from outside, as in the case history, "A Child Is Being Beaten." Certainly, the relationships outlined in the various sentence transformations above suggest not only that Effi is constituted in a set of unstable if not fantasmic relations, but that she cannot take place as a self-identical subject within them, but, as we will see, only as she is a phantom proxy.

Also characteristic of the fantasm, according to Lacan in *Le Séminaire XIV,* is that it is structured by repetition.[14] In *Effi Briest* there is no lack of such repetition. After all, Effi Briest is the phantom double of her mother and as such is bound too closely with her in a narcissistic relation.[15] Geert, meanwhile, doubles for Effi's father. Even Briest, the father, notes that Geert would have been better suited to Luise, a comment that suggests that Geert is being openly acknowledged as Effi's more legitimate father, though in actuality he is nothing but an old if not irrelevant suitor from the past.[16] When Effi marries Geert, she becomes not only his wife but also the phantom daughter Geert and Luise might have had. Since she also occupies the place of the mother and symbolically brings to consummation a relationship that was abrogated between her mother and this suitor, her marriage to Geert is itself a phantom proxy for a marriage that has taken place only in Luise and Geert's imagination. Indeed, Effi is excluded from the family into which she is structured and is brought more strongly as real daughter into relation with Briest, her father, who has felt similarly estranged in his marriage with Luise. Much of the novel focuses on this father/daughter relation and the inability of this couple to set matters right. At the same time, if Effi is excluded from the family

14. Jacques Lacan, *Le Séminaire XIV: La Logique du fantasme,* is available in transcript form from Éditions du Piranha, 32 rue René Boulanger, 75010 Paris. For a published summary of the seminar, one can turn to Jacques Lacan, "Pour une logique du fantasme," in *Scilicet* 2/3 (Paris: Seuil, 1970), pp. 223–73.

15. See Marie-Hélène Delanoë, "Le Fantasme de la femme dans la prime éducation au XIXe siècle," *Ornicar?* 22–23, (1981): 239–52. Delanoë's work confirms that the female fantasm is closely related to a repetition or doubling between mother and daughter which forecloses certain kinds of object relations.

16. Effi's father says at one point to her mother, "Überhaupt hättest du besser zu Innstetten gepaßt als Effi. Schade, nun ist es zu spät" ["You would have been altogether more suited to Innstetten than Effi. Pity it's too late"]. *Effi Briest,* p. 40; trans., p. 41.

into which she is married, she is actually supposed to act as if she were the proverbial good wife. But when she falters—that is, when Geert suspects resistance, something that given the situation was inevitable in any case—she is aggressively if not irrationally repudiated.

This repudiation, as we have noticed, concerns the sudden discovery of the letters in the sewing table. But given the rather curious set of relations into which Effi, as phantom proxy, is structured, we can see that the repudiation may have other motivations. Geert, who cannot help but confuse Effi with her mother, is almost certainly harboring hostility against Luise. She has betrayed him by refusing to declare and act on her love for him, and this betrayal is ambiguously repeated even as it is being rescinded in Luise's use of Effi as a substitute for herself. Quite clearly, Effi is being prostituted by her mother to Geert for the sake of symbolically completing a romance aborted long before. Indeed, Fontane subtly underscores the prostitute reference toward the beginning of the novel when Effi expresses bad taste in her desire to purchase a gaudy Japanese bed with a red light for the house in Kessin. Her mother chides her: "Aber meine liebe Effi, wir müssen vorsichtig im Leben sein, und zumal wir Frauen" ["But Effi dear, we must be careful how we live, above all because we're women"].[17] Again, furniture speaks, and it is ironic that Effi's mother is too obtuse to hear its innuendos. In addition to these immoral undertones, it is evident, from Geert's condescending speeches to Effi, that she is more like a daughter or child to him than a wife. Given that she may function in the role of the child that Luise and Geert might have had, there is a question of incest. Although neither the hint of incest nor even the suggestion of prostitution will play a major role in the novel, it is difficult to ignore that such suggestions are being raised and that cumulatively they may account for why Geert's reaction to the letters is so strong. Finally, there is the question of bad timing. As in the case of the discovered letters, the attempt of Geert and Luise to recover something from the past is futile and destructive. Indeed, the irony in Fontane's narrative is that Effi is perhaps a perfect fantasmic go-between that offers little resistance. One wonders: is this what Geert unintentionally refers to when he says that phantoms are a privilege?

17. Ibid., p. 32; trans., p. 35.

Given the problematic overlapping, Effi, as linguistic shifter (or "it") can stand in different places within various familial perspectives, provided that she does not declare herself a desiring agency in her own right. Rather, she must be the thing that binds, the unitary trait or signifier of desire that belongs to the demand of an other. Given such a context, Effi is both a thing (a shifter or place holder) and a phantom (or substitute). However, she is also a point of anchorage which binds even as it transgresses relations, since she is structured to break family relations while leaving them perfectly intact. The daughter/mother ambivalence with respect to Geert Innstetten is perhaps the strongest evidence that characterizes this sort of double-bind.

That the question of the fantasm is linked to the issue of woman's binding or tying relationships in *Effi Briest* can be best explained, I think, by referring to Lacan's topological knot of the Imaginary, the Symbolic, and the Real. Although much of Lacan has been considered within literary-critical circles, it is surprising the extent to which his teachings on the Borromean knot have been ignored. And certainly no consideration of the Lacanian notion of the fantasm would be satisfactory without mention that the fantasm does not appear in any one of the psychic orders of the Lacanian topology, but that it is constituted as the interlacing of the Borromean knot, which is the topology itself (see figure 4).[18]

Effi Briest is the go-between facilitating the appearance of specular doubles. As such, Effi is standing in for someone else's desire. Her marriage affirms not her own "I want" but the "I want" of her mother in relation to Geert, an affirmation that in itself comes into play far too late. A specular and fantasmic affirmation, it repeats an Imaginary relationship in another, which affirms the subjectivity of the desiring object as an object of desire. The relation between Effi and her mother, of course, is narcissistic—far too narcissistic—and results in Effi's lack of resistance, her ability to shift from one role to another. Like Lacan's speaking desk, she adapts too well. Yet this lack of resistance and mobility only demonstrates that Effi Briest does not affirm herself in

18. Lacan refers to this knot in *Le Séminaire XX* (Paris: Seuil, 1975). Also see *Ornicar?* which has numerous essays on the Borromean knot, Lacan's *Séminaire XXII: R.S.I.*, which is largely on the knots, and Alain Jouranville in *Lacan et la philosophie* (France: Presses Universitaires de France, 1984), pp. 367–437.

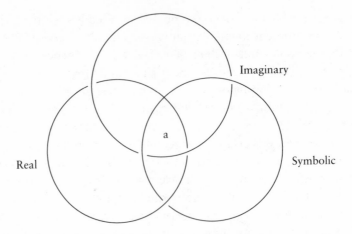

Figure 4. The Borromean Knot

the place of an object that could recognize the desire of an other. Rather, she has been expelled or ejected from the Imaginary order and jettisoned into the Real. Lacan, as we know, says in many places that the Real is that which cannot be penetrated (this, incidentally, may be why the sexuality of the young woman in Freud's case history takes to the side of things) and that it is inaccessible to analysis. But in the topological knot of the Imaginary, the Symbolic, and the Real, we learn that the Real is a loop that passes through the Imaginary, meaning that this is the point at which the "Freudian thing" and the "desired object" can be considered as bound or tied. Indeed, when we say that a woman withdraws into the Real, it is not in the absolute sense of the word, but in terms of this interlacing. In *Effi Briest* we notice that because the heroine is a "thing" in the Real she can function in the Imaginary as a shifter allowing for the fantasmic familial transformations listed above. In other words, the specular doubles in the Imaginary order depend on the phenomenon of there being a Freudian thing in the Real which mediates these doubles.

In addition, the Imaginary gets support from the Symbolic order, the social order of the family. And in this order Effi becomes part of property relations that are constituted in terms of patriarchal law. Without the regime of the Symbolic, the Imaginary spectral relations would fall apart, since at the level of the Symbolic an object of desire is definitively positioned in a structure that however much repeated or transformed always stays the same. In this context Effi acts as a signifier that constitutes a subject for another signifier, and it is this structure that Geert Innstetten activates when he discovers the letters. Indeed, only by way of the Symbolic can he determine his relation to Effi vis-à-vis the law-of-the-Father. Moreover, the Symbolic intersects with the Imaginary and grounds it in the law even as it crosses paths with the Real and determines mere things as agencies or signifiers of desire.

If there is pathology in the novel, it exists rather clearly in the structure of the Imaginary or narcissistic identifications that draw support from the Symbolic as well as the Real at the expense of Effi, who is being foreclosed by the Imaginary as one who can say "I am." Such a foreclosure ensures that Effi will always take place from a perspective that is eccentric to the affirmation of herself as a desiring being. This does not mean, simply, that she is ostracized, which would, in fact, give her a determinate position, but that she is being appropriated by others in such a way that she is essential for producing the very social bindings that keep her from coming into her own. Effi Briest, then, is put in the indeterminate position of being neither fully present nor absent in the very structure that articulates her as a social entity.

In order to understand how Effi can bind the three Lacanian orders, one needs to recall that in Lacan's topology "the Freudian thing" located in the order of the Real would, if transposed into the order of the Imaginary, function as the "desired object," and, if transposed into the order of the Symbolic, would function as the signifier of desire that positions the subject in relation to an Other. If Effi accedes to "the Freudian thing" in the Real, it is only because her mother obstructs her from occupying the position of "desired object" in the Imaginary, since she is already there where the daughter ought to be. Therefore, instead of situating herself as subject in the position of the desiring object as object of desire (*objet a*), Effi occupies the place of *la chose freudienne*. Yet, with respect to the order of the Symbolic, Effi is brought into relation with Major Crampas as Other whose desire puts Effi in the place of what it is that the Other wants. Geert, of course, quickly intuits this Symbolic economy at that moment he gains access to the letter as a signifier that positions his desire with reference to Crampas. Indeed, much has been said by readers of Lacan about what he calls the "agency of the letter in the unconscious," and Lacan himself has pointed out that one cannot determine whether the subject of a signifier is concentric or eccentric in relation to the place it occupies as subject of the signified. The possibility is quite likely, then, that one cannot determine Effi Briest's relation to the intercepted letters as a "subject" of the signified that would call itself an adulteress. In other words, no self-evident link between the signifier and the signified exists except as constituted by those others whose desire is positioned by jealousy. Here, once more, Effi takes place as a proxy of something and as such disappears.

We have now lost the "subject," Effi Briest, three times: she has disappeared into the Freudian Thing; she has quit the *objet a*, given that her mother already claims that position for herself; and she has disappeared as agency of the letter in the unconscious. Yet, were it not for all of these disappearances, the Borromean knot of Lacan's topology would fall apart. Moreover, what do we encounter in the repetition of these disappearances if not the coming to appearance of the fantasm as Lacan has defined it in his seminars?

Occlusion of *Objet A:* Of Anxiety, Inhibition, and the Symptom

It is well known that Lacan represented the fantasm with a short algorithm: $\$ \Diamond a$. In itself, $\$ \Diamond a$ stands for the alienation of the subject in relation to jouissance. With the diamond there is added the dimension of how the alienated subject either overvalues or undervalues that which appears in the position of the *objet a*. Rosine Lefort and Robert Lefort, in their authoritative *Les Structures de la psychose*, explain the Lacanian algorithm of the fantasm as delineating the evaporation of the object (a)—the desiring object as desired object—in terms of the subject's negation of the unconscious Other or law-of-the-Father.[19] This means, simply put, that the subject is alienated from the position of being wanted by an Other, and that the subject is thus

19. Rosine Lefort and Robert Lefort, *Les Structures de la psychose* (Paris: Seuil, 1988), p. 631. From the perspective of psychosis, this study is really the most outstanding survey of Lacanian theory we have to date by Lacan's followers.

radically alienated from jouissance. Yet given the deprivation of the *object*, it will come to appearance as something "greater than" ($>$) or "less than" ($<$) itself. In fact, the *object* will come into appearance by way of what the subject has foreclosed: the desire of the Other. What ensures that this return of the *object* will be spectral is the fact that the subject can no longer recognize itself in the *object* that bears on an Other's desire. For the alienated subject is working on the *object* both in a way that makes it less than and greater than what ought to be apprehended. That is, the subject encounters the *object* as a distortion. In *Effi Briest*, the *object* is clearly the mother, Luise, who is absent in the place that Effi comes to be as a surrogate who is alienated from jouissance but who nevertheless binds social relations as that "thing" which cannot come to appearance as the desiring object that recognizes itself as object of desire.

The *object* does not necessarily have the kind of spectral relation to a figure that we would find in a typical ghost story—that is, the substitution of a "living" phantom image for a "dead" physical figure— but may simply come to consciousness as a grossly distorted effect that for the alienated subject has no logical cause. In *Effi Briest* the noise of the phantom slippers might well fall under this rubric. Still, Effi herself is, even though living, the dead phantom double for her mother. If I suggest she is as if always already dead, it is because her existence is literally preempted by the mother, who sees to it that her daughter becomes little else than her phantom double, that "thing" which stands for her. From Effi's position, however, the substitution is not so simple, because it means that she is so radically estranged from her desire that she cannot come to be except as that "thing" which in its Freudian dimension points to the place where "it" hurts.

Let us return for a moment to Lacan's Borromean knot. The order of the Real, Lacan said in *Le Séminaire XXII: R.S.I.*, is that of anxiety. The order of the Imaginary is that of the inhibitions, and the order of the Symbolic is that of the symptom.[20] Put in terms of the logic of the fantasm, this suggests that the anxiety associated with things in the Real is a symptom in the Symbolic of an inhibition in the Imaginary.

20. Jacques Lacan, *Le Séminaire XXII: R.S.I.*, Lecture of May 13, 1975, in *Ornicar?* 4 (1975). Also see Jouranville, p. 373.

Considered in terms of the Fontane novel, this suggests that Effi's appearance in the Real as Freudian thing is a symptom of the *ça souffre* in the Symbolic that is connected to inhibition in the Imaginary, namely, an inhibition with respect to a relation to the *objet a*. Both the Freudian thing and the phantom would be linked according to this schema: the phantom being the thing.

Whereas we are accustomed to experience the literary fantasm as the representation of a purely imaginary construction (such as ghosts, spirits, gnomes), in Fontane we have a very good example of how the fantasm can be concretized in the person of a woman. Indeed, Fontane's novel shows that the fantasm does not simply appear because a simple substitution has been successfully made, but because the substitution is characterized by an inhibition. If we had the time, we could easily show that in Shakespeare the appearance of King Hamlet's ghost depends on a similar inhibition pertaining to Hamlet, which Ernest Jones has worked out in some detail. In Fontane, however, the substitution works well enough so that Effi can bring into relation the loops of the Borromean knot. Her ability to tie the knot of other people's desires but not her own is symptomatic of the extent to which substitution has failed. Effi Briest, then, is acting in the role of a symptom, the *ça souffre*. In her, as in the case of Freud's paranoid young woman, the lack of the *object* is badly supplemented because it is not in the "symptom's" repertoire to put the subject in the position of desiring-object as object-of-desire. If Effi is in the place where "it hurts," she is, as symptom, using that hurt to maintain the very system that produces pain. Not only that but her disappearance is both a prerequisite for the surfacing of what hurts in the novel and the consequence of what surfaces as symptom.

If *Effi Briest* is exemplary as a text that explicates the Lacanian fantasm, it is because for Lacan the fantasm is always constituted as repetition, and comes into appearance not simply because the Lacanian *objet a* is lacking, but because that lack is iterated with special effects in each of the Lacanian topological orders. Clearly the most extraordinary of such special effects is *la chose freudienne* in the order of the Real; however, from a broader perspective we have seen how the Lacanian fantasm concerns a disappearance that is repeated throughout the psychological topology (the R.S.I.) of the Borromean knot, a disappearance that conserves the very element that vanishes, in this case, Effi Briest. The fantasm, then, is the construction that accompanies or commemorates the repetition of disappearance and is what conserves the alienated "subject." In *Effi Briest*, we have the literary example of how the fantasm can be largely defined as the repetition of a disappearance evenly distributed within the Lacanian topology which articulates phony relationships of desire through the agency of the novel's heroine, Effi Briest, who is herself conserved as a fantasm and comes to pass as *la chose freudienne*.

Conclusion

"How is this ego that you treat in analysis better than the desk that I am?" Effi might ask. The clinical answer, of course, is that anyone who seriously asks such a question does so only because he or she has passed over into the realm of the Freudian thing where resistance is at once too weak and too strong. It is, and let there be no doubt about it, a pathological question, for if the desk speaks in place of the ego, that can only mean that the ego is sufficiently inhibited that it can only take place in the wake of its disappearance. In "The Freudian Thing" Lacan refers to this in terms of an object relation. "The object relation provides its appearances and this forcing has no other outcome than one of the three admitted in the technique in operation. Either the impulsive leap into the real through the paper hoop of the fantasm: acting out in a sense usually signifying the opposite of suggestion. Or transitory hypnomania by ejection of the object itself, which is properly described in the megalomaniac ebriety. . . . Or in the sort of somatization represented by hypochondria *a minima*, modestly theorized under the heading of the doctor/patient relationship."[21] The appearances of the object relation refer to how the ego sets up defenses or resistances against unconscious materials. The ego, whatever it is, does not exist independently of these imaginary object constructions or relations, and this ego is condemned to speak either (1) through the impulsive leap into the real by means of the fantasm (the paper hoop suggests that fantasm

21. Lacan, "La Chose freudienne," in *Écrits*, p. 429; trans., p. 139.

is akin to a screen through which a circus animal jumps); (2) through investing the object with such megalomania that the object is liquidated (objects incorporated in fantasies of power); or (3) hypochondria and somatization. "The whole thing," Lacan says, "would become banal if, after this prosopopoeia, one of you dreams that he is this desk, possessed or not with the gift of speech."[22] In other words, the Freudian thing is not a substitute for the adaptive ego of Hartmann or the *Cogito* of Descartes, but marks an object relation into which the ego vanishes as if it were what Muller calls a "black hole." The thing—or *ça*—is what speaks for the pathology of the subject rather than for the subject as "self."

Effi Briest pursues rather strongly at least two of the options listed by Lacan: the impulsive leap into the real by means of fantasm, and somatization or hypochondria. She dies, in fact, of somatization, and much of the novel concentrates on her relation with the doctor, a relation that once more poses the question of whether the ego is, in fact, better or worse than the Freudian thing that Effi has become. In the nineteenth century, the role of the doctor may well have facilitated the escape into the Real by means of treating the body as the site of the disease. In the case history of the young paranoid woman, written up by Freud in 1915, we can already see the extent to which psychoanalysis begins to understand the dynamics of somatization in relation to the subject's *parti pris des choses*. Not only that, but Freud is on the verge of understanding that basic to this phenomenon is the question of the temporality of desire. Lacan has gone much further than Freud in noticing how the dynamics of inhibition, the symptom, and anxiety function in relation to the construction of fantasm; and his work suggests how we might correlate the interrelation of the Lacanian orders with the production of a fantasm that is all too concrete. Still, the question of temporality is one that Lacan often ignores, even though it is he who has invoked the "time of the Other" in the seminar on *Hamlet*. In Fontane's *Effi Briest* it is self-evident that the dynamics of the phantom and of the *parti pris des choses* is almost entirely dependent on how life has been affected by the passage of time.

Indeed, it would be difficult to find many literary instances of this

22. Ibid., 422; trans., p. 133.

phenomenon in literature, though the *Lais* of Marie de France, *Perceval* of Chrétien de Troyes, and *Hamlet* by Shakespeare come to mind. In modern literature, such as Virginia Woolf's *To the Lighthouse*, time has its spectral accompaniments, too, though in "Time Passes" ephemeral shapes are brought into the foreground only to prepare us for a nostalgic recovery and apotheosis of the thing-as-lost—indeed, almost destroyed—object-of-desire. Again, in Marcel Proust's *A la recherche du temps perdu,* in which there is more than a little alienation, the disenchanted Marcel one day repeats a gesture from days of yore and remembers the shadowy things of an imaginary Combray, which reanimates his passion for life. And in James Joyce's *Ulysses,* after a lengthy hiatus, the time for sexual conjunction seems to be at hand in the yes of Molly Bloom, who, if the Homeric analogy is to be trusted, will embrace Leopold as Penelope did Ulysses. In Fontane, however, there is no such apotheosis. The novel ends after Effi has died and, as an afterthought, Luise asks her husband how it came to pass that things turned out so badly. "Ach, Luise, laß ... " Briest says, about to pick up a stock expression, "das ist ein *zu* weites Feld."

5

Disarticulations: Between the Sign and the Gaze

In *Blanchefleur et le saint homme,* Charles Méla is sensitive to an interplay between *merveille* and *malheur* in the *Conte du Graal,* the marvel or wonder of divine semblances and the misfortune connected with tracing or beholding them. He argues that the grail story of Chrétien de Troyes is a repetition of *semblances* whose scopic fascination disarticulates at once their likenesses and their traumatic features, since what appears to be at work in this dreamy repetition of *semblances* is the fading or decomposition of the image.[1] Indeed, the reading of such a work repeats that of disintegration, since the gaze of the reader appears only "en ces points de perte," at those places where the story is elliptical or blank. "To write is to efface and to read is to see nothing, since nothing is posited which isn't masked (cf. *Hamlet, Rosmersholm*)."[2] This is particularly relevant for the Perceval narrative in that one observes a hero whose gaze encounters answers for which he is unable to formulate questions, as if he were a dreamer who cannot articulate what he has envisioned, cannot analyze or bring into the full light of discourse the meaning of those very enigmas which fascinate but also terrify. What remains with Perceval are images, the mute representation of relics, whose coherence and power over Perceval are

1. Charles Méla, *Blanchefleur et le saint homme ou la semblance des reliques* (Paris: Seuil, 1979), p. 19.
2. Ibid., pp. 13–14.

a function of their reluctance to yield to the spoken word or integral text, whose force is that of remaining in suspension, of preserving a fragmentary network punctuated with points of loss or fading.

Although at great remove from Chrétien's *Conte du Graal,* in Lewis Carroll's Alice books one finds again an interesting opportunity to analyze a similar fascination with the scopic, in pictures. "Alice was beginning to get very tired of sitting by her sister on the bank and of having nothing to do: once or twice she had peeped into the book her sister was reading, but it had no pictures or conversations in it, 'and what is the use of a book,' thought Alice, 'without pictures or conversations?' "[3] If illuminations were significant for medieval texts, the illustrations of the Alice books are of essential importance, for not only did Carroll make his own drawings, which John Tenniel revised, but artists such as Max Ernst, Salvador Dali, and Peter Blake have continued to remind us that to picture Carroll's text is to dream over the lapse or fold that makes a tale out of what is impossible to tell, that in some sense, "reading" the Alice books constitutes a scopic experience that someone might call "spaced out."[4]

With that in mind I would like to begin by considering a pack of cards, keeping in mind that they too are illustrations whose enigmatic or puzzling features have a strong visual appeal. In the Alice books the fascination with the marvelous is always signaled by the phrase, "That's very curious!" Everywhere there is the sense of wonder or mystery before fresh sights whose enigmatic force Alice tries to unlock with a "proper" conversation.[5] Talk accompanies vision in the Alice books, though talk does not cure anything, does not clarify the enigmatic knots of perception. In that sense conversation is analogous to pictures, those very pictures Alice desired when she peered into her sister's book, but saw nothing. It is precisely such a sense of wonder before a tableau that Alice experiences when she enters into the Queen's croquet grounds with the bright flower beds and the cool fountains. Not unlike Perceval

3. Lewis Carroll, *Alice's Adventures in Wonderland* (New York: Schocken, 1978), p. 9.

4. See Graham Ovenden and John Davis, *Illustrators of Alice* (London: St. Martin's Academy, 1972), for a wide list of artists who have illustrated Carroll's texts.

5. See Tony Tanner, *The Reign of Wonder* (Cambridge: Cambridge University Press, 1965).

who is astonished suddenly to find himself in the chateau of Gourne-
mont, residence of the Fisher King, Alice "finds herself" in a wondrous
prospect of roses: "A large rose tree stood near the entrance of the
garden; the roses growing on it were white, but there were three gardeners at it, busily painting them red. Alice thought this a very curious
thing, and she went nearer to watch them."⁶ The gardeners are cards,
of course, and not only their unfamiliar act of painting the white rose,
of illustrating, but their very own "illustratedness" as cards creates in
Alice a sense of wonder, for she finds "this a very curious thing,"
engaging but puzzling. And just as she is made to articulate this, we
begin to enter into the conversation with the cards, a conversation that
illustrates all the illustrating Carroll has already presented. The conversation, too, is mysterious, and one cannot help noticing a mise-en-
scène of illustrations or semblances that circulate about a *point de
perte:* a wondrous mystery that is closely allied with another mysterious
experience expressed by the card known as "Five": "You'd better not
talk. . . . I heard the Queen say only yesterday that you deserved to be
beheaded." Such a cutting of the cards motivates this wondrous conversation as well as the act of illustrating the roses; and, indeed, it
signifies a *malheur* about which much circulates by way of repetition:
illustration on illustration, card next to card, the knowledge that a
deck can be cut anywhere, and so on.

Yet once Alice becomes familiar with the croquet grounds and the
court cranks she says to herself: "Why, they're only a pack of cards,
after all. I needn't be afraid of them!" As if the image were traumatic,
or at least potentially so, as if a dreamer were saying to herself that
she can stop the fantasmic production of signifiers whenever she wants,
that this is, after all, just dream. Again we notice *malheur* in Wonderland, and this feeling is but the dark, anxious underside of the word
"curious." Still, Alice keeps *malheur* under control by asserting along
with the recognition that the cards are only pictures the fact that her
name is Alice, as if a proper name had any more substance than "Five"
or "Seven."

Something similar occurs in the *Conte du Graal* when Perceval "intuits" his name to his cousin somewhat after he has seen the mysteries

6. Carroll, *Alice's Adventures*, p. 74.

of the lance and the grail at the Fisher King's residence, as if to say, I, Perceval, have survived the vision to which I have been submitted. My name is a stronger and more powerful representation than the one I experienced. Thus I am intact, whole, pure. Nevertheless, it is at this moment of intuition that Perceval learns about *malheur* and loss.

> He spoke the truth not realizing.
> But when the maiden heard, arising,
> she faced him, angry and estranged,
> and said, 'My friend, your name is changed!'
> 'To what?' 'To Perceval the wretch!'
>   (3581–84)[7]

At best, the name is but a psychic defense, not a cure for having failed to ask the question, to make the right conversation at table (Fisher King as Mad Hatter?), to articulate the mysteries in words to the wounded man suffering beside Perceval.

If the end of Perceval's quest is, as in the finished versions of the narrative, the naming of the enigma whose answer already gives itself like an open letter, the end of Alice's quest in Wonderland is restoring good authority to the region by dislodging the fierce temper of the castrating Queen of Hearts. This is achieved by a performative speech act that repeats what Alice has secretly known all along ... that *You* are merely a series of figures or illustrations. Indeed, Carroll emphasizes that cards have, like any painting, a front and a back and that when faced down, as they are when the King and Queen enter the croquet garden, they are effaced and cannot signify their class distinctions; whereas, when the cards face up, a hierarchy of values based upon a series of differences (color, number, portrait, suit) comes into play. A Saussurian Alice would have said, "You are nothing but a pack of signs!" or, better yet, "You are just language!" For like language, each sign has its recto/verso, and each sign is syntactically in play with every other sign, depending on the suit. The point is not so much to exploit the metacritical potential of the pack, but to say that in pronouncing "You are nothing but a pack of cards," Alice does not necessarily dispel

---

7. Chrétien de Troyes, *Perceval*, trans. Ruth Harwood Cline (Athens: University of Georgia Press, 1985), p. 99.

the "laws" of signification or syntax of the pack. Simple shuffling, the throwing of cards into the air, does not make the language of cards go away; it just initiates a new game. All Alice can do, like any other dreamer, is disrupt or silence the formidable chain of dream signification, of Wonderland, to disarticulate by recognizing that a representation must be put in its place, diminished in status vis-à-vis the ego. We will come to this shortly in terms of how Carroll diminishes the figure of woman in story and photograph. Yet to proceed in this way is to practice a certain Freudian denegation, to recognize the power of the decapitating Queen by taking decapitation into one's own hands, by throwing or scattering the deck of cards. To scatter the deck is not to abolish anything—a pack, a game, the laws of chance—but merely to ensure whatever is already and always there.

In Wonderland what is always already there is illustration, enigma, picture, representation, dream. There is also what Méla calls *semblance*. What needs to be stressed is that the semblance reveals itself as already disarticulated, at once dispelling its fascination along a serial chain, a chain along which image production is dispersed, morcellated, but a chain that also fixates and repeats, that also stages a fascination by means of an obsessive return to the same. What assembles the *semblance* is the series, the various moments of appearance, moments that are in themselves dispersed, cut, fading. The *semblance*, then, is structured like a language, though it evades translation into a plain discourse. As Jean-François Lyotard remarks, "The figure or form is itself not unified. The fantasm contains many forms that are simultaneously active."[8] In Wonderland the deck of cards is exemplary of such re-*semblance,* which is recuperated by means of dispersion, spreading, or cutting. Indeed, to shuffle the deck initiates a game or sign system, a significant series of relations; yet we know too that in Wonderland such spreadings or initiations never lead to games that make much ordinary or normative sense, that translate into the kind of "language" Alice can fathom. It is interesting that Lacan is most helpful to us here when he points out in *Séminare II* that the play of numbers in mathematics represents not so much a signification as a movement of the sign and that this slippage will circulate in a "universal machine that

8. Jean-François Lyotard, *Discours, Figure* (Paris: Klincksieck, 1971), p. 328.

is more universal that anything you could imagine." According to Lacan, "The world of signs functions, and it has no signification whatsoever." And yet "What gives it its signification is the moment when we stop the machine. These are the temporal breaks which we make in it. If they are faulty, we will see ambiguities emerge, which are sometimes difficult to resolve, but which one will always end up giving a signification to." Lacan argues that the halting of the machine, this temporal cutting or breaking, is the "intervention of a scansion permitting the insertion of something which can take on meaning for a subject."[9] And I would add at this point that such a scansion in the Alice books is nothing less than the insertion of the *objet a,* which is the gaze itself, that mirror reflection produced in the imaginary which facilitates the introduction or insertion of the self into language. This introduction asserts itself by no other means than a rupturing whose point is to disperse the deck of signs, to stop the movement of signification. ·

Notice that this insertion of the *objet a* is the insertion of an illustration, a mirror reflex that is itself the product of scansion as *coupure,* a reflection that is the Wonderful or Marvelous Alice who is "underground," as Carroll once put it. Here language, scansion, rupture, and illustration are closely allied and demonstrate to what extent Alice is articulated in terms of language and vision, sign and image. For she is herself a movement of the sign that arrests itself in a scansion that is the result of doubling or mirroring, the gaze, which is sign, object, illustration, the looking and looked at. Lacan notes that when one considers a universal language, one is already considering a machine or automaton or series that can arrest itself by means of a system that scans itself as it scans the whole. And this machine within the machine is produced by an accident, by an interference, like a slip of the tongue or a sudden fall down a rabbit hole.

The mirroring, reflection, or *objet a* that holds the subject's attention discloses itself most fittingly in the illustration or figure of the Cheshire Cat, who like the little girl and the pack is already "cut." If ever there were an opportunity to talk about metalepsis and an allegory of read-

9. Jacques Lacan, *The Seminar II: The Ego in Freud's Theory and in the Technique of Psychoanalysis,* trans. Sylvana Tomaselli (New York: Norton, 1988), p. 284.

ing, it is there for those who wish to make the application. For my part, it will be enough to say that the Cat is the rather mad and metaphysical character or figure who pronounces all the roads of Wonderland to be homologous or even homogeneous and in this way can stand in for Alice to the extent that it too has an investment in denying decapitation, though the Cat's denial comes at the expense of reason, sense, syntax, difference. The Cat's madness resides in the perception that the event of decapitation has not yet occurred, even when it is clear that the Cat is anything but in one place at one time with its entire body. The appearance of the decapitated Cat on the Queen's croquet ground raises what can only be called a decapitation riddle: (1) according to the executioner (Death), one cannot cut off a head unless there is a body to cut it off from; (2) according to the King (Law) anything with a head can be beheaded; and (3) according to the Queen (Castration), if something is not done right away, everyone's head will be rolling on the lawn. At the moment this mystery is articulated, the Cat's head slowly fades, magically resolving the problem even as it perpetuates its mystery.

The Cheshire Cat's (Alice's) body is not unlike what Lyotard calls the "erotic body," " . . . which is not the body experienced erotically but a surface on which is inscribed the localizations of desire, the opposite of a world, at least for the child, the pervert, the hysteric: a puzzle of regions where the charge and discharge of jouissance finds its places of privilege, but a puzzle no one or no thing can visually grasp in order to make a unified picture, since each zone itself must accept many simultaneous significations with respect to pleasure [plaisir]."[10] An erotic body, the Cheshire Cat is a figure representing a puzzle that is concerned with inscriptions of desire, not the least of which is the desire for omnipotence manifest in the wish to see without being seen, to be without being perceived, like a man taking pictures of little girls with torn dresses or in the nude. In that sense the disarticulating image is a function of its own desire to watch (the image as re-lapse), and the points de perte constitute an elaborate defense mechanism. The Cat is, of course, a metaphor for Alice's body, and may be considered her narcissistic double or just another instance of the objet a.

10. Lyotard, p. 338.

The Cat may well belong to the "child, the pervert, the hysteric." But this double, this enigma that is the Cat refuses to disclose itself "in order to make a unified picture" and, as Lyotard continues, "must accept many simultaneous significations with respect to pleasure."

The moment of the Cheshire Cat's vanishing head is not entirely unlike the procession of the mysteries at the residence of the Fisher King in the grail narrative, because the figures at the Fisher King's residence also evade the very articulation they elicit. Like the bleeding lance and grail, the Cheshire Cat's head is both marvelous and unfortunate, and whereas for Alice the Cat is rather engaging and appealing, just as for Perceval the lance and grail are wondrous, the Wonderland King is distraught by the Cat's uncanny presence above the grounds, for in it he sees *malheur,* misfortune, and even danger. Whereas the Queen shouts, "Off with their heads," the King is specific about executing only the Cat, for the Cat presents the enigma of cutting, the puzzle that cutting is its own negation and that therefore separation makes whole. Moreover, this figure raises the thought of an erotic body, the hysterical body or child body that belongs to not only Alice, but to the Queen, that lack in which the *objet a* finds itself. It is this Queen whom the King really wishes to decapitate, as if she were not already so.

For clearly at issue here is a castration complex concerning both the erotic and the question of points of loss. In *Alice's Adventures* this complex has to be read pictorially/linguistically in terms of woman's recognition that she has no phallus, in terms of the hysterical body. For what else is the castrating mother figure, this Queen of Hearts, but the enigmatic certainty that castration exists and that woman is its embodiment? Apparently the "subject," then, is woman. Alice for her part will deny such an articulation of the subject by attempting to cancel the bad authority of the mother, by means of a calculated rejection of the place of the mother as Lacan would situate it within an economy of imaginary and symbolic relations. Thus Alice denies castration, denies the fact that she has no phallus. And this denial occurs by way of Alice scattering the deck of cards by way of a performative speech act, an act that at once denies and maintains the law as it is conveyed through the Queen.

If Alice desires to repress the truth of castration in order to allay

penis envy, to suppress the trauma of her own woundedness, and if it
is the Queen's tendency to announce the "Law" of castration throughout Wonderland, it is the strategy of the Cat to show that the act of
decapitation evades temporality, spacing, and difference by making
undecidable the question of before and after. For the Cat, the event of
beheading never takes place, really, though its effects are everywhere
visible, and in that sense the Cat insists in a Derridean/Nietzschean
manner that truth as a function of deciding, limiting, or cutting is
suspended forever, and that the truth of castration, too, is always
averted, because similarly hung in uncertainty. It is an obsessive uncertainty, of course, one that fixates or pins down the "subject" before
a spectacle or movement of signification that mysteriously vacillates
between visibility and invisibility, the assertion of meaning and its
dispersion, articulation and dis-articulation.

Perhaps Derrida is right in *Éperons* when he says that castration "c'est
justement l'affaire de l'homme," and that woman does not have to
believe in it. And yet woman is saddled with this complex just the
same. That is, Alice Liddell has to play with castration in Wonderland,
since Victorian society proclaims this law so loudly. The more specific
proclamation comes from Carroll, the weak king of Wonderland, as a
consequence of what may well be a desire for someone who is not
touched or cut by the doom that the Queen of Hearts proclaims so
loudly; that is, Alice symbolically represents the phallic for Lewis Carroll. Indeed, she is the "key" to the Alice books and occupies that place
in which the entire opposition of whole and part, *merveille* and *malheur,* plays itself out. She can be viewed as the symbolic certainty that
castration can be denied and that Carroll's masculinity is not in jeopardy, a defense mechanism that insists that only by means of a phallus
can a little girl remain intact, that only by being touched by the symbolic
phallus can she remain a virgin. The "logic" for such a formulation is
already to be found in Derrida's "Double Séance" and also in Lacan's
"Signification du phallus" in which we are made aware of a phallic
mother posited by both sexes. Thus one might wonder whether Alice
as (ph)Alice is the signifier of desire by means of which man envies
woman's lack of a phallus, since such a lack always presents itself as

a phantom-phallus, a *semblance* whose mark is wholeness, completedness, or, as this is valorized in the West, virginity.[11] Such a phallus cuts and makes one, divides and sews, unifies and disseminates. From such a perspective one might wish to say that here a phallus is invaginated with a hymen, that in this marriage we see the difference of gender ambiguated.

❧

"During the Twelfth and Thirteenth centuries," Charles Méla writes, "la *semblance* concerns the body and, too, the enchanted body."[12] In romance the reference is not only to the apparition of fairies or enchanted castles, but to the metaphysical appearance of women such as Gwenhwyvar (the "Ombre Blanche") and Blanchefleur, whose face appears in the drops of blood that Perceval contemplates in the snow, if not, as Méla suggests, in the blood dripping from the lance in the grail scene at the Fisher King's residence. The sovereignty of such apparitions, Méla suggests, is asserted not simply as a symbolic force or significance, a meaning hidden within the appearance, but in terms of the image's birth in the very gaze of the viewer. When Perceval looks at the lance and grail, instead of seeing a symbolic meaning, he experiences the sovereignty of the apparition, its streaming out toward the one who looks. Similarly, the force of the image of Blanchefleur in the drops of blood on the snow is nothing less than her sovereignty, one that has been won by denying and accepting the phallus at once. For has not Blanchefleur slept with Perceval without compromising the sanctity of her body? "So they lay / the night together, side by side and mouth to mouth till morningtide." Has she not played at being Perceval's little girl in distress? Blanchefleur: "For each day is a grief to me, / and nothing brings relief to me" (2064; 1993–4). Blanchefleur's name, already a combination of virginity (*blanche*) and the phallic (*fleur*) gives us a clue to her power: that virginity ensures itself by

11. Martin Grotjahn, "About the Symbolization of Alice's Adventures in Wonderland," *American Imago* 4 (1947): 32–41. Translated in the *Revue Française de Psychanalyse* 14, no. 4 (1950). The article concerns symbolization in Alice's adventures and posits the equation between phallus and Alice.

12. Méla, p. 11.

sacrificing itself to the phallus, by acceding to the fantasmic condition
of phallic plenitude. Hence, if woman cannot have the phallus, why
should she not become it entirely? Why not allow the whole body to
detach itself from itself like the symbolic phallus, to present itself as
the signifier of desire which the other sex may never have, in short, to
become a *semblance*? Blanchefleur, we should recall, appears to Perceval like an apparition. She has left her bed and entered his room
without waking him.

> The maid sighed deeply, and she wept,
> and knelt beside his bed, and bent
> across him so her tears went
> upon his face and made it wet.
> She dared not be more forward, yet
> she cried so hard and with such art,
> the knight awakened with a start.
> He was astonished when he felt
> his face was wet and saw she knelt
> beside him with her two arms clasped
> around his neck and held him fast.
> He had the courtesy and taste
> to put both arms around her waist
> and draw her closer to inquire,
> "Fair maiden, what do you desire?"
> (1966–80)

We should not ignore the fact that on waking and seeing her as a lovely
apparition Perceval has, nevertheless, asked a rather psychoanalytical
question. Blanchefleur responds by saying she hopes she will not be
shamed for having come to Perceval. "Although I may be nearly nude,
my thoughts were never bold and lewd." Yet her entry into the room
is bold. As Chrétien says, she is "stouthearted," "courageous," "bold
and daring." And when Perceval invites her to spend the night with
him she says, simply, "if you prefer, / I shall do so" (1988–90). And
yet, even if they sleep mouth to mouth, they do not lose their virginity.

The word *sanblance* occurs in the Old French within the passage
where Perceval is transfixed before the three drops of blood in the
snow. Henri Rey-Flaud notices, too, that what Perceval sees in the

drops of blood against the screen of snow is the resemblance of that Blanchefleur "who joined Perceval in his room in Beaurepaire, nude, beneath a white gown over which she has thrown a red coat."[13] It is now that Perceval is made aware of the significance of Blanchefleur, the *malheur* in the *merveille* of the scene, the *malheur* that has everything to do with cutting, bleeding, pain, absence, though, as Méla would stress, nothing is cleared up, exactly, in this pause before the red stains. Nevertheless, in Blanchefleur's *semblance* Amfortas is inscribed, and of this there can be no doubt, because the bleeding lance and the sleeping Perceval are raised as sure markers that we are once more considering the mysteries of the Castle of the Fisher King. According to Rey-Flaud, "The blood on the snow marks, therefore, the emergence of the subject. And this subject emerges at that moment where for the first time the truth of his desire is articulated—truth, desire, and subject until that moment 'in abeyance' [*en souffrance*]."[14] Indeed, a subject manifests itself, constructs itself before the drops of blood. What counts for suffering is the stopping or abeyance of a narrative action before the spectacle, this rupture in which a man with a lance recalls a woman and discovers in that recollection or memory screen something about sexual difference and desire. It is he who has the phallus and she who bleeds. And yet she has not been touched: she remains whole, intact. Does Perceval marvel, having intuited "the truth" as Rey-Flaud calls it, that Blanchefleur is still pure, that having shared Perceval's bed she has vouchsafed her virginity? Is there not a certain undecidability in this *semblance* which hovers between cutting and wholeness, which makes impossible and obligatory the difference between parts and wholes? That would be to say, were we to affirm these questions, that she is and is not the hymen-phallus, a sexual construction in the imagination which is repeated in no one else but Perceval. And this would be another way of noting that the power of the image that is Blanchefleur rests in her appearance or manifestation as the *objet a*, as a fantasmic reference whose allure reveals itself in the gaze that recognizes the white and the red in terms of *merveille*

13. Henri Rey-Flaud, "Le Sang sur la neige: Analyse d'une image-écran de Chrétien de Troyes," *Littérature*, no. 38 (May 1980): 17.
    14. Ibid., p. 22.

and *malheur* respectively. But what is this fantasm, as Méla suggests, but the repetition of a recollection, the recollection of Perceval's mother, a figure Lacan situates in the region of the *objet a?*

Not unlike this Perceval who experiences a memory screen as he looks intently on the spots of blood on the snow, Lewis Carroll invokes the following in one of his texts, "Stand forth, then, form the shadowy past, 'Alice,' the child of my dreams."[15] Like a souvenir the dream-Alice remains and haunts Carroll from the shadowy past. The child friend: Alice Pleasance Liddell—this is the "full" name written out in the last poem of *Through the Looking Glass*. Her name inscribes jouissance, pleasure principle, a libidinal satisfaction, a kind of touch, of contact, of a coming together not only in a dream, but in reality, a coming together that in life is mediated by the social trope or figure called friendship. Indeed, the friend is the trope through which this narrative flows, the channel that allows the company of Carroll and his child friends to continue, to sustain itself on various dates. To meet: to narrate. The engagement occurs only with the possibility of story, only because narrative is there to provide a suitable detour or clearing or block between the writer and the little girls, that prevents close intercourse, such as touching, fondling, and sexual loving. Like a river—the Alice books are akin to the *roman fleuve*—the story separates two persons, one on each side of an embankment, and ensures that Alice and Lewis remain but good friends, stay apart as individuals, as intact, and yet remain in contact.

There are actually three people where we see only two. Alice, Lewis, and Charles [Dodgson]. The middle figure, like Alice, is phantomized, and for reasons that will become clear later; in any case, this Carroll connects the two figures on either side, for he is the Imaginary playmate not only of the Alices but of Dodgson as well. If anyone doubts this game, consider that Dodgson wrote to Dolly Argles on November 28, 1867, the following letter:

15. Lewis Carroll, "Alice on the Stage," in *Lewis Carroll: Lettres à ses amis enfants* (Paris: Flammarion, 1977), p. 278.

Dear Miss Dolly,
I have a message for you from a friend of mine, Mr. Lewis Carroll,
who is a queer sort of creator, rather too fond of talking nonsense.
He told me you have once asked him to write another book like
the one you had read—I forget the name. I think it was about
"malice."[16]

In the middle there is nonsense, Lewis Carroll, and on the two sides
or borders we have Charles and a little girl, communicating across
this chasm which separates and binds. And yet someone is saying "I
love you." Roland Barthes would have called this a figure of the
lover's discourse, and we can only agree that such a statement is
already the narrative that articulates itself in order to make sure each
figure remains isolated from the other, intact, even as it elicits a
means for touching to occur, for something like a physical union or
flaring up to take place, whatever that might be. In *Alice's Adventures*
"I love you" turns into the stream of words, a flood of adventures,
a peculiar proliferation of figures in which even the little child friend
is introduced, the "you" articulated at length within the nonsense of
Lewis Carroll, the phantom lover. What I find most intriguing is that
within the narrative line, Carroll develops what is an intermittent
breakdown between speakers. That is, the conversations or floods of
words that maintain friendly relations in the story between what
usually amount to two people keep falling apart as if the text were
trying to subvert the notion of the "friend"—as if it were trying to
break down that proper distance between Alice and the inhabitants
of Wonderland.

Certainly the figures Alice meets are unfriendly, if anything, most
of the time, and one could say that this failure to establish relations
is symptomatic of the fact that Dodgson wishes to cross the flood
of his own narrative, that he wants to disarticulate the narrative line
in order to get rid of that mediating story which keeps safe the
friendship between himself and Alice Liddell or any of the other child
friends who participate in this relation with a text whose proper
authorial name is Lewis Carroll. It is as if "I love you" must be

16. Ibid., p. 72.

followed with a silence, lapse, or disarticulation, the kind that in more mature relations anticipates physical touching. But since the text represses that silence through its own extension into a book-length story, a series of adventures, it contains within its very articulation that "wish" to dissolve and silence itself within a very contorted logic whose purpose it is at once to deny and yet achieve narrative progress, to negate itself at every point in protest to its own existence, which has to be there if Dodgson wants to maintain relations at all with his girl friends. Thus the narrative and the figures it contains comprise a limit between achievement and separation, being together or touching and being apart or remaining intact, and this means, finally, that the narrative itself is, if anything, a language of desire, the wish to be recognized by the child as a lover at the same time the demand for such recognition must be dissimulated.

What keeps and separates the simulacra is the figure of Carroll, the *semblance* of the subject as writer, Dodgson, and it is this *semblance* of which there can be found photographs that puzzle those who want to know "who" is being represented there. The figures of the child friends, too, not only fascinate in terms of narrative production but in terms of photographic production as well. And in this sense the child friends turn into images or figures situated within little *tableaux* that suggest narratives. For example, one photograph of Alice Tane Donkin is entitled *The Elopement* and shows a little girl escaping from a second-story window with the aid of a rope ladder. Actually, she looks like she is floating fantasmically, and this floating signifier, if you will, visually makes a statement such as "I love you" or "I want to be with you," whoever "you" may be, and her figure, placed precariously outside the window—the Lacanian *cadre du désir*—suggests the kind of being together (that of man and wife) that is immediately refused or negated by the figure's size and age, as if such a miniaturization represented an inhibition in the Freudian sense. If the photograph of the little girl represents a touch, an "I love you," or elopement wish, then the very distance that makes such a wish appear immediately available to the gazer—a distance between camera and power, scene and photographic place that makes possible the articulation of someone's desire—is repeated again by the inhibition of the figure, the reduction of a woman into a little girl. Especially in the photographs of the naked child friends,[17] the infantalization or inhibition of the figure is at once asserted as strongly as it is denied or interrupted by what are strong sexual references to adult females, and it is in this sense that the distance between the model and the photographer is at once maintained and denied, that a disarticulation of the image's overall sense occurs. "I love you" oscillates between "I seduce you" and "I cannot touch you."

But who is "I"? It is the figure of the child, whether literary or pictorial, a figure that is not simply an image but a dimension of a modality of seeing, even if the childlike eyes of these figures themselves are incredulous, themselves staring in disbelief, sometimes rendered inarticulate by the very spectacles they see. Indeed, the figure of the child embodies that dimension of the gaze whose visibility is impaired by incomprehension, wonder, fascination, fixation, entrapment, or ignorance; and whose gaze is that but the gaze of the one who constructs and reproduces the scenes in which these figures play, the gaze of the one hidden behind the desiring machine, the camera? It is the photographer's inhibited gaze we are really seeing in the photographs, though it is represented or seen only in the image or figure of a child, a face that cannot, even in life, properly "see" anything in the way the photograph would have it. At a later point we will see from a Lacanian position why this inhibition takes place, how the Lacanian Imaginary has orchestrated its role.

In "Inhibitions, Symptoms, and Anxiety," Freud writes, "Analysis shows that when activities like playing the piano, writing, or even walking are subjected to neurotic inhibitions it is because the physical organs brought into play—the fingers or legs—have become too strongly erotized. It has been discovered as a general fact that the ego function of the organ is impaired if its erotogenicity—its sexual significance—is increased."[18] This impairment occurs to "vision" when the organ of the eye or the scopic drive becomes too erotized. In Dodgson's gaze such an overly strong erotogenicity causes lesions, lapses, or fadings in the ego's comprehension of the erotic object. It is as if

17. See Morton N. Cohen, *Four Nude Studies* (Philadelphia: Rosenbach Foundation and Clarkson N. Potter, 1978).

18. Sigmund Freud, "Inhibitions, Symptoms, and Anxiety," in *The Standard Edition of the Complete Psychological Works of Sigmund Freud,* ed. James Strachey (London: Hogarth Press and the Institute of Psycho-Analysis, 1974), vol. 20, p. 15.

sight had become a violation of the visible, a violation that prohibits itself in its very expression. Perhaps it would be better to say that the gaze belongs to the imaginary playmate, Lewis Carroll, articulated at once as *objet a* and what Lacan calls the barred subject. It would be a gaze, then, that makes itself apparent everywhere in the Alice books, as well as in the photographs of the child friends.

We recall that in the Perceval story it is Perceval who is transfixed before the drops of blood and who sees there the semblance, who posits a memory screen in which not only Blanchefleur but Perceval himself is represented or mirrored. It is not simply a construction of figures but the establishment of a gaze, the stopping of a machine, as Lacan puts it, that allows for the interruption or punctuation of a subject by the establishment of an illustration or figure, a little or metaleptic imago who brings us closer to ourselves by bearing us away from ourselves. If Carroll is himself a semblance produced in the gaze of one who has a desire to possess a little woman, the children whom Dodgson photographed are part of that reductive fantasm or semblance known as Alice, who is herself a reflection of a girl who lives above ground or on this side of the looking glass. Like Blanchefleur, this semblance is everywhere invested with both *merveille* and *malheur,* plenitude and lack. But if Perceval recognizes in his memory screen the object of his desire, if he finally sees Blanchefleur miraculously virginal because he sees in himself a man who would, given the chance now, violate her chastity, Dodgson recognizes only Carroll with his young girl friends, sees even more than Perceval a female figure who is inviolate and protects that inviolability by photographing it. It is in the photographs that the children will be touched by the phallus as manifested in an imaginary looking known as voyeurism but who will remain chaste, pure, whole. And we must ask: is it not only by means of a photograph of a little girl that such a child can be touched, her being cut by a stare, and only for the sake of proving that she is intact, that she attain a sovereignty by herself acceding to the fantasmic condition of phallic plenitude? Being unable to receive the phallus, does the semblance of the child not substitute for it?

༕〜◎

"To photograph people is to violate them," Susan Sontag writes. "By seeing them as they never see themselves, by having knowledge of them they never can have; it turns people into objects that can be symbolically possessed."[19] It is as if a photograph can look through a person, can see a person stripped, naked, can, as in the photographs of Diane Arbus, demythologize people by merely exposing their covered surface to our tacit and perhaps endless scrutiny. Carroll's photographs of children similarly demythologize the figures of Victorian children by pointing out a certain freakishness: the knowledge that these children are not what they appear to be, that these figures are in some sense disturbingly other. And what disturbs is not so much their mere appearance, but their gazes, the knowledge of themselves they can never have and yet represent or possess in any case, that gaze they have appropriated almost completely for themselves.

If the figures Arbus photographed present themselves to us as freaks, as unselfconscious surfaces, uninhibited in outlandish display, such figures also manifest a cruel gaze that violates what at first seems an innocent,

---

Eric Rohmer's film *Le Genou de Claire* restages the scene between Perceval and Blanchefleur. A film that carefully balances *merveille* and *malheur,* it is set on Lac Leman, Switzerland. Jerome, a cultural attaché in his late thirties, owns property on the lake, and as the film opens he is on holiday and comes across Aurora, an old flame who likes to write about kinky sexual situations. It is she who brings Jerome into proximity with two very young women who are vacationing with their mother by the lake. The younger of these adolescents is a fifteen-year-old brunette named Laura. She has an older half-sister who is seventeen, a blonde named Claire. Rohmer is intrigued with the nineteenth-century contrast of brunettes and blondes, though in his films their coloring does not correspond to any fixed symbolism. Rather, the contrast exists in order to counterpoint moods that reflect ways of being in the world.

It is Aurora, of course, who plants a seed in Jerome's mind about experimenting with adolescent desire. Those of us familiar with psychoanalysis know that Aurora's motivations are not merely analytical or in

19. Susan Sontag, *On Photography* (New York: Farrar, Straus & Giroux, 1978), p. 11.

blind self-presence. And that cruel gaze is certainly that of the photographer, but a gaze that is lost or given to the space that is the figure, held by the image as the image's own; call it a dispossessed look, if you like.

Such a gaze separates the art of photography from mere picture taking and marks the point at which the "I" turns "eye," a modality of seeing free from the enclosure of a self in which censorship manifests itself. That is to say, perhaps photography becomes art when the photograph discloses the photographer's inhibited gaze, which cannot see but is seen, a gaze whose object is nothing less than the seeing as freak, other, or *objet a.*

"Woman is presented to man by means of a symptom; woman is a symptom for man," writes Lacan.[20] And according to Freud, "A symptom is a sign of, and a substitute for, an instinctual satisfaction which has remained in abeyance; it is a consequence of the process of repression."[21] Of course, the instinctual impulse finds a substitute in spite of repression, "but a substitute which is very much reduced, displaced and inhibited and which is no longer recognizable as a satisfaction. And when the substitutive impulse is carried out there is no sensation of pleasure; its carrying out

---

any sense very benign. She is a voyeur who derives pleasure from encouraging others to act out her fantasies, particularly when these others are of the opposite sex. Jerome is another matter. About to be married, he thinks he can allow himself to flirt with these girls, suspecting that with them nothing too serious can happen. Like some of Rohmer's other films, this one is roughly divided into two unequal divisions: one presided over by the brunette mood, and the other by the blonde mood. The younger of the two girls, Laura, is an especially precocious gamine and, in fact, has a crush on Jerome. Melancholic, philosophical, introspective, and overly sensitive, Laura is both fascinated and put off by Jerome. He, for his part, relays back to her the desire she wishes to arouse in him and, at the climax of this part of the film, the two walk in a mountainous area, embrace and kiss. As is usual in Rohmer, there is something very awkward about two different people holding or kissing one another. It has none of the automatic qualities of Hollywood sex. In fact, the embrace and the kiss—I think it is the only passionate kiss Jerome experiences during the film—curiously conveys a mixed feeling of attraction and repulsion. Some-

20. Jacques Lacan, *Scilicet* 6/7 (Paris: Seuil, 1976), p. 60.
21. Freud, p. 17.

has, instead, the quality of a compulsion."[22] In short, the symptom is accompanied by anxiety. Against Freud's comments one immediately notices the radicality of Lacan's formulation that woman is a symptom for man. For example, in terms of Carroll, the photographs could be seen as symptoms or substitutes that mark an inhibition. That Carroll had numerous notebooks filled with such photographs and that his biographers mention his strong absorption in photography as almost an obsession fit with the notion of a symptom as having "the quality of a compulsion." And, too, the intersection of *merveille* and *malheur* points to the strife between pleasure and anxiety which attests to the symptom's damping the pleasure that instinctual satisfaction ordinarily would attain. That Carroll substitutes images for the real erotic body, the real flesh and blood of woman, only makes this dampening effect more evident. Carroll's photographs are symptoms or displacements, perhaps what one might call part objects for a privileged object that can never make itself present in the full sense of the word. As such the symptoms are obsessive signs or signifiers that repeat themselves over and over again in the service of

---

thing like but not like child molestation insinuates itself here—which is to say, we are viewing the preliminaries to what some might view as a crime. That both Laura and Jerome feel quite uncomfortable and suspect that some kind of law of the emotions has been transgressed marks the end of their close relationship, though they remain friends. He and she have both experimented with physically embodying attraction for one another, but Laura keeps her distance. It is not that she is supposed to feel shame; rather, she feels something more like repulsion. Jerome is old enough to be her father. Jerome himself, however, feels something else: for him the kiss does not just reveal or disclose his distance from Laura, but the impropriety of his feelings and actions towards her. His act is one of deliberate molestation, however much he has pretended to be emotionally transported. Yet, here too, there is a conflation of *merveille* and *malheur,* of the marvelous and unfortunate moment of contact between two people so distant; here the modern experience of adolescence emerges as something which expresses an abyss dividing generations. Although Laura likes to think that she might be more suitable with an older man than the clumsy

22. Ibid., p. 21.

repression. That the photograph constitutes its own erasure is not surprising, for the photograph's purpose is to manifest an object in what looks
like a real world that is rejected in the register of the Lacanian Symbolic,
and therefore the photograph must disarticulate itself even as it facilitates
the prolongation of an impossible gaze; it must make possible that look
which is a function of a self-concealing or self-canceling desire. To reproduce or restore the object of an instinctual impulse on this register of the
apparent or appearance, what amounts to presentation on the Lacanian
register of the Imaginary, is to submit to the erasure commanded by an
imperial Other, to submit to a forced censorship initiated or relayed by
the unconscious. A fantasm, then, is produced, that is to say, a dreamlike
object that we can contemplate in a conscious state, a symptom that recalls
the return of something the mechanism of repression has failed to cancel
entirely.

In *Le Séminaire XI,* Jacques Lacan calls considerable attention to the
idea that central to the issue of visualization is not only fading but the
annihilation of the subject that in Hans Holbein's *Ambassadors* is represented as a skull. "Holbein makes visible for us here something that is

---

boys of her own age group, there is a curious feeling of repulsion that
occurs when fantasy is realized in a kiss. The physical touch or caress is
a holding, staging, or framing that converts *merveille* into *malheur.*

In the second part of Rohmer's film, wherein the genius of Claire's
passive blonde spirit prevails, we are made to notice three appearances of
her knee. First, Jerome sees the knee straddling a ladder as Claire picks
fruit with her boyfriend, Gilles. Second, Jerome notices it as Claire is
putting medication on her finger while sitting in a chair. Her left foot is
propped up on the chair as she is sitting on it, hence raising her knee.
Aurora, who never misses a beat, particularly when it relates to the erotic,
hands Jerome a glass of lemonade and holds it out just far enough so that
Jerome in reaching over Claire's body can "accidently-on-purpose" take
hold of her right knee and clasp it. "Pardon," he says. This gesture, I
should add, is done very quickly, and Rohmer cuts the scene just at the
moment Jerome touches Claire. The third holy manifestation of the knee
appears to "St." Jerome in what is the climax of this part of the film.
Jerome is taking Claire by speedboat to Annecy where she wishes to leave
a letter for Gilles. Earlier that day, Jerome has concluded that Gilles is

simply the subject as annihilated—annihilated in the form that is, strictly speaking, the imaged embodiment of the *minus-phi* φ of castration, which for us, centers the whole organization of the drives through the framework of the fundamental drives."[23] What Lacan points out, then, is that this annihilation passes unseen even though it is most clearly represented by Holbein. We look at this fantasm—a phallic fantasm, no less—but see nothing. "What, then, before this display of the domain of appearance in all its most fascinating forms, is this object, which from some angles appears to be flying through the air, at others to be tilted? You cannot know—for you turn away, thus escaping the fascination of the picture."[24] The skull in the Holbein is distorted; we might say faded or erased, and Lacan's belief that Maurice Merleau-Ponty was right in thinking that the gaze is not entirely something constructed or invented by a subject, but something originating in the "flesh of the world," leads Lacan to posit the notion that when we "see," we "see" through an other. In the Imaginary register this "other" is the *objet a,* whereas in the Symbolic register it is

---

two-timing Claire, and for some unacknowledged reason—one assumes jealousy is the cause—he wants to punish and humiliate her. Shame is very much at issue here. He gets his chance with her on the lake when it begins to rain so heavily that he must put into shore and wait out the storm in a little wooden shelter. The scene in the shelter is itself quite undramatic by Hollywood standards, but is one of the stronger scenes in the history of cinema. Everything is simple, perhaps even a bit static. None of the emotion is exaggerated. None of the movement is stylized.

In the lengthy first sequence the camera never shows Jerome and Claire in the same frame. When film critics see such disjunctions, they interpret them as meaning that the characters exist on different planes. It is interesting that whereas in the scene with Laura in the mountains the camera pans around the couple as if to embrace or caress them with the camera eye, in this the only intimate scene between Jerome and Claire the camera refuses to hold both figures in the same frame.

Here I would like to propose that one could think about a phenome-

23. Jacques Lacan, *The Four Fundamental Concepts of Psychoanalysis,* trans. Alan Sheridan (New York: Norton, 1978), p. 89.
24. Ibid., p. 88.

the large Other. It is this vision of the overlapping big Other on the little other that the "I" as "eye" tries to capture and yet fears to see.

Roland Barthes, in *La Chambre claire*, notes that "photography is unclassifiable. I will ask myself then to what this disorder could cling," and again, "a photo is always invisible; it's not that which one sees."[25] For what one sees is a phantom double whose enterprise is not to indicate what surely it must, "At the end what I see in a photograph taken of me ...is death."[26] In this sense, Carroll's photographs of children visualize what is narrated in Alice's adventures, the stories of little girls (his Alices) underground. Like Persephone, the child is at once dead and living. But this suspended "death" is but the arrest of the subject's gaze, of Dodgson's looking. It is the overlapping of *objet a*, the gaze, with the large Other who raises the pertinent existential question: are you dead or alive? In the *Adventures* this can be rewritten to read: are you sleeping or waking?

Dodgson's photographs are a writing that remarks on the Lacanian Symbolic register at the same time that they function within the narcissistic

---

nology of cinematic holding in terms of the shot. Whereas we are used to thinking in terms of how characters on screen may hold or frame one another, yet shots or frames also do some holding as well. In the scene with Claire and Jerome, the shots actually resist holding or touching. That is, the camera refuses that totalizing space wherein both figures can be included and hence brought into a relation that puts them on the same plane. Of course, the failure (perhaps even the disarticulation) of a visual embrace is itself a gloss on Jerome's act of caressing Claire's knee. Just before he touches her, there are two medium-shot sequences in which the two figures are seen together in the same frame but not visually revealed as directly communicating. After these sequences, the camera focuses primarily on Claire, as Jerome suggests that Gilles has been unfaithful. After she has run out of self-defeating reasons to defend him, she breaks into tears and tells Jerome to shut his mouth. The camera zooms back from Claire's face, though still not far enough to hold both Jerome and Claire in the same shot. It is now that the assault on Claire's knee is made, a

25. Roland Barthes, *La Chambre claire* (Paris: Seuil, 1980), pp. 15, 18.
26. Ibid., p. 32.

economy of exchange in terms of the register of the Lacanian Imaginary. What sustains the fantasmic production of the child figures may be still another question posed at the Symbolic level that asks the subject something analogous to the questions just formulated, "Where is your phallus?" And such a question, already posed clearly in the Holbein painting in which a skull represents itself phallically, refers on the register of the Symbolic to the annihilation of the subject, an annihilation that can be warded off only if the subject can convince himself that annihilation can be defeated by overcoming time, that is, by image formation, immortalization in terms of photography as well as by neutralizing the effects of castration by imagining that one is, after all, not a male who has been castrated, but a female all along.

In this there may be some affinity (not necessarily psychotic) with Judge Schreber who was absolutely convinced that he was becoming a woman, that if one watched him half-naked before a mirror for some time, one would notice the transformation. Here too the feminine turns into a "symptom" for man, because woman is an imaginary substitution or signifier experienced on the level of the physical (an imagined reality, cer-

---

touching that the camera isolates and holds for a long time. As Jerome touches Claire, who is almost too distracted with grief to notice, he begins willfully to massage her. That Claire happens to be wearing a mini-skirt and that the upper part of her thigh is fully exposed makes this massaging gesture visually ambiguous. As Jerome will say of this later, what was intended as an act of desire she took as a gesture of consolation. In fact, we can see that Jerome's touching of the knee is the beginning of a seduction that avoids both the embrace and the kiss, an avoidance of holding already encoded into the shot sequences. But as in the first half of the film with Laura, the woman remains chaste. There is something mysterious if not wondrous about this maintaining of distance, something reminiscent of Perceval and Blanchefleur, except that the modern world is hardly one where sexual innocence or ignorance plays a very large role. Claire is already quite experienced in matters of lovemaking.

This is the account Jerome tells to Aurora in her sitting room immediately after the scene, which ends with Jerome's pulling his hand away and the resumption of the boat ride to Annecy.

tainly) by the subject, and what counts for him is visualizing that sign which marks his transformation. Like Schreber, Carroll wards off the Symbolic threat of castration, the Oedipal law of the Father, by becoming a little Alice, or to put it more aptly in terms I have already used, a little (ph)Alice, for what object is the little girl replacing, what privileged object is being restored by means of substitution if not the PP: the pleasure principle which is also the penis? The fixation on the child is a fixation on one's own body and the girl child's gaze is nothing less than a look at once accusing, "Where is your phallus?" and consoling, "It's right here: I am (ph)Alice." The phantom phallus is anamorphic: at once intact, large, present, and at the same time impaired, vanishing, absent, like the skull phallus in the Holbein painting of two ambassadors mirroring one another, or like the growing and shrinking child, Alice. The child as (ph)Alice, then, marks the coming to pass of a fantasmic structure in which, once more, *malheur* is brought into relation with *merveille*.

So much then has to do with the figuration of a gaze, the construction of *objet a* in which the arrest of a signifying movement is punctuated. What has concerned us is the appearance of a fantasmic aspect of Lacan's

---

She sat facing me, one leg bent, the other stretched out, her knee was sharp, narrow, smoother, delicate, within reach. Touching her knee was the most extravagant thing and at the same time the easiest.... It took courage, you know; I've never done anything so heroic or at least so willful. It's the only time I accomplished an act of pure will.

A bit later he says,

I had to open her eyes. This was my good deed. What I took as a gesture of desire she took as one of consolation. Then a sort of peace came over me mixed with the fear of not controlling the moment. But the results couldn't be more moral. On the one hand I broke the spell, on the other, the girl's body no longer obsesses me. And I did a good deed. I got her away from that boy for good.

Aurora, characteristically, responds with: "She'll find someone worse." But Jerome concludes, "Je suis comblé" ["I am fulfilled"].

phallus notion in a region of the schema from *Le Séminaire V: Formations de l'inconscient* (figure 5) bound with Imaginary substitutions, constructions, and destructions. This relation or figuration of the gaze may be quite significant, because it helps to demonstrate the mistakenness of the kind of thesis advanced by Gilles Deleuze in *The Logic of Sense*, which looks forward to a schizoanalysis pairing Carroll with Artaud, as if they were mirror images. In the section "Of Schizophrenia and the Little Girl," Deleuze argues that in the difference between Alice and Humpty Dumpty one can find two ambivalent poles, "fragmented organs—body without organs, body-sieve and glorious body"[27] This kind of description brings one close to the Schreber case, though for me the reference was with an eye on narcissism and not psychosis. It is the psychotic reading of the Alice books that I am challenging with the less spectacular though perhaps less considered view that these narratives are not saturated with psychotic behavior, that schizophrenia is not the topic of the Alice stories.

If we consider Lacan, we immediately recognize that psychosis is a malady that occurs when the relays of narcissism fail, when the Imaginary

---

Aurora, who is amused by the story, treats it with detachment, since she realizes the entire account is predicated on the man's attempt to be in the place of woman so that he can calculate the effects of his desire and actions on her. And essentially this same dynamic motivated Jerome's flirtation with Laura as well. Thus when he says, "This was my good deed," he is assuming quite a bit on the part of a woman he hardly knows or cares about. But if Jerome tries to assert Claire's autonomy in the name of his own desire, Claire's knee retains its own sort of autonomy or remoteness even as it has been revealed or exposed in such a manner that Jerome can be said to have taken complete possession of it.

This exposure is really quite complex because it not only represents Jerome's access to the woman's body (and her sexuality) but also her body's privacy and autonomy, its inaccessibility to him. Most interesting, this does not take place at the level of refusal—that is the whole point of the scene—but at the level of distance and difference. For Jerome the perception of this appearance of the knee is nothing if not that of the withdrawal of the erotic. And this leaves the knee up in the air, as it were,

---

27. Gilles Deleuze, *The Logic of Sense*, trans. C. V. Boundas (New York: Columbia University Press, 1990), p. 92.

splits into two zones, resulting in the foreclosure of both the law and the
barred Subject. In fact, such a split results in two selves: the ideal ego of
what Freud called primary narcissism and the ego ideal of secondary narcissism. With such a splitting, the sense of the Real is expelled, foreclosed,
since this, too, is ruptured when each narcissism goes in its own direction.
Apparently the two selves do not know they are related to each another,
even though they exist or manifest themselves in discourse. In schizophrenia there is no longer a master code to unify, no Law to pin down or
anchor the movement of the signifier, to articulate a desire rather than
many desires that have become autonomous. Such a Law is manifested in
the place of the large Other, but is acknowledged by the self whose existence is "stupid" and everyday.

Everyone knows that Charles Dodgson is Lewis Carroll and vice versa,
but what is most important is that one figure knows about the other, sees
a relation and a metaphorical one at that. In the letter to Dolly Argles,
quoted earlier, we notice that Dodgson tells her about the strange Mr.
Lewis Carroll. If we read to the end of the letter, we discover him telling
her that if she has anything to request of Mr. Carroll to make sure her

---

in a somewhat ambiguous manner, its position being at once very fetishistic
and very moral.

We are now in a good posture to see to what extent a highly questionable
scene between an older man and a teenage girl substitutes the moral for
the erotic and in that way attempts to forge a connection where, in fact,
there is none at all to be made. Also, we can appreciate the extent to which
a man's rather immoral interest in girls is rationalized on moral grounds,
as if his rather questionable interactions with them could suddenly be
turned into some kind of moral tale. Too, it must be said that whereas in
the first episode with Laura, *merveille* gives way to *malheur,* in the second
malheur gives way to *merveille* and that, to this extent, each episode holds
or embraces the other even though in each an embrace or holding misfires.
This misfiring, of course, bears very much on the framing of the relation
between Jerome and the very young women, a framing that approaches
what Jacques Lacan calls the *cadre du désir* wherein one of Lacan's later
maxims is staged, namely that no relation between the sexes inherently
takes place. What the man relates to is merely the *objet a,* and therefore,
as Lacan says in *Encore,* the whole of his realization in "the sexual relation

correspondence goes through Mr. Dodgson as insurance that Mr. Carroll receive it. There is nothing schizoid here because the specular doubles recognize each other within the Imaginary. Moreover, we discover in Carroll's correspondence a very strong sense of what we could call reality. Carroll knows much better than some of his biographers that his desire to photograph "nude studies" of little girls was not entirely for the good of either the children or their families. In the instructions Carroll left to the Executors the following appears with respect to the nudes: "Please erase the following negatives: I would not like (for the families' sakes) the possibility of their getting into other hands. They are best erased by soaking in a solution of washing soda." The idea that the plates can be washed clean does suggest that perhaps there is something unclean about them. Then, too, there is the suggestion that these images are fantasmic insofar as they can be made to vanish. Particularly the nude image lends itself to disarticulation. Its reality undergoes *ces points de perte.*

One might say that reality, in this case, is made up of the Imaginary

---

comes down to fantasy." Claire's knee, of course, is that object and, for Lacan, would answer the question of how neurotics make love. As he puts it, "How do neurotics make love? That was where the whole thing started. It was impossible not to notice that there was a correlation with perversions—which lends support to my *object a,* since, whatever the said perversions, the *a* will be there as their cause."[28] The failure of Rohmer's film to frame or hold this fantasmic object in such a way that it maintains Jerome's fantasy exposes the bankruptcy of the object's value in and of itself and that neither the filmic window of desire nor the erotic or moral constructions posited in the script, prevent us from realizing the Lacanian principle that, in the default of the object, the absence of a sexual relation is made manifest from the side of the woman who does not give that object support, or, to put it another way, who does not allow that object anaclitically to prop his desire.

In the case of Lewis Carroll's picture of his girl friends, the fantasy is maintained by providing an isolated space within which the figure achieves

---

28. Jacques Lacan, "A Love Letter," in *Feminine Sexuality,* ed. Juliet Mitchell and Jacqueline Rose (New York: Norton, 1982), p. 157.

and its relation to the large Other or Symbolic order, which dictates that the nude photographs, at least, be erased after the subject's death. Yet, while the subject lives, these photographs occupy the role of the *objet a* which fills in for a lack the subject experiences. In the seminars of Lacan there is mention of the minus phi, or gap in which the phallus itself is missing, and it is here that so many gadgets will appear, in which a lure will punctuate the movement of the signifier with a sudden arrest and the manifestation of a subject, the ego ideal as "I." Whereas this ego ideal (Lacan's *objet a*) stands in relation to the large Other (the law of the Father), it finds its scopic fulfillment in the place of the *objet a*. It is at this scopic locus, moreover, that there is a demand for a phallus or completer of desire initiated by way of the Mother, a signifying agency who lacks and possess the phallus, depending upon how one takes her. Thus the ego ideal will see by way of a gaze or moment of recognition produced in the locus of *objet a* a phantom phallus or representation of that which can never be had, of that which belongs to both Mother and Father. Hence we are broaching the Oedipus relation, since at issue is the child's desire for Father's phallus in order that he can provide Mother with what she

---

plenitude and becomes a totalizing entity that is itself the completion or fulfillment of desire. Still, the famous pose of Alice Liddell as a waif in torn clothing reminds one of how the body becomes accessible to the desire of an other by exposing or focusing on certain parts of the body. Of course, the tears in the dress are quite overdetermined: the figure is at once abject, pitiable, solicitous, seductive, vulnerable, controlling, and violated. And yet, all this is represented in terms of child play or pretense. Even though Alice is being dressed down, she is, at the same time, being dressed up. And this game, if one can call it that, is what frames or holds Alice in a perceptual field whose contradictory horizons are moral rectitude and sexual exploitation. In other words, the pose is suspended somewhere between charity and violation, the moral and the immoral. What differentiates this from Rohmer's film, of course, is that Rohmer inserts the male into the violate/inviolate space of the woman as an actant and explores the physical dimension of what happens when the man physically, sexually approaches a young woman who inhabits quite an other experiential world quite different from his. What is so interesting about Rohmer's "Genou de Claire" is the fact that even when Jerome touches the

wants, a wanting which is articulated not only in the locus of the maternal (the Imaginary) but in the locus of the paternal (the Symbolic).

We could go further in pointing out that in terms of the following Lacanian schema a fantasm can be constructed when one likens the *objet a* with the Law, then diagonally crosses the graph in order to link the Other with the barred Subject and then, finally, connects that barred subject with the "a" prime or ego ideal (the Imaginary Me). (See figure 5.) This N pattern translates as follows: the ego ideal is articulated not only by means of a narcissistic relationship to the Mother (a-prime to *objet a*) but is also articulated by means of an intercession of the Law, of a phallic mode of substitution to which the ego ideal itself wants to accede ("I wish I were my Father"). In this way the Imaginary (whose master trope is metonymy) is repeated in the Symbolic (whose master trope is metaphor), and these two registers can be said to be tied together. Obviously, the a-prime or ego ideal cannot simply see itself without any mediations in the locus of the law, the Father, the large Other, but has to receive a message or letter in the form of a Name or phallus, a forwarded letter, as it turns out, that has knocked at some doors before arriving at its destination.

---

young women, he is not able to enter into a shared world of experience wherein the touch might make any erotic sense to both of them at the same time. And this, of course, is where one can detect a certain difference between Rohmer and Carroll. For Rohmer men and women can only satisfactorily approach one another sexually when their relationship makes erotic sense. For example, in *La Femme de l'aviateur, Le Beau Mariage, Le Rayon Vert,* and *Nuits de la pleine lune,* this is crucial to all that transpires, since at issue are relationships that are fundamentally out of synchronization and in terms of which the touch becomes extremely difficult to negotiate—even, as in *Le Beau Mariage,* to the point of considerable misery on the part of the young woman who is trying to make a big catch. In the photographs of Carroll, however, the erotic proceeds much more neurotically without any appeal to an other; there, the erotic only has to make sense to the photographer's desire and the girls are, of course, kept entirely ignorant of the photographer's pleasure. In Carroll's photographs, therefore, the erotic does not have to be negotiated between model and spectator: in fact, it is only conceivable from the side of the male spectator, since the girl doesn't take place in the very scene where

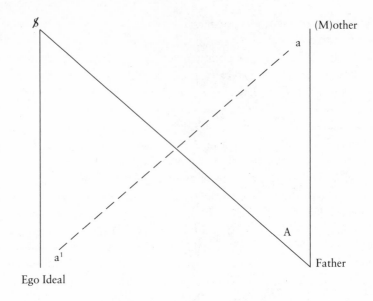

Figure 5. The narcissistic relation between the ego ideal and the (M)Other is mediated by a trajectory that passes from the (M)Other as lack (castration anxiety) to the law-of-the-Father, to the barred subject, and finally to the ego ideal.

Specifically, this letter comes via the barred Subject before it can arrive at a-prime—the ego ideal. This forwarding movement is nothing but the Symbolic at work, yet notice how strangely the Symbolic has wormed its way into *another* narcissistic relationship, one that we have not yet considered. This is the relationship of a-prime to the barred Subject. (See figure 6.)

her sexuality is being appropriated. For Carroll, then, the representation or photograph itself becomes the *objet a,* an imaginary object proffering a sexual relation. In Rohmer, to the contrary, the woman manifests herself as Real (as some Thing apart—Lacan's *la chose*) if only to withdraw from the man in such a way that his imaginary relation with her is put into jeopardy.

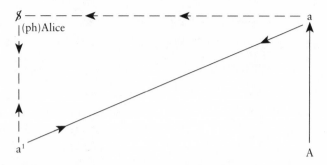

Figure 6. The barred subject identifies with the (M)Other: $ \not{S} \diamond a $. The result is that the fantasmic figure of the child appears in the place of the phallus. In other words, the narcissistic relation of a–a' is short-circuited.

This is a very significant relation because without it the psychotic becomes everywhere manifest, and for the following reason: in order for the ego ideal to withstand the pressure of the Law, it must sublimate the Law into part of an Imaginary construction. Thus instead of saying, "I want to be like Father," it is necessary to say, "I want to be me." The incorporation of the Law into a narcissistic relation reduces the Law's threat, diminishing or transforming the Father as leader of the primal horde into just another brother, just another version of myself to which I have access and right. In the mollification of the unconscious Law by the Imaginary, the voice of the Other is allayed, neutralized, incorporated, within a system of relations in which the Mother occupies a preeminent place. Were it not for such accommodation, the Other would announce itself directly to the world as in psychosis where one has imposed speech, the telepathy of voices.[29]

29. In "A Lacanian Psychosis, An Interview with Jacques Lacan," a certain Mr. Primeau suffers from telepathy. "On the radio I had the impression that someone was listening to me, was making fun of me. I was really at the end of my rope with this telepathy." But the radio speaks to Primeau, too, and says things under its breath which he knows are intended only for him. At other times Primeau hears certain "emergences" such as "*You killed the bluebird. It's an anarchic system.*" As the patient himself says, an "imposed speech" structure has developed. In this instance, the Real, Imaginary, and Symbolic are not interacting with one another; in particular, the Imaginary and Symbolic are not properly interacting. Jacques Lacan, in *Returning to Freud,* ed. Stuart Schneiderman (New Haven: Yale University Press, 1980), pp. 20, 37.

If I have strayed from Carroll, it is to make the following observation: in Carroll the relation between the ego ideal and the barred subject is reflected or mirrored in the relationship of the ego ideal (a-prime) to ideal ego (*objet a*). And this doubling is deviant, since in the confusion of these two narcissisms a transposition takes place in which the locus of the Mother (*objet a*) finds itself in the place of the barred subject, as if it had been shifted over. If the relation of the barred subject to a-prime is usually mediated by the intrusion of the Symbolic, as in figure 5, in figure 6 repression has taken place and the Mother intercedes on the behalf of her little boy. It is as if Carroll does not listen to the Law as it is forwarded through the barred subject by the Father, a forwarding or maturing that would give some clue where the ego ideal ought to find itself temporally and in terms of its masculinity. Instead of listening to the law of the Father, Carroll puts in place of the barred subject an image of woman with which he speculates.

But this image of woman, what is it exactly? It is *objet a,* the locus of the Mother as well as the locus of the gaze. And when this small object other is transposed in the place of the barred subject, the ignorance of the subject, as Lacan has reminded us, has to be maintained. And therefore when the Mother comes to occupy the place of the barred subject, she turns into a child, a subject that can be looked at in a narrative or through a camera but which itself "doesn't know." And this is not all. For the barred subject is in the place where the phallus is posited and also in the place where a fantasm will appear, for the *objet a* has all the qualities of trompe l'oeil or photography, according to *Séminaire XI.* So it should not surprise us to see a "phantom phallus" in place of a real one, which is to say, a certain (ph)Alice.

It follows, too, that if the *objet a* is shifted over to the place of the barred subject, this will influence what the ego ideal thinks of itself, how the ego ideal or Imaginary self constructs its identifications. Indeed, this may account for how we get both Charles Dodgson and Lewis Carroll, since Carroll, who mediates Dodgson and the child friends, is but another ignorant or empty subject who is prone, as he says over and over again in the letters, to talk nonsense. It should be said that Carroll can be at both the locus of barred subject and ego ideal at the same instant, for Carroll is the Imaginary me or ego ideal whose famous name will accede to the position of the Law (logic, rebus, literature), which considers Carroll a certain Father of the word, of a Truth that even if we cannot always decipher it remains, all the same, a Truth to be reckoned with. Yet if Carroll manages the Imaginary in such a way that he becomes a strong writer, a Father of language, that ego ideal is still compromised by the *objet a* in the place of the barred subject. For in that gaze wherein the *objet a* installs itself there occurs the production of a fantasm that at once turns Carroll into an immortal at the price of his own sexuality—the sexuality of Charles Dodgson. Here again there is *merveille* and *malheur* as well as a fading, lacking, losing out, here in this scopic fascination with naked little girls in poses that attempt restitution of the Mother, of their mothers. And all this in the place of the Mother, which has slipped too far towards the locus of the barred subject.

Can we say that Carroll's triumph as a writer occurred because of what we might call an early misrecognition, that *Mother is more like Father than me, and that I am more like my Mother than my Father?* It would comprise a metaleptic movement in which by way of a feminine image the subject brings itself into a certain relation with the Law, produces an Imaginary resemblance where none, perhaps, ought to be so pronounced. And (ph)Alice? She is suspended, phantomized, phallicized over the barred subject, like a Cheshire Cat in a tree. It is a way, perhaps, for Carroll to be both the son of his Father and his Mother, and a way to answer what Lacan thinks is the fundamental question the analysand is fated to ask: "Who am I?"

6

Permission Granted,
or Beyond the Fantasm

In *La Bataille de cent ans: Histoire de la psychanalyse en France II* Elizabeth Roudinesco chronicles events that led to the famous break between Jacques Derrida and Jacques Lacan. Of interest are two conceptual issues that distinguish this so-called history, the question of granting oneself permission, and that of respecting the impasse. In "Pour l'amour de Lacan," Derrida comments: "As usual Lacan had left me the greatest liberty of interpretation, and as usual I would have taken it even if it had not been given to me, such as it will have pleased me."[1] This comment parodies Lacan's strategy, outlined by Derrida, of a theoretical call forwarding, as in the following example from "Raison d'un échec," in which Lacan accuses Derrida of ripping him off. "This is why my discourse, so slight as it may be beside that of a work such as my friend Claude Lévi-Strauss, marks out differently, in that ascending wave of the signifier, the signified, the 'it speaks,' the trace, the gramme, the lure, the myth, nay of the lack, of the circulation with which I am myself now dispossessed. The Aphrodite of this foam, having this last time raised *la différance*, with an *a*. And this [*ça*] leaves hope for what Freud consigns to the silt of catechism."[2] In other words,

1. Jacques Derrida, "Pour l'amour de Lacan," in *Lacan avec les philosophes* (Paris: Albin Michel, 1991), p. 406.
2. Jacques Lacan, *Scilicet* (Paris: Seuil, 1968), p. 47.

184

even as Lacan modestly compares himself to Lévi-Strauss, whom Derrida stringently criticizes in *De la grammatologie,* it is to be recalled that Derrida has expropriated a whole vocabulary from that very lesser critic, the Aphrodite of which, rising up from the foam or silt of Lacan's catechism, is *la différance,* its little letter *a* owing its genealogy to Lacan's seminars on the *objet a.* Derrida's response to such charges has been that Lacan has left himself the greatest liberty of interpretation, and as usual has taken it without permission and as he pleases as if he were operating beyond the laws of any scholarly decorum or protocol.

Whereas in certain respects Derrida's point may be apt, Lacan's attitude concerning Derrida has not been without foundation, contrary to what Derrida and his followers have suggested. Indeed, Derrida's emphasis upon Lacan's theoretical call forwarding into a future anterior as well as upon Lacan's arrogating permission without asking consent of the other could be viewed as an elaborate diversion that is intended to deflect our attention away from a much cruder cover-up by no one other than Derrida's apologist, Roudinesco, who like Derrida himself takes a certain delight in reading Lacan from the seamy side of psychoanalysis. In other words, I intend to challenge the more or less familiar account that Lacan's egregious and unforgivable misbehavior toward Derrida is the source of their antinomy. I also intend to consider certain implications in Lacan's work that make Derrida's objections to his behavior vulnerable. In particular, I reevaluate Derrida's recent criticism of Lacan's willingness to take permission as it pleases him, by showing that Lacan's taking license has some very important theoretical ramifications, among them recognition of a trait of jouissance that takes us not only beyond the impasses of a deconstructive understanding of Freudian psychoanalysis but also beyond the fantasms or imaginary constructions that are posited there, for example, the daughter/mother, Sophie Freud, in Derrida's rereading of *Beyond the Pleasure Principle.*

In Elizabeth Roudinesco's *Bataille de cent ans* the following account is given of Lacan and Derrida before their first encounter.

In the fall of 1966, Jacques Derrida had not yet met Lacan. The latter had, nonetheless, devoured *De la grammatologie* as soon as it appeared in *Critique* and let the philosopher know, through Miller and François Wahl, how highly he thought of the text. No doubt he expected to see him come to his seminar, taking up the place that had gone vacant since his dispute with Ricoeur. But Derrida was distrustful, and hesitated to throw himself into the seducer's arms. Jealous of his independence, he experienced Lacan's interest in him as a threat.[3]

Like many journalists in the popular press, Roudinesco uses considerable license of her own when filling in the narrative holes in her own psychological observations. She accuses Derrida of suspiciousness, of feeling threatened by Lacan, and of being jealous for his own independence. In turn, she characterizes Lacan as "capricious in his whims," "frail," and as a man "settling unconscious scores."[4] She sets her observations in the present and provides such motivations to explain reductively how and why the estrangement between Lacan and Derrida took place. In a word, she simplistically provides closure.

In her account of their meeting in Baltimore during the famous "Structuralist Controversy" conference, Roudinesco notes that Lacan informed Derrida that he had been conceptually preempted, and we overhear Lacan saying to Derrida: "You can't bear my having already said what you want to say." Again, instead of invoking a notion such as *destinerrance* (the errant destiny of what has been said), Roudinesco searches for fairly ordinary psychological motivations such as Lacan's supposed "fantasy of owning concepts" and his "narcissism of priority."[5] Of course, because Roudinesco's tactic of giving closure by invoking seamy motivations is so transparently inadequate, given, for example, Derrida's remarks in "Pour l'amour de Lacan," one is tempted

3. Elizabeth Roudinesco, *La Bataille de cent ans: Histoire de la psychanalyse en France II* (Paris: Seuil, 1986). Trans. Jeffrey Mehlman, under the title *Lacan and Company* (Chicago: University of Chicago Press, 1990), pp. 409–10. I cite the Mehlman translation.

4. Ibid., pp. 411–12.

5. Ibid., p. 410. Derrida's neologism, *destinerrance,* is equated with *Verstimmung* in the work of Martin Heidegger. See Jacques Derrida, *D'un ton apocalyptique adopté naguère en philosophie* (Paris: Galilée, 1983), p. 86.

to simply dismiss Roudinesco's book as intellectual soap opera. Yet scattered in it are some important clues that suggest less arbitrary motivations.

In another part of *La Bataille* Roudinesco notes that in 1966 Derrida delivered "Freud and the Scene of Writing" to the Institut de Psychanalyse, presided over by André Green. In this paper Derrida touched many of the hot buttons in Lacan's seminars and, given the context of the group, we discover that he did so self-consciously. Roudinesco also mentions that Derrida's wife, Marguerite, was undertaking a training analysis with members of the Institut and that she was studying the work of Melanie Klein. Because we are considering a recondite politics, it is helpful to point out that the Institut de Psychanalyse was an organization sponsored by the SPP, the Société Psychanalytique de Paris, from which Lacan and Daniel Lagache broke in 1953. Although the SPP would continue to make Lacan's life difficult, Lacan did communicate with one of its analysts, André Green, whose own work was very much influenced by Lacan's seminars. Green was invited to join the SFP or Société Française de Psychanalyse to which Lacan belonged, but Green preferred to keep his SPP affiliation, since this association was recognized by the IPA, the International Psycho-Analytic Association, whereas the SFP could get no such legitimation. During the very early 1960s, Green led an intersociety group that brought the SFP into contact with the SPP, but as political tensions rose within the SFP, Lacan ended this joint venture. After Lacan's "excommunication" in 1963 by the SFP as a prerequisite for recognition by the IPA, Lacan formed the École Freudienne de Paris. Green, however, continued to offer seminars under the auspices of the SPP, the organization that Marguerite Derrida had now joined and under whose institutional sponsorship Jacques Derrida was delivering a brilliant paper close to Lacan's interests which, curiously enough, made no reference to Lacan—as if to say that within a serious analytical context it was neither necessary nor proper to mention Lacan's contributions to the field.

Given this history, there is reason to think that Derrida's actions may not have been meant to ingratiate him with Lacan and his school. Intentionally or not, Derrida had given a signal to the Lacanians that he was declaring loyalty to a group interested in Lacan's thinking but, at the same time, interested in revising it in such a way that Lacan himself could be ignored. The gesture of appropriating and expropriating Lacan at one go by an enemy camp was, no doubt, something that would have deeply galled Lacan, and given past history, it was not unthinkable that the SPP might very well have been trying to write Lacan out of the very theory he had developed. Lacan, no doubt, considered Derrida a threat insofar as Derrida was brilliant enough to carry such a project off. Moreover, Lacan was already in his mid-sixties when he finally emerged as a stellar figure, and he must have been very sensitive to those who would deny him credit, who would, in Lacan's own terms, deny the Name-of-the-Father.

Roudinesco's failure to reconstruct this slant (and, of course, it is necessarily a *slanted* view, namely the "other" slant) suppresses the possibility that Lacan's angry reaction may have been justified from a certain political perspective and that Derrida was by no means targeted for criticism solely on the basis of mean-spiritedness. In short, there is a way to read Roudinesco's history that allows us to see that Derrida had positioned himself within the context of a psychoanalytic politics with a stormy history. In this context, Derrida's account of Lacanian *destinerrance* appears in some respects at least to be insufficient, particularly since it too is based on a latent assumption concerning petty motivations—Lacan's unquenchable thirst for self-aggrandizement. In other words, neither the determinacy of Derrida's assignment of petty motives to Lacan nor the indeterminacy established by his theory of destinerrance is sufficient to discredit the much more plausible argument that Derrida took actions in 1966 which ran contrary to the politics of Lacanian theory. This is most curious, of course, since during that same year Derrida published an extract from *Of Grammatology* in *Cahiers pour l'analyse,* a journal published by the Cercle d'Épistémologie at the École Normale Supérieure that was founded by Jacques-Alain Miller and others who were dedicated to an understanding of Lacan's teaching. Hence even while Derrida's work was appearing within a publication allied to Lacan, Derrida was at the same time maintaining a certain distance from the Lacanians.

That Derrida may have had reservations about Lacan is also suggested by Roudinesco's understanding that already by 1959 Derrida had become friends with Nicolas Abraham, an analyst affiliated with the SPP, who like his eminent colleagues, Marie Bonaparte among them, had considered Lacan, in Bonaparte's terms, a bit fraudulent, a bit mad, and quite dangerous.[6] But it is with the Confrontations group emerging out of the SPP in the 1970s that Derrida himself would later become a kind of rallying point along with Nicolas Abraham, his wife Maria Torok, and René Major. Thus Derrida's affiliation with the SPP in 1966 was by no means one that happened in passing. Retroactively, it signifies an alliance with analysts who were either ambivalently attracted to Lacan, establishing distance from him, or openly hostile to and dismissive of him.

Roudinesco tells us that the irreparable break between Derrida and Lacan did not come until 1968 when Lacan published a number of remarks in the serial *Scilicet,* supposedly to embarrass or denigrate Derrida. The greatest offense, according to Roudinesco, was Lacan's publication of some remarks that Derrida had made at a cocktail party concerning his relation to his son, Pierre. We are told that Lacan had not reacted to Derrida's story in person and had decided, instead, to publish his interpretation, as if he were treating a case history of one of his patients. It is no surprise that this interpretation is theoretically very canny and contradicts the account given by both Roudinesco and Derrida that Lacan was merely motivated by bad conscience and that his remarks are so much rubbish.[7] Roudinesco tells the story in *La Bataille* as follows:

> One evening, as his son Pierre was beginning to fall asleep in his mother's presence, he asked his father why he was looking at him. "Because you're handsome." The child reacted immediately by saying that the compliment made him want to die. Somewhat troubled,

6. Jacques Derrida, "Nature, culture, écriture (de Lévi-Strauss à Rousseau)," *Cahiers pour l'analyse* 4 (September/October 1966): 1–45.

7. When I presented this chapter in a truncated form at the Modern Language Association, the question came up whether Derrida might not have baited Lacan with a story fabricated for that very purpose. In short, is *Derrida's* account fictional? I contend that its literality is almost beside the point, since it operates as a text countersigned by Lacan. That is, the text, whether true or not, functions symptomatically and, as I show, is significant in terms of its own relays of *destinerrance.*

Derrida tried to figure out what the story meant. "I don't like myself," the child said. "And since when?" "Since I've known how to talk." Marguerite took him in her arms. "Don't worry, we love you." Then Pierre broke out laughing. "No, all that isn't true; I'm a cheater for life."

Lacan did not react. Some time later, Derrida was dumbfounded to read the anecdote in the text of a lecture by his interlocutor delivered at the French Institute at Naples in December 1967. Lacan recounted it as follows: "I'm a cheater for life, said a four year old kid while curling up in the arms of his genetrix before his father, who had just answered, 'You're handsome' to his question. 'Why are you looking at me?' And the father didn't recognize (even when the child in the interim pretended he had lost all taste for himself the day he learned to speak) the impasse he himself was foisting on the Other, by playing dead. It's up to the father, who told it to me, to hear me from where I speak or not."[8]

In "Pour l'amour de Lacan" Derrida says of these remarks that "I am not sure even today of having correctly understood the interpretation risked in what was, don't forget, a publication signed in *Scilicet* [where Lacan was the only one to be authorized to sign]." And Derrida then adds that he had the impression Lacan really wanted to insert *son* in the place of *father,* so that Lacan would be saying "It's up to the son, who told it to me, to hear me from where I speak or not."[9] In other words, Derrida feels sure that Lacan's barely suppressed desire was for Derrida to acknowledge him as his true intellectual father, an interpretation that Roudinesco independently offers, as well. But what neither Roudinesco nor Derrida are willing to acknowledge is that Lacan's comments are much more perceptive than they are willing to suppose.

A sensitive listener, Lacan has heard the anguish of the child when he denegates to his parents "I'm a cheater for life" ["Je suis un tricheur de vie"]. Lacan knows that it is a serious matter when a child verbally imagines his own self-loathing and can believe he has located it at the moment he has begun to speak. Lacan knows too that this self-loathing may have a source in his parents, one of whom is playing the dead

8. Roudinesco, p. 411.
9. Derrida, "Pour l'amour de Lacan," p. 406.

father, and not only in real life, which, of course, is Lacan's main point. Concerning the connections between personal and professional life, it is important to recall that a month before Lacan published his trenchant observations, we can already read the following remarks from the first installment of "La Pharmacie de Platon" in *Tel Quel* in which the concept of the father is being put to the test: "A logos indebted to a father, what can that mean?" To that question Lacan is already posing the answer by pointing to its effect, namely the foisting of an impasse onto the son, identified by Lacan as the Other. Most uncanny, in this respect, is a passage in "La Pharmacie de Platon" which seems to be under attack by Lacan, even though it appeared just four weeks before Lacan's essay was published in *Scilicet:* "[Thoth] is thus the father's other, the father, and the subversive movement of replacement. The god of writing is thus at once his father, his son, and himself. He cannot be assigned a fixed spot in the play of differences."[10]

This is precisely what Lacan is calling the impasse, an impasse in which the son as other of the father finds himself by being denied the Name-of-the-Father. And no doubt it is an impasse insofar as the son, in Derrida's words, is put in the role of being "a sort of joker, a floating signifier, a wild card, one who puts play into play."[11] In short, Thoth, like Derrida's son, sees himself as "a cheater for life."

At this point one could conduct an analysis of "Speculating—On Freud," in which the impasse between Freud and the grandson is figured in the bobbin, not to say the legs of Sophie Freud. Such an analysis— and readers familiar with Derrida's *Post Card* can already see it quite clearly in advance—would show how the bobbin closely resembles Lacan's *petit objet a*, which, we recall, surfaced as a kind of fantasmic Aphrodite in the backwash of Lacan's catechism, though, in this case, within a text by Derrida. Here, for example, is Derrida's description of that object: "No longer an object which would re-present itself, but re-presentation, the return of itself of the re-turn, the re-turn to itself of the return. This is the source of the greatest pleasure . . . that the re-turning returns, that the re-turn is not only of an object but of itself,

---

10. Jacques Derrida, *Dissemination*, trans. Barbara Johnson (Chicago: University of Chicago Press, 1989), p. 92.
11. Ibid., p. 93.

or that it is its own object, that what causes to return itself returns to itself."[12] Those who recall the opening pages on the *petit objet a* in Lacan's seminar, *Le Séminaire XI: Les Quatre Concepts fondamentaux de la psychanalyse,* recall its opening words: "To continue. *Wiederholung.*" Repetition will lead Lacan to consider the question of returning, which leads to young Parque's observation that "I saw myself seeing myself."[13] This passage is analogous to Derrida's remark about the bobbin returning to itself not as an object of itself, or as its own object, but as that which returns as return. Lacan situates this return in the scopic relation: "The object on which depends the fantasy from which the subject is suspended in an essential vacillation is the gaze." Moreover, "of all the objects in which the subject may recognize his dependence in the register of desire, the gaze is specified as unapprehensible."[14] Like Derrida's reading of the bobbin from *Beyond the Pleasure Principle,* Lacan's consideration of the gaze as *petit objet a* concerns that "thing" through which the subject sustains himself or herself in a function of desire, a "thing" that like Derrida's understanding of the bobbin has fantasmic properties for the subject. We should not be surprised, Lacan demonstrates, if this function is going to have fantasmic effects such as anamorphosis, since the gaze is itself "that point of vanishing being with which the subject confuses his own failure. Furthermore, of all the objects in which the subject may recognize his dependence in the register of desire, the gaze is specified as unapprehensible."[15] Yet, for all that, the gaze is that which is very much subject to repetition, repeated looking.

Derrida himself approaches the gaze when in "Speculating—On Freud" he quotes Freud's remark, "One day I made an observation which confirmed my view. The child had a wooden spool." Yet Derrida remarks that the scene is one of "an incompletion (in the object, or its description) all the more in that: 1) this is the scene of an interminably *repeated supplementation,* as if it never finished completing itself, etc;

12. Jacques Derrida, *The Post Card,* trans. Alan Bass (Chicago: University of Chicago Press, 1986), p. 318.
13. Jacques Lacan, *The Four Fundamental Concepts of Psychoanalysis,* trans. Alan Sheridan (New York: Norton, 1978), p. 67.
14. Ibid., p. 83.
15. Ibid.

and 2) there is something like an axiom of incompletion in the structure of the *scene of writing*. This is due at very least to the position of the speculator as motivated observer. Even if completion were possible, it could neither appear for such an 'observer,' nor be declared as such by him."[16] Lacking from this fantasmic scene—a scene that is by no means completely representable—is a "trait" that may be "on the side of the scene described, or on the side of the description, or in the unconscious that binds the one to the other, their unconscious that is shared, inherited, telecommunicated according to the same teleology." This trait "speculates on the return" and is "completed in coming back: the greater pleasure, he says, although this spectacle is less directly seen, is the *Wiederkommen*, the re-turn. And yet, that which thereby again becomes a *revenant* must, for the game to be complete, be thrown away again, indefatigably."[17] The key word is *revenant,* the specter, ghost, or fantasm that keeps returning or coming back. And it is this ghost or fantasm which is the absent but returning trait symbolized by the bobbin that takes us beyond the pleasure principle even as it maintains the Freudian (but also Derridean) scene of writing as an impasse of incompleted returns or destined errancies. It is in this sense that Derrida posits the scene as a spectacle that takes us *beyond the fantasm* in so far as it is endlessly prohibited from coming to appearance.

Of course, Lacan would have asked whether the bobbin or the Name-of-the-Father has to necessarily swallow up one's entire psychology in an impasse of call forwarding that cheats us by never reaching its destination. In other words, Lacan's resistence to *destinerrance* puts the brakes on the impasse that *destinerrance* throws onto the subject. In the abrogated *Séminaire XI: Les Noms du père,* which Lacan gave on November 19, 1963, the day after Jean Laplanche and his cohorts had "excommunicated" him from the SFP, he spoke of the trait or trace of the father's name which gives us access to a jouissance that precedes the fall of an object from the mantle of anxiety, as in, say,

16. Derrida, *The Post Card,* p. 313; my italics.
17. Ibid., p. 314.

the way a golden ball rolls away from Princess Nausikaa and comes to rest near father Odysseus. Pleasure, in this instance, is *not* a function of the impasse and its fantasies, which turn us into counterfeiters of our own legacy (as in Homer), but is the bliss introduced by the trait of the name that divides itself in a manner akin to the names of God one finds in the Bible. In this sense, Lacan's notion of the trait stands for a trace that is not of the stuff of fantasy and fantasm. To make that point, Lacan gives a close reading of the Abraham and Isaac story in which the knife at Isaac's throat breaks the impasse of anxiety in such a way that one can accede to a jouissance that is beyond representation or fantasy. This, Lacan says, is the significance of the rite of circumcision; it breaks the impasse the father throws onto the Other by marking the difference between the father's bliss and desire. The circumcision, "that little piece of flesh sliced off," is what constitutes the *objet a,* and what serves as the trait of the name which binds a people and gives to each man the pass, the rite to pass as the right to pass. It is this little piece of flesh that has been stolen from even before the subject can remember, a theft that promises that a son will not grow up wanting to die under the loving gaze of his father. To speak of this lack as the metaphysically determined absence that requires infinite supplementation even as it supplies the ground for whatever system it is designed to prop up is to experience the lack as what falls out as an all-consuming anxiety whose fixation on the father is only too palpable. And it is this representation or fantasy of circumcision which Lacan rejects.

In the Abraham and Isaac story, the *objet a* falls away from that hole in being where the entrapment of pleasure is expressed as frustration in the Imaginary, castration in the Symbolic, and absence in the Real. In fact, the *objet a* discloses itself as that *tranche* [or trench] in which something is given so that it may be taken as it pleases us "beyond the name." It is not, as in Derrida, the construction of an impasse or obstruction whose scene of writing demands the *revenant.* Hence the painting of Abraham and Isaac by Caravaggio, of which Lacan speaks to his audience, is the *tranche* (as seance and slice) in which the law is given so that a son may have access to a jouissance beyond desire (beyond the impasse), a jouissance beyond fantasy (the fantasms associated with sexuality), and beyond the law (the Name-of-the-Father, of identity): in order that the son can take without permission, which is to say, as it pleases him; as it makes, for him, pleasure; as it gives him pleasure; as it is his wont to take it; or, again, as it is that he wishes it to be.

That this pleasure bears on the pleasure of the father of the primal horde is very much uppermost on Lacan's mind; however, whereas in Freud's writings that primal horde was itself a "primal scene" or "fantasm," for Lacan it is the designation of what comes before such notions of representationality. More striking, Lacan realizes that the trait of pleasure he is talking about moves beyond the pleasure principle of what we might call civilized behavior, since the pleasure of which Lacan speaks has no respect for the pleasure of the one whose consent is not being requested and whose permission, it would appear, doesn't matter. In fact, there is the suggestion that in such cases permission is always already granted in advance, since the "as it pleases us" concerns a relation that has not yet been introduced to anxiety, in short, to the concept of violence. Yet, from the subject position of those who have come after the prelapsarian father, the "as it pleases us" would appear to condone violence against women in the name of prelapsarian bliss, a violence that one could characterize as rape, a patriarchal rape that is held back by the primordial trait of the father so that it may be inherited as the legacy of a pleasure from before that imaginary time when women were shared and families established within tribal and, later, less bounded structures of family life.[18]

And yet, this rape, though it is given to the son as a certain birthright or rite is, nevertheless, experienced as the trait or arche-trace of the primal father's pleasure, a trait or trace that is fixed even in the destiny of the law of desire whose charge is to express pleasure in the form of a demand that the other can consent to or not. Here, of course, the aesthetic pleasure of works such as Rubens's *Rape of the Sabine Women*

18. It is interesting to compare this violence to that of St. Teresa, who, in Lacan's estimation, is an erotomaniac who allows the orgasm to be detached from the field of the demand of the Other. The difference between the primal father's pleasure and that of St. Teresa must be, in Lacan's mind, that for the father the Other is not metaphysical and, hence, absent in the place where jouissance is experienced.

or Correggio's *Jupiter and Io* would necessarily have to be mediated by the *différance* between bliss and desire which Lacan has posited as precisely that mark which takes us beyond the impasse.

In contrast, Derrida's account of the bobbin appears as a masturbatory impasse that articulates a relation to the *legs* of Sophie constructed to deny any permission that bears on the trait of the primal father's pleasure. The legs or legacy of Sophie is indeed the construction of a fantasm—really a taboo—that throws the impasse onto the son and would make of him a cheater for life, what Lacan would have viewed as an inhibited being incapable of taking things as he pleases. Derrida himself institutes this inhibition in "Pour l'amour de Lacan" when he points to the scandal of Lacan simply taking whatever he wants from whomever he wants without permission or license. From a Lacanian point of view, however, this is little else on a Symbolic order than a turning away from that necessary violation of the other which at least has to be psychologically imaginable in order for the deadlock of desire to be lifted. From a Lacanian perspective, Pierre, Derrida's son, may well be the name for a deadlock insofar as he is a stone or object that has fallen from the mantle of anxiety, the fear of giving oneself the pass, of permitting oneself to enjoy the trait of the primal father's claim on women. Pierre, in other words, is the stumbling block if not the *revenant* of desire, and in his name the impasse is given whose Freudian domain is that of inhibition, anxiety, or, to put it another way, *destinerrance:* the falling of the object away from any assured destination, which in Lacan's terms would be the Name-of-the-Father.

In case one thought Lacan had himself never worked through the question of *destinerrance,* or simply rejected it, one should consider the phrase on which Lacan developed *Le Séminaire XXI: Les Non Dupes errent*—the nondupes err or go astray. This phrase is Lacan's expression for destin-errance and speaks to what was broached in the abrogated seminar *Les Noms du père.* The unconscious of that phrase on the hitherside of the mirror of language, *les non-dupes errent,* is intended to suggest that those who dismiss the Names-of-the-Father or arrogate the names for themselves are fated to wander around aimlessly in the impasse and scenography of an Other's permission of yes or no. Indeed, for Lacan this errancy marks a determinate relation to a yes and no that defines one's position and hence turns that impasse into a legacy. Derrida, whose writings are *always* written from the perspective of the philosopher as nondupe, is one who will greet *destinerrance* or errancy as part of deconstruction's entelechy.

It would be far better for us, Lacan suggests, to act the fool or dupe who accepts or inherits the Name-of-the-Father in such a way that its yes or no is accompanied by the unitary trait of a primal bliss that grants permission in advance to supersede the impasse of the father's desire, an impasse that constructs what Derrida calls the *revenant,* the fantasm of an Other whose allure depends on her saying no. Ironically, to go beyond that fantasm one must be a willing dupe of the father, someone like the grail knight Perceval, who habitually takes license by not heeding symbolic scenes rich in fantasmic effects. In the well-known scene, rendered by Chrétien, in which Perceval encounters a sleeping beauty in a tent whose handmaidens are away picking flowers, he announces to her that given his mother's teachings, he will pay his respects by kissing the maiden. She informs him, "I'll never give a kiss to you, of my own free will." Chrétien informs us of Perceval's response: "The young man had strong arms; / instead he crushed the maid in his embrace, / not knowing how to act with grace. / He stretched her out beneath him, lying / upon her, and she struggled, trying / to fend him off and to get loose, / but her best efforts were no use."[19] Because Perceval is a dolt who hasn't understood his mother rightly, he simply enacts the primal trait of the father's jouissance rather than the Oedipal no or taboo, which is, of course, handed down through the mother's teaching. In keeping with this abrogation of Oedipus, Perceval, who doesn't even know his own name, does not ask the Name-of-the-Father when shown the grail cup and lance, even though he is in a chapel or house of the Father. Once having been shown the door of the Fisher King's castle, however, Parsifal starts to ask questions, and, as we know, it is as a nondupe that he will wander for so many

19. Chrétien de Troyes, *Perceval*, trans. Ruth Harwood Cline (Athens: University of Georgia Press, 1985), lines 699–706.

years. Yet when, in von Eschenbach's version, Parsifal returns to the Grail Castle, it is clear that he has achieved the Name-of-the-Father not so much because he wandered as a nondupe in the wasteland but because by his very nature he was fool enough (that is, enough of a dupe or, what amounts to the same thing, pure enough) to circumvent the impasse—that yes and no—of Amfortas's wound. So that when Parsifal finally asks Amfortas, "What ails you, uncle?" he does so more or less unself-consciously or nonchalantly as an awkward aside, having taken for granted that the grail is now in his possession. Fundamental to that accession is the grail as a manifestation of the unitary trait, which Parsifal has achieved in advance as the trait of the father's bliss.

In underscoring the nonchalance with which Parsifal obviates the name with a "What ails you, uncle?" the name is at once surpassed as a condition of its being maintained. It may be in part for this reason that von Eschenbach is motivated to relate to us the story of Lohengrin, Parsifal's son, who is sent by the Templars to marry the devout and very wealthy duchess of Brabant. Lohengrin will say in earshot of all the people that he will be devoted to her as long as she never asks him his name. But of course she is a nondupe who will ask in the hopes that the name will put her wandering mind to rest. Consequently, Lohengrin leaves her and returns to the grail castle. Were she capable of sustaining the shame of the dupe or lover who is so taken in that she doesn't even know her husband's name—like a woman forced by a man she doesn't know—she would have achieved the grail (not to say its bliss), whose mystery exceeds *les noms du père (les non-dupes errent):* the symbolization and self-certainty of genealogy, lineage, family, ethnicity, and political identity. In this transcendence, the fantasies of the family would have all been surpassed for the sake of a pleasure that concerns the trait of original jouissance, a jouissance *beyond* fantasy and the fantasm.

It is *this* jouissance that Amfortas has lost and which can only be returned to him if a young fool does as it pleases him. Yet, in the scene in which Perceval is shown the lance and the cup a complex double bind is in effect: if he asks about the lance and the cup he will, in effect, be the sort of subject who is bounded by what Lacan would call the Symbolic, those things which belong to the Father. If he doesn't ask, he is merely someone who cannot give himself permission, in short, someone who is inhibited from gaining access to primal bliss because he is, again, bounded by the Name-of-the-Father. The brilliance of Chrétien was to have seen beyond this impasse by means of having Perceval ejected from the castle by giving himself the license of being a dupe and of not having asked the question. In other words, redemption in *Perceval* lies not in the grail templar's expectation of what the subject was supposed to know, but in the freedom of Perceval to be a fool, to exercise a liberty whose primal trait does not even look on the grail castle, the grail, or the lance as symbols of paternity but merely as things to do with as one pleases. The contrast to this orientation is quickly supplied by Perceval's cousin, who foists the impasse of the Symbolic on the knight by explaining the meaning of all that he saw. " 'Tell me, my friend, what is your name?' " The narrator remarks: "Not knowing his real name at all / he guessed his name was Perceval / of Wales and said so, but the youth / did not know if it were the truth . . . / 'My friend,' she says, 'your name is changed!' 'To what?' Perceval asks. 'To Perceval the wretch!' "[20]

Such, then, is the *abject object* that is foisted onto the nondupe, who necessarily wanders in a forest of paternal symbols in which the Name returns like an accuser in order to stand in the way of the primal trait of pleasure. And it is in this sense that we can grasp the extent to which Lacan's notion of going beyond the pleasure principle differs from that of Freud's, which Derrida adheres to much more closely in "To Speculate—On Freud," in which the name, Freud, keeps returning in order to pose the question of the bobbin and of whom it serves. It is no surprise that Derrida will conclude that "paralysis: the step beyond the PP [pleasure principle] will have remained interdicted." Moreover,

> If it is to assure its mastery, the principle *of* pleasure therefore first must do so *over* pleasure and at the expense *of* pleasure. Thus it becomes the prince *of* pleasure, the prince whose pleasure is the conquered, chained, bound, restricted, tired subject. The game is necessarily played on two boards. Pleasure loses in *measure* itself: in which it brings its principle to triumph. It loses on every turn, it wins on every turn *by measure* of its being there before being there, as soon as it prepares itself for its presence, by measure of

20. Ibid., 3572–80.

its still being there when it reserves itself in order to produce itself, invading everything beyond itself. It wins on every turn, it loses on every turn *by measure:* its unleashed intensity would destroy it immediately if it did not submit itself to the moderating stricture, to measure itself. Death threat: no more principle of pleasure therefore no more *différance* that *modifies* it into a reality principle. What is called reality is nothing outside this law of *différance.* Reality is an effect of this law.

Somewhat later, Derrida remarks that "irresolution belongs to this impossible logic" and that irresolution is "the speculative structure between the solution (non-binding, unleashing *absolute* untightening: absolution itself) and the non-solution (absolute tightening, paralyzing banding, etc.)."[21] What distinguishes this from Lacanian analysis, and what distinguishes Lacan in general from Freud, whose *Beyond the Pleasure Principle* speculates with the bobbin according to Derrida's formulation, is adherence to a religious perspective alien to Freud, in which thinking the primal trait of the father's pleasure is possible according to a logic of permissibility and of the Name, which, as Charles Méla has also noticed, we find clearly delineated in the grail stories of Chrétien and von Eschenbach.[22] It is at this juncture that one could examine the antinomy of faith and speculation in psychoanalysis, an important juncture elided by the history upon which Roudinesco and Derrida have speculated.

At the very least, exploration of the question of permissibility or license raised by Roudinesco and Derrida point to a number of major theoretical issues that have been occluded in the very politicized manner in which the rift or falling out between Lacan and Derrida has been portrayed. Moreover, problematic for those who would station themselves with either figure is that in each case one is left with an unsatisfactory consequence: inhibition or sexual frustration in Derrida,

21. Derrida, *The Post Card,* pp. 400–401.
22. Charles Méla, *La Reine et le Graal* (Paris: Seuil, 1984). The emphasis in this lengthy study of the medieval grail narratives is on the mirroring of scenes in whose displacement a primal or originary fantasm is held in abeyance. Méla, who is quite aware of Lacanian theory, has subordinated it to an interpretation of the grail that supports an iconoclastic and antifetishistic understanding of religious symbolism during Chrétien's time.

violence or sexual aggression in Lacan. No doubt, it is in relation to these alternatives that the work of Luce Irigaray, Hélène Cixous, and Julia Kristeva takes on added meaning, particularly Kristeva's point that the primal trait is that unnamable remnant whose jouissance takes to the side of the mother. All that lies beyond or ahead of this primal maternal trait, Kristeva tells us, is père-version.

PART II

ECHOES
OF THE
FANTASM

7

Geoffrey Hartman and
the Spell of Sounds

We are in the realm of the passions, perhaps of their
tenuous sublimation; and it is the stricken ear rather
than stricken eye that leads us there.
> —Geoffrey Hartman, "Words, Wish, Worth:
> Wordsworth."

One might say that human consciousness possesses a series
of inner genres for seeing and conceptualizing reality.
> —P. N. Medvedev and M. M. Bakhtin, *The Formal
> Method in Literary Scholarship*

In a paper delivered at Ann Arbor in 1978, Roman Jakobson discussed
the sound shapes of language and pointed out that for the child the
sound of language is already a transitional substance in D. W. Winnicott's sense: a phatic buffer, separating psyche from world, self from
other. The sound shapes of language are redundantly spread out in
sentences, Jakobson said, because sound is the matter of the text, but
also the protective envelope within which the subject comes to be and
through which the subject can penetrate the world while never leaving
what is one's coverlet of words.[1]

In the sound shapes of language, the subject finds a safe berth, and
it is to this safety that the subject later returns, a safety that like the

---

1. Also see Roman Jakobson and Linda R. Waugh, *The Sound Shape of Language*
(Bloomington: Indiana University Press, 1979). Unfortunately, this study says almost
nothing about psychological defense formations, nor does it discuss transitional phenomena and split-brain studies, something Jakobson talked about at length at a semiotics
conference at the University of Michigan in May 1978.

Heideggerian house of Being (*Sprache*) has restorative possibilities. Although Jakobson was talking about a subject, it is clear that this subject is not something that idealistically precedes language; rather, the subject is constituted within the linguistic, since it is, as Jacques Lacan has pointed out, structured like a language. For Lacan, too, the crucial condition for language is that signs are not merely fixed as in a society of bees but that they are *expressed*. Lacan has said, in this regard, "As language becomes more functional, it becomes improper for speech, and as it becomes too particular to us, it loses its function as language." For Lacan and Jakobson, speech (*parole*) or language cannot be considered apart from the inevitable recognition of the role of enunciation. "What I seek in speech is the response of the other. What constitutes me as subject is my question. In order to be recognized by the other, I utter what was only in view of what will be. In order to find him, I call him by a name that he must assume or refuse in order to reply to me. [...] If I now place myself in front of the other to question him, there is no cybernetic computer imaginable that can make a reaction out of what the response will be."[2] Language, then, is not an autonomous system of signs but speech, and the subject is constituted in the appeal or evocation of this speech, this communication whose horizons are, as Jakobson pointed out, the addresser and the addressee, or *destinateur* and *destinataire*.

In *Semiotikā: Recherches pour une sémanalyse*, Julia Kristeva calls these poles *sujet* and *destinataire*, preserving some psychoanalytic resonances, and she speaks of the relation between these poles as being dialogical, since the "code" transmitted in the "message" never belongs to the *sujet* or *destinataire* proper but is appropriated from what Mikhail Bakhtin calls the polyglossia of linguistic formations in culture.[3] Of course, the sound shapes themselves are part of the polyglossia, and if they are used by the subject as a phatic buffer or shelter, it is a protective covering that is inherently part of the speech of an other, a covering that is identified with the voices others have spoken. When Lacan writes that "the function of language is not to inform but to

2. Jacques Lacan, "Function and Field of Speech and Language," in *Écrits*, trans. Alan Sheridan (New York: Norton, 1977), pp. 85–86.
3. Julia Kristeva, *Semiotikā: Recherches pour une sémanalyse* (Paris: Seuil, 1969), pp. 145–54.

evoke," he has in mind, certainly, the evocation of an other's speech.[4] Perhaps such evocation might be considered in terms of pulling speech over oneself in the way that a child might pull a blanket over the head—speaking as a blanketing with words.

When Sigmund Freud moved from the practice of hypnosis to that of analysis, it was by discovering that in place of working directly with the primary process in hypnosis, one could work more effectively through the resistances the patient encountered with words when conscious. That is, Freud noticed in the diachronic analysis of the analysand's relation to words a dialogue with the unconscious marked by impasses, intolerances, inhibitions, and sudden revelations. Through the sound shapes of language, the analysand breaks down and establishes particular defenses, thereby discovering in the coverlet of words both traumatic and therapeutic dimensions. In analysis, the sound shapes of words articulate a relation between *sujet* and *destinataire* which is protective as well as destructive, and thus ambivalence is detected in what for analysis becomes a text/context relation.

Exemplary is Serge Leclaire's case study, "Le Rêve à la licorne," in which slippages between the name, Liliane, and *licorne* (unicorn) take precedence.[5] Leclaire determined that the dream of the unicorn defends against a trauma—a phobia of sand—and that the sound shape *li* helps to constitute an address between the *sujet* (Phi*li*ppe) and the *destinataire* *(Lili)* as mediated by the *li*corne. These *li* sounds allow Philippe to articulate the phrase "j'ai soif" or "I'm thirsty" evoked by the figure of Lili. In this way, "Philippe, j'ai soif" becomes an ambivalent phrase that thanks to the sound slippages traverses the *sujet* and *destinataire* in two directions: from Philippe saying, I'm thirsty, and from Lili who is mocking him by saying you, Philippe, who are always thirsty, I dub you, "Philippe, j'ai soif." Yet as Leclaire is quick to point out, "Philippe, j'ai soif" also means that Lili is saying "Philippe, I want you, I'm thirsty for you." In other words, the sound shape *li* not only evokes the *licorne* in order to mark where the sand phobia is encountered and warded off, but it marks the subject as a virginal figure who is expressing desire for a woman or women ("Liliane" is a condensation for Lili, his cousin,

4. Lacan, "Function," p. 86.
5. Serge Leclaire, *Psychanalyser* (Paris: Seuil, 1968), pp. 99–117.

and Anne, his sister) whom he, in fact, may be fleeing. No doubt the sound shapes allow the subject to seek shelter in a wish and a fantasm while at the same time marking the trajectory of traumatic instances of which one is the perimeter of a phobia. Indeed, Leclaire's analysis demonstrates a moving back and forth between the axis of *sujet/destinataire* (Philippe/Liliane) and text/context (the dream/the family; the text of the analysis/the recollected experiences of the patient; *parole/langue,* and so on). And it is the articulation of these axes which are maintained by clues disclosed by the sound shapes themselves. These function like passwords that suddenly stand out from the polyglossic realm of linguistic interactivity in order to establish an intimate channel between an addresser and an addressee. Not only that, but the sound shape has the capacity to bind the addresser/addressee relation to text/context relations of which only one is the *parole/langue* relation out of which the sound shape comes to prominence as a privileged feature.

No doubt, one could argue that the sound shape *li* is a Lacanian *point de capiton,* which Slavoj Žižek defines as "the point through which the subject is 'sewn' to the signifier, and at the same time the point which interpolates individual into subject by addressing it with the call of a certain master-signifier ('Communism,' 'God,' 'Freedom,' 'America')—in a word, it is the point of the subjectivation of the signifier's chain." In Leclaire's case study, the unicorn interpolates the individual into a subject by addressing it with a call of a religious symbol for chastity. The unicorn is the master signifier; but the *li* is actually the *point de capiton* in the signifying chain that is working at a syllabic level to pin down the subject's desire. Žižek is correct to emphasize that the pinning down or quilting of the signifying chain is something that occurs retroactively, just as the defenses against trauma are always achieved retroactively. "Signifiers which are still in a 'floating' state—whose signification is not fixed—follow one another. Then, at a certain point—precisely the point at which the intention pieces the signifier's chain, traverses it—some signifier fixes retroactively the meaning of the chain, sews the meaning to the signifier, halts the sliding of the meaning."[6] By "fixing" Žižek means that the *point de capiton*

6. Slavoj Žižek, *The Sublime Object of Ideology* (London: Verso, 1990), pp. 101–2.

retroactively submits the signifiers to some code, which he identifies with an Other. In the Leclaire study this Other would probably be the Virgin Mary (the Holy Mother), who can be both accusative and conciliatory. The *licorne*, which symbolically substitutes for her, furnishes the *point de capiton* (the sound shape *li*), which both establishes addresser/addressee and text/context relations, and these, in turn, function to articulate defensive constructions that guard against anxiety reactions. Retroaction is significant insofar as the point of anchorage is furnished only after a trauma has been experienced, for only then is the diachrony of the "chain of signification" (that is, the narrative [conscious and unconscious] of what the subject can remember of his or her experiences) converted into a synchronous signifying structure (or dream text), which is then repeated with numerous variations. In other words, thanks to the syllable *li*, addresser/addressee relations are attached to text/context relations—for example, the relation of Virgin or Other as addresser and Philippe or Subject as addressee is put into relation with a mise-en-scène (that is, a dream text) and its everyday experiential contexts.

Leclaire notes that a major role of the sound shapes in the dream is to allow the dreamer to keep on sleeping through his thirst. Yet no one can say that the dreamer is sleeping well. Masud Khan has argued, in "Dreams and the Analytic Situation," that dreams are already a wish for a cure and that the aim of analysis should be to allow the patient to sleep well. This means, from our perspective, that the sound shape as *point de capiton* may function as part of a therapeutic process that wants to fulfill the aim of sleeping well. At the same time, it is expressing another wish that is being inhibited, the wish to possess Liliane, and, hence, the wish to be woken up sexually. Perhaps such contradictory impulses are already situated in the space between "Li" and "li," the repetition of wishes in sound.

Geoffrey Hartman has been very sensitive to the sound shapes of language, particularly in terms of psychological defense formations. He recognizes with respect to the "timely utterance" of Wordsworth that such poetry absorbs thoughts that could unbalance the mind. In

"Words, Wish, Worth: Wordsworth," Hartman explores the wish work of a poet who speaks with the voices of his predecessors, searching for safe poetic attachments in order to gain access to his own voice. It is as if Wordsworth were looking for a shelter in the words of others. "Wordsworth's antiphonal style—his version of 'echoing song'—limits by quotation or self-institutionalizing commentary a potentially endless descent into the phantom ear of memory." Wordsworth does not want to be capsized, or swamped by the phantom ear of memory, or over-whelmed by the superfluidity of the voices. Yet "Wordsworth's voice has lost, or is always losing, its lyric momentum; formally it is hesitant, disjunctive, 'dark steps' over places in nature or scripture aware of the 'abrupt abyss' that may, again, open up."[7] Perhaps this is why William Wordsworth makes an abrupt appeal to Dorothy, his sister, in *Tintern Abby,* saying, "in thy voice I catch / The language of my former heart, and read / My former pleasures in the shooting lights of thy wild eyes." The emphasis is on the recognition of the sister's voice as that medium in which movement to a happier and more protected state is facilitated. This is not so far removed from Leclaire's "Rêve à la licorne," because there, too, Liliane marks the voice or sound shape of a relative through whom one finds shelter and protection. Similarly, in *Tintern Abbey* voice assuages pain. Just as Philippe is voice dependent on Lili, William is voice dependent on Dorothy. Indeed, he appropriates her voice that his own might take shelter in it. It is what one might call the activity of a therapeutic consciousness. Indeed, if J. Hillis Miller has written about textual parasitism and Harold Bloom has talked about the anx-iety of strong precursors, through Hartman we appreciate in the wish for words an intervocative worth and an intertextual or dialogic bless-ing. As Hartman writes concerning "timely utterances," "Lyric is a speech act between vowel and passionate wish," and this suggests an intertextuality greatly indebted to the "surround of sound."

Of course, not all texts are blessed by the sound shapes of language. For if the sound shapes of language facilitate a restoration of the self in some literary contexts, such as the poetry of Wordsworth, they also have the potential for trauma. In "Wordsworth and Goethe in Literary

7. Geoffrey Hartman, "Words, Wish, Worth: Wordsworth," in *Deconstruction and Criticism,* ed. Harold Bloom et al. (New York: Seabury, 1979), pp. 195, 196.

History," Hartman asks, "What does voice want? What is the point or hidden intent of the supposed narrative? Why does it haunt this place?"[8] Voice is not located in the subject but *around* the subject, and, moreover, these voices traverse, suddenly call out, summon, or evoke. In Goethe's *Erlkönig* this summoning is particularly ominous. It marks not the assuaging of pain but pain's ghostly and ghastly penetration into a mise-en-scène, one reminiscent of that moment in Freud's *Interpretation of Dreams* when a voice calls out, "Father, can't you see that I am burning?" In Goethe, of course, the child asks its father, "Mein Vater, mein Vater, und hörest du nicht, / Was Erlenkönig mir leise verspricht?" Here the voice does not console; rather, it terrifies the paternal ear through the prattle of the child.

In "Wordsworth and Goethe" Hartman makes two crucial suggestions for literary theory. The first is that through an analysis of the intervocative in literature one can uncover oppositions that go beyond traditional genre differences. "I have tried to uncover an opposition which goes deeper than that between lyric and narrative," Hartman says. The second point is that "just as we have used poetry to analyze the notions of 'voice' and 'character,' so we could use it to analyze the notion of 'psyche.' A psychoanalysis should emerge from this more adequate to art than any so far devised; and these concepts of voice, character, and psyche may then allow us to explore the history of the poets: the relation between the works of an artist and the role he plays or desires to play in literary history."[9]

These points parallel somewhat the thoughts of Julia Kristeva in *Semiotikā* when she argues that we can read literature in terms of a synchronic or text/context relation emphasizing ambivalence and a diachronic or *sujet/destinataire* relation emphasizing what she calls the dialogic. Indeed, sound shapes would be situated in the register of the *sujet/destinataire,* and it would be here that such linguistic formations would infiltrate a spectrum of cultural genres with which we are familiar on a synchronic text/context axis: tragedy, comedy, lyric, song, novel, and so on. In *Semiotikā,* Kristeva writes,

8. Geoffrey Hartman, *The Fate of Reading* (Chicago: University of Chicago Press, 1975), p. 190.
    9. Ibid., pp. 195, 196.

A description of the specific function of words in different literary genres (or texts) requires a *translinguistic* approach in terms of 1) the conceptualization of a literary genre as an impure semiological system which "signifies underneath language but never without it"; and 2) as an operation carried along by the overall groupings of discursive sentences, questions and answers, dialogues, etc., that without slavishly following the linguistic model is justified by the principle of semantic expansion. One could thus posit and demonstrate the hypothesis that *any evolution of literary genres is an unconscious exteriorization of linguistic structures at their different levels.*[10]

In particular, Kristeva focuses on "linguistic dialogue" in order to develop the idea of "semantic expansion," which, in her view, necessarily comes about in the conjunction of the *sujet/destinataire* and text/context axes. And, recalling the work of Russian formalists such as Eikhenbaum, she stresses that dialogue cannot be considered without first recognizing an oral level that is "equivalent to a psychic state." With Lacan in mind, however, she notices that this oral register "relates to a discourse of the *other* in terms of which the oral discourse is but a secondary consequence (the other being the carrier of oral discourse)." In her later writings this "other" is identified with both the father (the symbolic) and the mother (the semiotic), and the subject's "voice" will enter into a relation with these others which is expressed as both "dialogue" (*sujet/destinataire*) and "ambivalence" (text/context). In *Semiotikā* we are already told that "dialogue and ambivalence lead to an important conclusion. In the interior space of a text as well as within the space between *texts* poetic language is a 'double.' "[11] Within one text there is dialogue and between two texts there is ambivalence, but also vice versa. Of major importance for Kristeva is that in each instance there is a certain transgression that implies a negation of the other's voice or text and that the laws of genre are established in terms of these practices of negation, even if they cannot altogether escape identification.

Hartman, in "Wordsworth and Goethe," also wants to pursue in-

10. Kristeva, *Semiotikā*, p. 146.
11. Ibid., pp. 147, 150.

tertextual, intersubjective, and dialogic systems of linguistic formation which cut through traditional genre forms. Unlike the early Kristeva, who ignores linguistic features at levels below the morpheme, Hartman seeks oppositions through the analysis of the sound shapes of language which, in his view, transcend distinctions like the lyric and the narrative. Like Kristeva, he reads literature with an emphasis on the *sujet/destinataire* register, which invalidates genre distinctions posed simply in terms of a text/context model of conventional and formal features. But he does not develop the kind of detailed linguistic descriptions that one finds in Kristeva's earlier work, because his interest is in listening to the errancy of sound shapes in poetic language rather than attempting to establish a rigorous account of how negativity functions in systems of signification. Of interest to Hartman is a "psychoesthetic" that will lead to a psychohistory within which one might be able to discern specific types of dialogic formations that will reveal the psychic defenses as particularly important for a historical understanding. Already with respect to Goethe and Wordsworth, Hartman suggests he has uncovered in the analysis of voice some distinctions that would allow one to begin a psychohistoric research, one in which the axis of *sujet/ destinataire* is stressed.

At this point I wish to offer four examples in which we can begin to see how psychological defense formations are part of a dialectic between the dialogic or diachronic axis and the formal or synchronic axis of Kristeva's model. We notice how psychological defense formations can be organized so that we may distinguish works in which words succeed in bringing about a felicitous defense from those works in which words or sounds fail to protect the subject from an overspillage of trauma. The works to be discussed are Virginia Woolf's *To the Lighthouse*, Herman Melville's *Moby-Dick*, James Joyce's *Finnegans Wake*, and Alban Berg's Violin Concerto. In none of these works do we find unambiguous sources for psychological typing; no analysand is unambiguous. One can try, however, to initiate a comparative analysis of psychological defense formations as they are disclosed in the spell of sounds. What is to be of interest is not so much a saving of the text as cultural artifact, but a saving of consciousness as the performance and behavior of sound shapes, a saving we find more troubled as we proceed. For certainly by the time we consider Alban Berg, the performance or behavior of sound is a performance of the composer's dying. What is saved or treasured up is sound, a saving that in Berg is a symptom of a sickness, abscess, or, as Lacan would say, a *hole* in being by means of which he finds melodic completion in his own passing. This is very different from the consolations of voice in Woolf, where the melodies of the dead can still comfort and heal, however precariously. Finally, our approach to considering these texts exposes how the poetic cuts across generic distinctions even as great as prose and music.

We recall that in *To the Lighthouse* Lily Briscoe asks what the voice of Mrs. Ramsay wants. The novel is a mixture of leitmotifs that in large part pair emotionally aggressive statements such as "No going to the lighthouse," or "Someone blundered," with defensive and therapeutic ones. "But it may be fine tomorrow," Mrs. Ramsay said, "I expect it will be fine." Here a little boy is spoken to, and the sound shapes defend and ward off the inevitable truth that Mr. Ramsay wants his children to know, that "it won't be fine." The whole novel, it seems to me, is a struggle with this defensive voice of Mrs. Ramsay, that is, the wish that she may be right after all. James wishes nothing more than to prove his mother correct, a wish later fulfilled in the father's guilty completion of a ritual that suggests itself to him from the grave. The voice is ghostly, a mixture of memory and desire for a restitution that history and quotidian time deny. Mrs. Ramsay's voice or voices speak from the grave in order to mark that wish for a return to childhood or to a past when words could still console even in the teeth of a threatening storm out of the West. In the last section of the novel everyone returns to Mrs. Ramsay's wish that all will be well, and this is the novel's great vision as well as its transcendental lie. " 'Mrs. Ramsay!' Lily cried, 'Mrs. Ramsay!' But nothing happened. The pain increased. That anguish could reduce one to such a pitch of imbecility, she thought!"[12] In this last section of the novel words fail Lily Briscoe,

12. Virginia Woolf, *To the Lighthouse* (New York: Harcourt Brace, 1927), p. 269. A passage worth developing in a more detailed account of the novel would be the moment when Mrs. Ramsay covers the pig's skull with her shawl while putting Cam to bed. Here the defenses against death are overtly thematized with respect to vocal

and she feels terribly cheated. In their place she paints and wonders what the voice of Mrs. Ramsay really meant. This is the dark side of feminine consciousness, the feeling that there are not enough shelters in which a feminine consciousness may seek protection, that there is perhaps no feminine voice or only very few that speak truly, only the empty defenses of so many manic housewives catering to philosophically obstreperous blockheads. In calling out the name, "Mrs. Ramsay," Lily expects some answer, some presence, some sign. But there is nothing. And yet, there is the scene in which reconciliation takes place, in which Lily has her vision when James, Cam, and Mr. Ramsay, a man now in his seventies, reach the lighthouse. Suddenly the voices become vision, the painting of Lily a "touching compulsion" of the eye, that symbolic articulation fixing what Kristeva in *Polylogue* calls the chora. And still, Lily's feeling that the painting will rot in an attic suggests that even here we feel the obverse side of an anxiety of influence: the sense that the voices may inevitably fail us.

To the Lighthouse is filled with melody and accompaniments, as the characters themselves notice, and this offsets the dark premonitions, fills in for the lack that Mrs. Ramsay and Lily Briscoe feel so poignantly and pointedly. Moreover, this melodic structure, in which phrases take on the resonance of motifs—one thinks of "Minta's glow" or "the atheist Tansley"—quickly sound themselves out as an ambience for reverie. Surely, it is in the melody of the text, its chora, that thought is supported, carried forward, pushed to associative crescendos that coincide with the crashing of the waves. At one point Mrs. Ramsay says, reflecting on some lines of poetry recited by her husband, "The words (she was looking at the window) sounded as if they were floating like flowers on water out there, cut off from them all, as if no one had said them, but they had come into existence of themselves."[13] Here, too, there is profound awareness that voice may fail us, though perhaps not wholly. For the words, the sounds, do come into existence of themselves. These words are homeless, restless, their existence saturated

---

and visual allayings of fears. " 'But think, Cam, it's only an old pig,' said Mrs. Ramsay, 'a nice black pig like the pigs at the farm.' But Cam thought it was a horrid thing, branching at her all over the room. 'Well then,' said Mrs. Ramsay, 'we will cover it up' " (p. 172).

13. Ibid., p. 99.

with loss, with what Lily and Mrs. Ramsay both understand as the alien habitat in which feminine consciousness finds little support, and yet they come into existence, they precipitate, for they are of the sea and its soundings, its melodious roar. It is this roar which fills the novel with the bass of being, as Irving Massey might put it, the soundings, tissue, or woof within which the textually sonorous interlacings establish themselves as homes for reverie and dream. It is in this sound-space, this timbre, that the novel replicates an analytic situation to the degree that these sounds allow the agents of voice to come to terms with their resistances, disappointments, repressions, and fears. "Always, Mrs. Ramsay felt, one helped oneself out of solitude reluctantly by laying hold of some little odd or end, some sound, some sight. She listened, but it was all very still; cricket was over; the children were in their baths; there was only the sound of the sea."[14]

The intervocative is strong in Woolf, and Hartman calls it the antiphonal in Wordsworth when he cites it there. I think that in Woolf's novel the antiphonal allows for a fragile and tenuous reconciliation between *sujet* and *destinataire,* that the restorative properties of voice are saturated with the knowledge that we must accept what blessings we can, that finally there is a consolation and great beauty of vision, however tenuous and momentary. Here voice opens onto symbolization or thematization in which a restoration of the self is possible while homage to the dead is paid. It is a symbolization that facilitates the capacity to dream well and, perhaps, to sleep knowing that the voices protect and save us.

In *Moby-Dick,* a much more strident work than *To the Lighthouse,* the defenses of voice are handled much differently. We recall Pip, who after having watched the sailors interpret the hieroglyphs on the Ecuadorian doubloon, says only, "I look, you look, he looks; we look, ye look, they look." Stubb, the second mate, remarks, "Upon my soul, he's been studying Murray's Grammar. Improving his mind, poor fellow!" It could be a Jakobsonian comment in that Stubb acknowledges grammar is not independent of the sound shapes, that syntax and voice

14. Ibid.

are intimately related. Stubb's comment also implies that sound shapes improve the mind, and this is reinforced by his comment, "Here's the ship's navel, this doubloon here," a navel that is most accurately described by Pip's grammatical recitations.[15] This is, one can only suppose, an anticipation of Freud's notion that the dream has a navel. And in Pip's slippage of the pronoun, as well as within the pun, Lacan would almost certainly have noticed the production of a *logique du fantasme,* that articulation which Freud notices in the transformation of "a child is being beaten," a phrase that in itself reminds one of Pip.

But this is only a small instance of the sound shapes of language in *Moby-Dick,* the residue of one who has been capsized and driven mad in the infinity of the sea. There is also the intensity of the parodic, the weaving of many discourses: scripture, science, navigation, geography, history, anthropology, folklore, and much else. When Ahab speaks, we hear a parody of Lear and Hamlet. Similarly, the cetology chapters mimic sources well known to specialists concerned with the "try-works" of the novel. Indeed, the "try-work" of the book is an attempt to appropriate these discourses in order to break away from a fixation, to drown out the trauma of Moby-Dick (that Mrs. Ramsay of Melville's text) by means of speaking about whaling and whales generally. Like Lily Briscoe, Melville's narrator is painting pictures in order to make voice visible, something that has been taken to extremes in the Arion edition of Melville's text, as if the antiphonal is somewhat antiphonic, perhaps a defense against drowning in the streaming of voice. Still, the antiphonal and the antiphonic repeat an appointment with the cataclysm that is Moby-Dick, one we see in the painting Ishmael sees of a whale impaled by a ship's masts, or, in Chapter 45—"The Affidavit"— the numerous accounts of the stoving in of boats by whales, and, again, the various accounts by passing vessels of encounters with the phantom-like whale of which the story of the Town Ho is most chilling. In all these examples, the voices or antiphonal play points to a desire to escape trauma, a primal scene, while at the same time meeting it head-on. Here restoration implies destruction.

An emblem for this condition is Jonah sleeping below the water line

15. Herman Melville, *Moby-Dick; Or, The Whale* (Berkeley and Los Angeles: University of California Press, 1979), p. 445.

while storms toss the ship. In part, Jonah represents someone who finds a safe berth in words, who allows the spell of sounds to transport him to a land of calm. But in another sense, Jonah also represents the sleeper who journeys to the navel of the dream and enters it. He returns to the womb of words, and not only once, but twice: first in the ship, and then in the whale. It is a troubled passage, because Jonah's descent is a defensive tactic countering the call of God's words—escaping the prophetic history of Nineveh—while striking it head-on by entering God's watery temple. This is a "complex," as some have called it, which struggles between acceptance and rejection of the voice. No doubt it is here that Kristeva's perception of the voice as a transgression against the law of an Other becomes extremely pertinent. Within the defensive appropriation of the sound shapes, that covering which allows Jonah to sleep, there is revealed a negativity expressed as trauma. At issue is not so much the failure of voice, that nothing which Lily Briscoe intuits in *To the Lighthouse,* but the Otherness of words which makes itself known from a fixation that is that fixation's very appearance.

The sound shapes of language provide a home, however troubled, for consciousness in which a wish-work can be conducted, an "analysis" undertaken. And in *Moby-Dick,* as in Woolf's novel, the water is not so much an image, merely, but a cascading of sound as well as a topos for wishing. As Melville puts it, men are drawn to the sea because "meditation and water are wedded forever." Melville calls the sea a "wonder world," meaning both an astonishing medium as well as a topos where we read "signs and wonders." It is here that Ahab wishes to slay the trauma, that Pip intuits his own madness in the infinite watery plain, that Ishmael wishes for deliverance, Queequeg for wisdom, and so on. The sea, one could say, has therapeutic elements. Even little Pip is delivered from his cowardice and is safely berthed in the sound shapes of words. Starbuck says of Pip, "in this strange sweetness of his lunacy, [he] brings heavenly vouchers of all our heavenly homes."[16]

16. Ibid., pp. 488–89.

In "Christopher Smart's *Magnificat*" Hartman writes, "Smart's anxiety about 'tongues' may have produced too good a poetic defense mechanism."[17] The suggestion is that poetic language may well be pathological. This is a point I want to develop further with respect to James Joyce's *Finnegans Wake*. A psychoanalyst would have little trouble noticing that in *Finnegans Wake* the voice marks a destabilization of ego formations and the overrunning of the primary processes. The text itself is more like what one might expect in hypnosis than in analysis, since under hypnosis the analysand is directly involved in the over-spillings of suggestion. We notice too in sections such as the "Study Chapter" that *Finnegans Wake* is similar to *Moby-Dick* in that we have again a "try-works" aimed at triangulating a traumatic zone, a "try-works" characterized by the intertextual collision of many discursive systems: geometry, science, anthropology, and so on. In part, the trauma of *Finnegans Wake* concerns the vagina of A.L.P. which is, if one thinks about it, but another watery berth. In *Finnegans Wake*, however, this kind of fixated symbol has been more or less successfully desymbolized in the overspillings of suggestion whose medium is the channel or current of the sound shapes of many blended languages. Here the anxiety has been channeled into sound and has produced a poetic defense mechanism that many readers would consider far too effective.

This defense mechanism follows the psychopathology of everyday life, which Margot Norris has focused on in her study, *The Decentered Universe of Finnegans Wake*.[18] But the poetic defense mechanism is also highly developed in terms of Joyce's sexual inhibitions, which Mark Shechner has documented from a clinical perspective in *Joyce in Nighttown*. At one point, Shechner relates that these inhibitions were accompanied with elaborate fantasies written out at length in letters to Nora when Joyce was far away from her but that they were converted into something more like sleep when he was with her. "I am so tired after all I have done here," Joyce writes, "that I think when I reach Via Scussa I will just creep into bed, kiss you tenderly on the forehead,

17. Hartman, *The Fate of Reading*, p. 90.
18. Margot Norris, *The Decentered Universe of Finnegans Wake* (Baltimore: Johns Hopkins University Press, 1977).

curl myself up in the blankets and sleep, sleep, sleep."[19] In *Finnegans Wake* the spell of sounds is perhaps the expression of a wish for sleep that at the same time supports sexual fantasies akin to what Shechner documents as part of Joyce's sexual life. This is relevant in terms of the water imagery in the novel.

Joyce invokes water with respect to Anna Livia Plurabelle, and it is this watery invocation that supports a sexual fantasy even as it drowns it in sleep. In doing so a disarticulation of a mise-en-scène takes place which is recovered as a spell or hush of sounds, a therapeutic current that at the end of the Anna Livia Plurabelle chapter, for example, assuages what Margot Norris sees as the trauma of the text: the fault of the father as primal scene. In the passage that follows, there is a fading brought about by sound as the scandals of the text are diluted and washed away by the blessed water that is woman.

> Can't hear with the waters of. The chittering waters of. Flittering bats, fieldmice bawk talk. Ho! Are you not gone ahome? What Thom Malone? Can't hear with bawk of bats, all thim liffeying waters of. Ho, talk save us! My foos won't moos. I feel as old as yonder elm. A tale told of Shaun and Shem? All Livia's daughter-sons. Dark hawks hear us. Night! Night! My ho head halls. I feel as heavy as yonder stone. Tell me of John or Shaun? Who were Shem and Shaun the living sons or daughters of? Night now! Tell me, tell me, tell me, elm! Night night! Telmeatale of stem or stone. Beside the rivering waters of, hitherandthithering waters of. Night![20]

Two washerwomen are speaking from bank to bank on the river Liffey, and as the dusk darkens, they turn into stem and stone. And between flows the stream of words, the antiphonal stream of textual confluences and the dissipation of voice into voices and sounds, a plurality of narrative residues reclaimed in the power of sleep, the wish to dissolve into debris and droplets of watery wit. But too there is a wish to stay awake and entertain lascivious fantasies, to keep the dirty gossip going

19. Mark Shechner, *Joyce in Nighttown* (Berkeley and Los Angeles: University of California Press, 1974), p. 92.

20. James Joyce, *Finnegans Wake* (New York: Viking, 1939), pp. 215–16.

about the daughters and sons of A.L.P. The washerwomen, who clean the dirty linen of these "daughter-sons" (the phrase suggests incest), turn into stem and stone (the tools for cleaning laundry), become the stuff out of which dreams are made, and yet not unlike children they resist sleep by asking for more narrative. It is as if parents are saying "night, night" while the children play "tell me a tale." As in Woolf, there is the fear that voices may fail us, that the spell of sounds is the charm preventing us from liquidation or dissipation.

In the quoted passage there is a fine balance between sounds determining what appears as represented and the representation determining the course of sounds. The spell sustains the course or chorus of voice but also sedates and allows these sounds to suggest metamorphic distortions in which agencies of voice turn into visible or concrete things, not to mention, a framed mise-en-scène of the river Liffey at dusk. In themselves these things, so much like ghostly mutterings, become sonorous densities that later take on identities as the Mookse and the Gripes, Glugg and Chuff, St. Patrick and the Archdruid. Here the ambivalence of text/context comes into play, just as it does when we realize that "Night! Night!" reminds us of T. S. Eliot's bar-closing scene in *The Wasteland*, a poem in which water also plays an important role. But there is also the dialogic relation of *sujet/destinataire* in the movement of a disarticulating relation between enunciation and the enunciated, a relation in which the agent of voice fades into vocal stammerings, natterings, or sonorous glides into the silence. In part, the famous passage quoted above does not turn so much on what these voices mean or even how they present the very trauma they wish to flee, a primal scene of transgression articulated in relation to parental "others." Rather, it raises a defensive means of desymbolization, depersonalization, and desexualization made possible through the syntax, rhyme, leitmotif, crescendo, retard, voicings, and resting of antiphonal tonalities, this texture of sounds in whose vocative tracings we can appreciate ghostly effects of the intervocative medley of sound shapes, ghostly effects that Lacan notices in the unconscious.

When Hartman writes that Christopher Smart produced too good a poetic defense mechanism, he suggested that the spell of sound was the medium where the symptoms of madness and the aesthetic infiltrated each other. Similarly, Harriet Weaver believed that *Finnegans*

Wake was symptomatic of Joyce's madness, and Clive Hart has asserted that this charge has been all too easily dismissed. Hart argues there may, in fact, be some truth to it.[21] According to this view, Joyce's text marks a serious failure in artistic communication since the poetic defense mechanism worked all too well. Moreover, Joyce's madness, such as it was, can be seen in terms of a fetishistic investment of emotions in sound, something Jacques Lacan touches on in "Le Sinthome," his seminar on Joyce, wherein Lacan conflates the symptom with sin and *homme* (yet notice other particles: sin, tho, me) in order to force a relation to the father which, in fact, Joyce lacked, a disconnection that, in Lacan's opinion, leads to something like "imposed speech" in *Finnegans Wake*.[22] Hart notes that Joyce had a magical theory concerning sound, and this theory worked in favor of a desymbolization that many Joyceans have never seriously considered. It is a desymbolization that Masud Khan would see as typical of "alienation in perversion," that is, the maintenance of fantasy structures in the service of depersonalization. If Lacan noticed that Joyce "stuffed the signifier," meaning that words became thing-like—sound as matter, word as object, and so on—Masud Khan shows us the relevance of this assessment. In perversions, he says, "The object occupies an intermediary position: it is not-self and yet subjective ... it is needed as an actual existent not-self being and yet coerced into complying with the exigent subjective need to *invent* it."[23] Although this could define literature in general, we must bear in mind that in perversion the relationship to the object is marked with an incapacity to relate to the object and that this failure is compensated for by magical investments and the kinds of regressive

21. Clive Hart, "*Finnegans Wake* in Perspective," in *James Joyce Today: Essays on the Major Works,* ed. T. F. Staley (Bloomington: Indiana University Press, 1966), pp. 135–65.

22. For installments of Jacques Lacan's *Séminaire XXIII: Le Sinthome,* see *Ornicar?* 7–11 (1975–76). Also see installments in Jacques Lacan, *Joyce avec Lacan,* ed. Jacques Aubert (Paris: Navarin, 1987).

23. Masud Khan, *Alienation in Perversions* (New York: International Universities Press, 1979), p. 21. Elsewhere, Khan says, "In my clinical experience perverts are not persons who impress one with being endowed with a biologically high or intense natural sexual appetite and drive.... It is all programmed in the head and then instinctual apparatuses and functions are zealously exploited in the service of programmed sexuality" (p. 15).

identifications typical of the well-known passage from *Finnegans Wake*. Here the magical investments mark the failure of poetic voice. And sound becomes a perverse object, a *sinthome*.

Hartman acknowledges such a condition in "Christopher Smart's *Magnificat*" when he writes, "Should we feel that words are defective, or else that we are defective *vis-à-vis* them (words becoming the other, as is not unusual in poets who have a magnified regard for a great precursor or tradition), then a complex psychic situation arises. It is fair to assume, however, that the distance between self and other is always disturbed, or being disturbed; that there is always some difficulty of self-presentation in us; and that, therefore, we are obliged to fall back on a form of 'representation.' "[24]

If we recall Kristeva's *Semiotikā*, we notice that *Finnegans Wake* exemplifies an instance in which the sound shapes of language are determined in negative relation to parental others—and, more specifically, to a primal scene—and that the orality of Joyce's language is situated in what Hartman calls the distance between self and other where self-presentation becomes troubled. Clearly, in *Finnegans Wake* the sounds concern a wish and a wound, a wish to repair the defectiveness of words, that wound which distances or alienates the author. Moreover, the difficulty concerns a self-presentation or re-presentation suppressed on the register of text/context relations and compensated for by a polylogue on the diachronic register of the *sujet/destinataire* in which a certain disarticulation is bound to occur.

My last example concerns the vanishing of words and the sustaining of the sound shapes themselves. Since I have discussed the precarious relations that the spell of sounds articulate, especially with respect to psychic defense, I consider now an example of how sound prepares the artist, still in his prime, for a premature and mysterious death. The Alban Berg Violin Concerto was written and dedicated to the passing of Manon Gropius, a beautiful young woman who lay in bed for about a year with polio. The Violin Concerto was begun before Manon died, and Berg finished it rather quickly upon learning from her mother,

24. Hartman, *The Fate of Reading*, p. 74.

Alma Mahler Gropius, that an angel had passed away. Not long after the piece was completed, Berg himself died. He never completed his opera *Lulu*, which had been suspended for the sake of the Violin Concerto. As we know, music has its affiliations with death; the *Dies Irae*, requiems, funeral marches, and so on are all prominent in the repertoire. Berg's Violin Concerto is not any of these, which is to say, it is not distanced by membership in a specific musical genre appropriate for mourning. Rather, the Violin Concerto is an unmediated vision, the reflection of a severely depressed consciousness which strains against melody. Indeed, the death of Manon is investigated in the initial playing of open fifths in the violin and harp parts, a series of pitches that pose as so much tuning. It is an initial tuning of the instrument that ordinarily would come between silence and performance, a transitional object, perhaps, carrying one from the inarticulate to the articulate, though not without resistances. For these open fifths are merely sound shapes, a kind of found musical object. The Violin Concerto fixes on this object as something belonging rather distinctly to the musical portrait of the girl, to the beauty of an association between a child and her practicing, her beginning to play. The fifths suggest a mise-en-scène, then, of someone learning music or of someone starting to play. These notes also outline a romantic direction taken within the atonal sequences or rows that Berg develops, as if the Violin Concerto were stuffed into the sound shapes of the fifths. Thus it is out of these notes, this raw sounding on the violin, so suggestive of a ghostly presence, that a *Trauermusik* is born, a music in which the composer does not, as figures do in Woolf and Melville, find a safe berth in sound. For Berg contemplates death in the margins of the music, in that spell of sound not yet music, though in every sense, music proper.

It is from these margins climaxing into sweeping chords based on the interval of the fifth that Berg attempts to bring Manon back from the dead even as this passionate reach takes account of itself as a groping in the margins where music ends and silence begins—this land of the dead. Indeed, Manon slips into the darkness, is reclaimed by the low woody timbres of the clarinets, which in the Adagio play a Lutheran chorale, "Es ist genug." Musicologists never cease to be amazed by how quickly Berg worked the chorale into the Violin Concerto, not much unlike an afterthought that, it seems, was always already intended. Even the shape of the Chorale's Melody curiously fits exactly into part of Berg's main tone row which was, oddly enough, its last four notes. "It Is Enough ... " In the sounding out of the chorale there is the desire to end, the wish-work of the sounds to die, of the composer to lie down and be himself claimed by the afterworld.

"O Ewigkeit, Du Donnerwort." So J. S. Bach titled his Cantata 60, from which Berg borrowed the chorale. "Oh Eternity, You Thunderous Word." In the Violin Concerto the word of the eternal thunders in the climaxes of the second movement, though it is never far from the structure of the open fifths, that sustaining agency of the concerto. Indeed, the fifths maintain the illusion that in music the voices will not fail us, and yet Berg's composition reminds us that the voicings and voices are, in fact, failing, fracturing, breaking off. The open fifths testify that the music threatens to turn into mere sound shapes or noise, and the atonal rows struggle abrasively against their harmonic contexts, marking a dissonance indicating that in this piece music is in trouble. Even if the last bars offer a restatement of the fifths as a ray of hope, it is a reconciliation tainted with soft bitter dissonances, a reconciliation haunted by the memory of Manon, by that mise-en-scène of a child's tuning on the violin, a tuning, *Stimmung, Trauermusik* in whose dis-illusioned scale or clime the composer expresses his wish to leave off, to end quietly where the tuning stops and the hush which follows the thunder starts. The music is no longer a defense against death but an acquiescence to it. The composer has, in a word, wrecked. He has, to recall a leitmotif from Woolf, perished alone.

These four examples form a brief introduction, then, to the study of psychological or attitudinal aspects relative to the sound shapes of language as they are interpreted from the perspective of psychological defense, what Roman Jakobson saw as a determining factor in the understanding of sound in relation to sense, and what Hartman has seen in terms of a psychoesthetic. We are moving, as well, toward an intertextual understanding that appreciates the significance of sound shapes in terms of the infiltration of dialogical elements that impact on both the axes of *sujet/destinataire* and text/context. What has in-terested me, in particular, is how psychological defense (and by exten-sion, questions of pathology) might be considered a major factor in discussing linguistic relationships that are usually treated in ways that leave out such subjective modalizations. That generic distinctions made solely along text/context lines might be strongly affected by various subjective or psychological formations that involve the relations of *sujet/destinataire* is a perception that few theorists and commentators on the arts have followed up.

In the last decade or so, Kristeva has worked in this direction, and her *Pouvoirs de l'horreur* touches on Céline and the pathology of abjection in order to gain better insight into literary language with respect to the dialogic or *sujet/destinataire* axis. In *Soleil Noir* she extends these researches into the pathology of depression. It is here that sound shapes are directly encountered, though, oddly enough, still not investigated per se. In discussing a patient, "Helen," Kristeva writes the following:

> Like an Alice in distressland, the depressed woman cannot put up with mirrors. Her image and that of others arouse within her a wounded narcissism, violence, and the desire to kill—from which she protects herself by going through the looking glass and settling down in that other world where, by limitlessly spreading her constrained sorrow, she regains a hallucinated completedness. Orally assimilating the mother who gets married, who has a man, who flees. Possessing her, holding her within oneself so as never to be separated from her. Helen's almightiness shows through the mask of aggressiveness and shores up the other's nonexistence in her daydream as well as the difficulty she experiences in deciding who she is when facing a person different from herself, separated from herself in actual life.[25]

Not surprisingly, a sound shape will emerge here too, one given from the side of the (M)Other. "I forgot to tell you," Helen tells Julia Kristeva: "I've had sex and I was nauseated. I vomited and I saw, as if I were in between sleep and wakefulness, something like the head of a child falling into the washbasin while a voice called me from a distance, but mistakenly calling me by my mother's name." And Kristeva comments, "She had locked up a fantasy, the representation of her mother,

25. Julia Kristeva, *Black Sun*, trans. Leon Roudiez (New York: Columbia University Press, 1989), pp. 74, 75.

within her body.''[26] The sound shape of the mother's name—interestingly, Kristeva fails to provide it, hence saving it as *mot tabou*[27]—marks, as in Leclaire's case history of the unicorn, a dialogical site in which the subject is divided into conflicted subject positions where the sound shape emerges at once as a defensive or phatic buffer and as a mark of where a trauma has manifested itself. That is, in Kristeva's later work, we see specific attention to the oral word and how it affects what she calls asymbolia and what, in our own investigations, we cited as desymbolization, the effect that accompanies a pathology of the sound shape. Furthermore, we noticed that such desymbolization is most likely a response to traumatic vulnerability.

This seems to be Hartman's view, as well. In *Saving the Text,* Hartman returns to language in its relation to the conscious ear. He suggests that no investigation of *écriture* can wholly escape accountability in the recognition of an "ear-fear": "I return to my initial hypothesis, that the ear is vulnerable, or passes through phases of vulnerability. Its vulnerability is linked—the actual causes being obscure—to real or fantasied words, to an ear-fear connected with overhearing, or to the word as inherently untrustworthy, equivocal, betraying its promise of immediacy or intimacy.''[28] It is this intimacy of language which Hartman reads in Shakespeare, Goethe, Keats, Wordsworth, Melville, Baudelaire, Joyce, and Genet, but also in the philosophers Nietzsche, Heidegger, and Derrida. In *Saving the Text,* the ear-fear of Derrida is interrogated from the perspective of the sound shapes of language. "For many readers *Glas* does emanate an incomprehensible or intolerable music. 'Klang und nicht Sprache' is the wound attributed by Hegel to Memnon's colossus.''[29] And yet, for Hartman this music is decipherable in the slippages of verbal sounds, in the intimate sonorities heard in the echoland of psychic defense sensitive to that awful vulnerability of the ear.

As Hartman knows, this defensiveness is revealed most brutally by Jacques Derrida in "Limited Inc abc ... " in which the name of John

26. Ibid., pp. 76–77.
27. See Chapter 3, "*Jane Eyre* and the *Mot Tabou*."
28. Geoffrey Hartman, *Saving the Text* (Baltimore: Johns Hopkins University Press, 1981), p. 157.
29. Ibid., p. 72.

Searle is molested with the power of a curse, hence impugning the credibility of the author's claim to his own thoughts, that imaginative copyright transmitted by the voice through the text. Derrida calls him "Sarle" ("société à responsabilité limitée"). In "Limited Inc abc ..." Sarle snarls. And Derrida asks in a similar tone, "And how do the 'common,' 'generic' elements, which always exist even in a proper name, withstand contamination in and by foreign languages?"[30] Which is to ask, how can the ear decide the *translinguistic?* How can the ear not deconstruct the signature of a snarling opponent whose words participate in a collective slandering of the name, Derrida, of not a restricted but an unrestrained and general attack mounted through collegeal mutterings, those frantic and heated telecommunications between academic "friends"? Who is real? Who fantasied? What is the *genre* of this transmission, these words, this essay, this signature, this muttering, this debate, this writing? As Hartman so rightfully notes in *Saving the Text,* deconstruction is trapped in this labyrinth of the ear, in this genre of hearing that goes *beyond genre.* And it is in sympathy with such a deconstruction that Hartman bids us to listen to the sonorities and seductions of that "Klang" in "Sprache," to those slips of the tongue which molest the certainties of a generic imperative for whom the sound shapes of language can never be much more than a lyric impulse chained to the labor of form.

30. Jacques Derrida, "Limited Inc abc ...," trans. Samuel Weber, *Glyph* 2 (Baltimore: Johns Hopkins University Press, 1977), p. 167.

8

Tonalities of Apocalypse

All life
Is as a tale told to one in a dream
In tones never totally audible
Or understandable, and one wakes
Wishing to hear more, asking
For more, but one wakes to death, alas,
Yet one never
Pays any heed to that, the tale
Is still so magnificent in the telling

        —John Ashbery, "Litany"

"Il y a la cendre...." Has the phrase simply been ringing in Jacques Derrida's ears ever since it came to him at the end of *La Dissémination?* Or did it come from somewhere else, perhaps from a distant apocalypse? Which is to ask, Who or what is ringing or speaking in *Feu la cendre?* Is it the remnant of a fantasy that has returned to Derrida's psyche in the form of an "imposed speech," or is it of a different order altogether, say, an apocalyptic tone that is sent as the trace or trait of an event that, as Vladimir Jankélévitch points out, is extremely difficult to recover. "All we have in common is being here, all of us, the survivors. Everything that is most common and essential to us, you will admit, is summed up in our being alive; by accident, we are here ... each one of us, individually, is here ... we don't know how! ... through an oversight on the part of the Gestapo ... we don't know what happened, but we came back."[1] Such remarks remind us that the Holocaust is something of an expulsion story, a hideous inversion of Genesis.

---

1. Quoted in Emmanuel Levinas, *Difficult Freedom* (Baltimore: Johns Hopkins University Press, 1990), p. 162.

What can be known about it, Jankélévitch suggests, depends entirely on the condition of having survived or come after the event, that is to say, on the *après coup*. And this requires us to meditate on the fact that this event has to be conceived from the perspective of an expulsion, a living-on that does not give us access to "what happened to us." Derrida's notion of the cinder, I believe, is crucial to this problematic. Indeed, the phrase, "Il y a la cendre," which derives from Emmanuel Levinas's formulation of the "il y a" as horror in *Existence and Existents*, suggests that as *après coup* or aftermath of disaster, the cinder nevertheless intones something—that it rings in the manner of a death knell or *glas*. Yet, this ringing is a tone that "comes after the subject" in the sense that Jankélévitch's notion of living on or surviving comes after the kind of subjecthood that could possibly recount or represent itself as anything other than *revenant* or coming back.

When Jankélévitch says that only his being alive is most essential, he is already suggesting that the survivor exists beyond some notion of subjecthood which cannot be recovered because the disaster was characterized by so many forgettings, the "forgetting" of the Jews by the European population, generally, but then too the "forgetting" or oversight of the Gestapo. "We were forgotten," Jankélévitch says, meaning that the subject, as such, has vanished and cannot be recovered in what lives on. But who or what, then, returns? And how are we to conceptualize questions of ethics in terms of such an existential condition?

Edmond Jabès's writings are an attempt to answer this question: "...a voice? perhaps mine?—perhaps only the ghost of a voice, of a word. Perhaps a few words from a word so lonely that it slips away from both the I and the You. Word of a different absence, a stranger even to absence; word of a different silence ... Perhaps just the inkling of a word coming after the word, after even the after-word." It is, again, "A word coiled up in its voice, useless, useless except for the voice, for the uncertain burial of an unseen word. Aely's voice and word."[2] Expelled from the subject, the You and I, consigned to a different unspeakable absence, the word accedes to a voice very rem-

---

2. Edmond Jabès, *The Book of Questions: Yaël, Elya, Aely*, trans. Rosmarie Waldrop (Middletown: Wesleyan University Press, 1983), p. 221.

iniscent of Derrida's irreducible cinder, the "il y a la cendre." That is, the word is no longer anyone's in particular, but is the return of something exterior to or beyond the subject that is, at the same time, very intimate and close to what Jankélévitch calls being and which Jabès associates with what remains, "Aely's voice and word." It is this word Jabès will identify with the Law of God.

For Derrida the voice and word is also difficult to estrange from that unspeakable absence, that different silence of which Jabès speaks.

—Why Cinders 'there'? The place of burning, but of what, of whom? As long as one does not know, and you will never know, the sentence says what it said earlier, the incinerated is no longer nothing, nothing but the cinder, the innermost cinder furnace, the remnant that must no longer remain, this place of nothing that may be, a pure place was marked out.

—Pure is the word. It calls for fire. Cinders there are, this is what takes place in letting a place occur, so that it will be understood: Nothing will have taken place but the place. Cinders there are: Place there is [Il y a la cendre: il y a lieu].[3]

The cinder testifies or bears witness to the destruction of which it is itself the effacement. And one may wonder how such notions, if they go so far as to deconstruct the subject, make it possible for us to maintain an ethical relation to the victim? Recently Derrida addressed this kind of question by asking, Who comes after the subject?: "Responsibility is excessive or it is not a responsibility. A limited, measured, calculable, rationally distributed responsibility is already the becoming right of morality; it is at times also, in the best hypothesis, the dream of every good conscience, in the worst hypothesis, of the small or grand inquisitors."[4] Even though genocide was carried out according to some procedure, there is no principle of reason, no calculative strategy, that is capable of measuring our ethical relation to this terrible catastrophe. We cannot adequately address this disaster by reducing or limiting our

3. Jacques Derrida, *The Cinder*, trans. Ned Lukacher (Lincoln: University of Nebraska Press, 1991), p. 37.
4. Jacques Derrida, " 'Eating Well': An Interview," in *Who Comes after the Subject?* ed. E. Cadava, P. Connor, and J.-L. Nancy (New York: Routledge, 1991), p. 118.

ethical sensibility to a traumatic mise-en-scène, a personal phobia, a sociological theory (banality of evil, male fantasy, abjection, and so on), or even a rational historical account. When Derrida intones "il y a la cendre," he is taking note that the phrase is like the cinder, a disembodied aftereffect, a spectral phenomenon that is left over, survives, and, most important, calls to us collectively "from what is not, in order to recall at the delicate, charred bottom of itself only non-being or non-presence." This call of the cinder is mirrored, of course, in the tonality of Jankélévitch's remarks. Similar, too, with respect to Jankélévitch, is the following statement, which refers to a double expulsion, first from society and second from the scene of the crime without which it is difficult for the survivors to make sense of what happened and of who one is: "I have the impression now that the best paradigm for the trace ... is not, as some have believed ... perhaps, the trail of the hunt, the fraying, the furrow in the sand, the wake in the sea, the love of the step for its imprint, but the cinder (what remains without remaining from the holocaust, from the all-burning, from the incineration the incense)."[5] The cinder, in other words, is not what points to a path or road that one can follow or track down according to the logic, say, of Plato's Stranger in *The Sophist*. Rather, as trace the cinder speaks from beyond an event to which we cannot retrace our steps, an event from which the subject is foreclosed, despite the fact that this historical moment was exceptionally determined and had determinate consequences. The cinder, in that sense, is an apocalyptic ringing or death knell that marks the distance from and proximity to a moment that resists the kind of recoverability that Jankélévitch refers to in his remarks even as it has left its traumatic and determinative mark not only on Jews but, it has to be said, on the West as a whole.

The American poet John Ashbery, however distant from Derrida's concerns, is attuned to similar buoyant voices on the winds of the *après coup* recalling a distant catastrophe. In Ashbery this uncontrolled calling is absorbed in the decor of suburban tameness in which violence is everywhere suppressed. Indeed, Ashbery's poetry is so understated and matter-of-fact that often the distinctions between gravity and levity are difficult to determine, as if in a postmodern culture the difference

5. Derrida, *The Cinder*, p. 43.

is unlocatable in a vernacular tongue. The effect is that cataclysmic events sound commonplace and even silly, that, conversely, faintly whimsical occurrences sound menacing. Ashbery is suspended between consciousness of decentered tonalities, an "Echo divisé," as Derrida has remarked about such writing. And it is through such tonal unfocusings that ethical considerations are raised, for such tonalities reveal the collision and collusion of attitudes as they are found in a discourse that belongs to no one and everyone, a discourse in which the ethical floats like so many fantasmal echoes that refuse to take on a stable identity or point of view. And it is within this wash of ethical nuance, this tolerance for every conceivable attitude, that the question of victimage is posed in a way that goes beyond any primal scene of victimage. Note Ashbery's poem "A Wave."

> Enough to know that I shall have answered for myself soon,
> Be led away for further questioning and later returned
> To the amazingly quiet room in which all my life has been spent.
> It comes and goes; the walls, like veils, are never the same,
> Yet the thirst remains identical, always to be entertained
> And marveled at. And it is finally we who break it off,
> Speed the departing guest, lest any question remain
> Unasked, and thereby unanswered. Please, it almost
> Seems to say, take me with you, I'm old enough.

These lines close "A Wave" and comprise but one of the vast number of sea changes—sudden scenic shifts—in the poem. Here the speaker is momentarily disclosed, as in some other parts of the poem, as a prisoner whose consciousness is suspended in a texture of attitudinizing and intoning through which a disaster is recollected. It is not so much that a victim is making moral determinations or has merely gone mad, but that this consciousness is beyond good and evil and inhabits the waviness of unfocused ethical nuances, finds its home in an unsynthesized and multiple texture of verbal tones flattened only by an anonymous colloquialism that gives the language an informal appearance, one that is, of course, posed and itself indicative of a society that permits an ethical latitude. It is within this latitude of permissibility that Ashbery sounds notes of neutrality, as the beach of consciousness where the shocks of the waves can be felt.

And the mind
Is the beach on which the rocks pop up, just a neutral
Support for them in their indignity.[6]

The whole of "A Wave" can be read as this permissive neutral plain or beach on which is felt the tonal residues of catastrophe or indignity. The rocks, themselves unsignifying, thingy, are washed up on a sandy neutrality, "A luminous backdrop of ever-repeated / Gestures, having no life of their own, but only echoing / The suspicions of their possessor." It is, at best, the effect left by an average, everyday scatter of thoughts. "And the issue making sense becomes such a far-off one." For the issue is not focusing the scatter of thought into a point of view but of inhabiting far less decided "suspicions" that surround the indignity of the things about which nothing can be properly said, about those "unsayable" rocks thrown up on the beach.

The waves are "the reflexive play of our living and being lost / and then changed again," a reflexive play that makes up a passive intoning and attitudinizing that acquiesces to the voicing of its discomfort to the changes brought by the waves so rich in monotony. This is the same monotony of cinders and ashes, and it is of a similar flake-like structure, of a certain peeling off, a decomposition and scattering. It is perhaps not merely coincidental that the book jacket for *A Wave* is a reproduction of Vija Celmins's "Untitled (Big Sea #1)," whose ashen and almost silvery waves manifest a luminous and yet flat hyperreality whose monotony suggests collapse into mere grayness, an agoraphobia of dullness. As if to say, with Ashbery, "No, the / Divine tolerance we seem to feel is actually in short supply," or "All those days had a dumb clarity."

If there is an "apocalyptic tone" in works like "A Wave," it is the reflexive play of tonal saturations as they mediate sudden changes of thought, an attitudinizing that makes up suspicions concerning the end, an end that is itself not some thing occurring at some time but an end in whose violence consciousness always already lives through as an unfocused sensitivity that marks the horizon of a day-to-day living with others. It is an ethical attitudinizing through which our relation to

6. John Ashbery, *A Wave* (New York: Viking, 1984), pp. 89, 70.

others is derived from the casualness of speech rather than from direct encounter, as if it were the faint tonalities embedded within language that determines our inconsistent and undecidable relationship with others.

In Derrida's work *La Carte postale* this ethical attitudinizing extends to calling into question the identity and possibility of an addresser and addressee. "Au nom de quoi, au nom de qui publier, divulguer ... ?"[7] In whose name, publish, divulge, in the name of what? Derrida, at every point, questions the determinations of the name, the univocality of its properness, the consistency of its address to a readerly horizon that is itself awash in a wear and tear of linguistic tolerance inhibiting the proper reception of the proper name. "En vue de qui, auprès de qui accepter de divulger?"[8] That is, with whom can one allow oneself to tell all? But more appropriate, is it possible to conceive of an addressee for whom one can, indeed, write, one who is not, in any case, oneself? And if one receives one's own postcards, is the recipient at one with the sender? Is it a "me" or "self" who is the stable ground for the delimitation of what the postcard says? Derrida suggests that even a closed circuit in which cards are sent to oneself is no insurance against the divisibility of the writer and the name, for the arrival of the letter always discloses something else of the writer's destiny, an event in which the written says something else about the name that has preceded its coming and which is not easily recoverable by even a reader who has authored the message. But what is this something else the message says? It is, among other things, the tone the message accrues in its arrival or coming, the resonance it takes on after having passed through the mail, through its *being sent,* its *transmission.*

"Il y a la cendre," what does it mean once it is sent back to Derrida from *La Dissémination?* Is it the same phrase anymore? What occurs in the turning of such a phrase? A catastrophe?

> As soon as there is, there is différance ... and there is postal maneuvering, relays, delay, anticipation, destination, telecommunicating network, the possibility, and therefore the fatal necessity of going astray, etc. There is strophe (there is strophe in every sense;

7. Jacques Derrida, *La Carte postale* (Paris: Flammarion, 1980), p. 89.
8. Ibid., p. 89.

apostrophe and catastrophe, address in turning the address (always toward you, my love), and my postcard is strophes).[9]

As soon as one can assert the arrival or thereness of the postcard one has *différance,* and perhaps even the cinder, given that Derrida does not hesitate to burn some of these cards.

In *La Carte postale* there is a rather complex play with the notion of turning in words such as *détournement, à tourner, strophe* which suggests that the relationship between addresser and addressee is subordinated to the inclinations or directions established through the process of a message's transmission, its sending. The Ancient Greek term *strophe* itself literally means to turn, and it is here that from within the inclination of a routed message that strophe takes on apostrophic or catastrophic inclinations. Addresser and addressee are but the effects of such erratic turnings and routings, effects of the inclinations of messages en route. Part of Derrida's interest in talking at length about the postal network is that through it the existential assumptions about dialogue between selves and others are put into question by the medium of something as trivial as a postcard, whose routings alter the manner in which the messages are to be taken, affect the tone of the strophe, a tone made up of the inclinations or turns the text achieves by the directions afforded it by the postal service, its physical journey through the mail, the telegraph, or, in another sense, over the telephone lines. Such a transmission of tone (or destin-errance), what is it but the condition of any text's receptivity?

For Ashbery such receptivity is perhaps itself the major topic of many of his poems. For example, in "I Might Have Seen It," a poem from the collection *As We Know,* Ashbery writes,

> The person who makes a long-distance phone call
> Is talking into the open receiver at the other end

9. Jacques Derrida, *The Post Card,* trans. Alan Bass (Chicago: University of Chicago Press, 1987), p. 66. "Dès qu'il y a, il y a différance... et il y a agencement postal, relais, retard, anticipation, destination, dispositif télécomunicant, possibilité et donc nécessité fatale de détournement, etc. Il y a strophe (il y a strophe en tous sens, apostrophe et catastrophe, adresse à tourner [toujours vers toi, mon amour], et ma carte postale ce sont des strophes)" (Derrida, *La Carte postale,* p. 74).

> The mysterious discourse also emerges as pointed
> In his ear there are no people in the room listening

This poem forecloses the relationship of an addresser/addressee while heightening the sense of a mysterious discourse characterized as pointed, emergent, distant, and audible in the openness of the receiver at "the other end." But this end, is it not always already the final end, too?

> As the curtain bells out majestically in front of the starlight
> To whisper the words This has already happened
> And the footfalls on the stair turn out to be real
> Those of your neighbor I mean the one who moved away[10]

Abruptly, the poem ends, like a conversation that has been "hung up" at the "other end." The starlight, the whispering, the recognition "This has already happened," all suggest the mood of an apotheosis reinforced by the thought of a neighbor who has moved away (died?). Too, the lines run on like phone conversation lines, though here they are not framed by dialogue, only dissipated through the open receiver at the other end. Apostrophe and catastrophe modulated in an ordinary long-distance call.

This living through of the end in Ashbery becomes a day-to-day awareness marking the withdrawal of the end. Maurice Blanchot, who has himself written at length of the "disaster," notes that as a community with the capacity to annihilate all living things we generally live beyond the horizon of mortality, a living beyond which eludes closure, ending, finality, the determination of any one primal fantasm. As in Ashbery, the end is not something to come but something whose realized potential we have philosophically transcended, an apocalyptic moment that postmodern consciousness survives as a "turning" between apostrophe and catastrophe.

Perhaps we could say that for Derrida "There is strophe" means "Cinders there are." For it is a living through to the beyond of a rationalism concerning the ground of addresser and addressee, a living

10. John Ashbery, *As We Know* (New York: Penguin, 1979), p. 83.

through that gives way linguistically to tonal resonances whose saturations play havoc with traditional values, syntaxes, or mise-en-scènes such as voices talking through an open receiver. Indeed, it is through an apocalyptic tone that values are not merely revalorized but scandalously inhabited by delicate attitudinal transgressions. Ashbery demonstrates the scandal within informal English, whereas in Derrida the scandal is reflected in the ambiguity of resonances from a slightly more academic clime. Still, these writers are sensitive to the conduit of a neutral voice that has passed through the catastrophe to the hitherside of the end, "Those of your neighbor I mean the one who moved away."

❧

One does not have to read far into John Ashbery's poetry to recognize that system is usually collapsing if not always already disarticulated. And Ashbery himself is quite obliging in discussing this feature of his work. At one point in *Three Poems* he admits,

> The system was breaking down. The one who had wandered
> alone past so many happenings and events began to feel,
> backing up along the primal vein that led to his
> center, the beginning of a hiccup that would, it left
> to gather, explode the center to the extremities of
> life, the suburbs through which one makes one's way to
> where the country is.[11]

Although addressing a conceptual system, Ashbery analogically refers us inside of what appears to be an urban space as well as a living body, and it is, oddly enough, the levity of a hiccup that threatens to annihilate the entire system, as if an occurrence in one analogical register bears on the others. In Ashbery, one can only suppose, analogues somehow do not metaphorically refer to one another but inhabit each other and hybridize. But rather than describe at length this peculiar use of catachresis, I will focus merely upon the hiccup itself, since this little explosion or outburst, at least in the very beginning, has an apocalyptic

---

11. John Ashbery, *Three Poems* (New York: Penguin, 1972), p. 53.

tone, a ring that can be heard yet once more in the syllables of Jacques Derrida's *Glas*.

In *Glas* the *gl* is neither voiced entirely, nor voiceless either. Derrida says of the *gl* that it is

> a voiceless voice stifling a sob or a clot of milk in the throat, the tickled laughter, or the glairy vomit of a baby glutton, the imperial flight of a raptor that swoops down at one go on your nape, the name gluing, frozen, a cold pissing of an impassive Teutonic philosopher, with a notorious stammer, sometimes liquid and sometimes guttorotetanic, a swollen or cooing goiter, all that rings in the tympanic channel of fossa, the spit or plaster on the soft palate, the orgasm of the glottis or the uvula, the clitoral glue, the cloaca of the abortion, the gasp of sperm, the rhythmed hiatus ...[12]

Gl, the occasion for a Rabelaisian catalog that quickly loses its humor, the sticking in the throat of a sound, the death rattle, the last gurgling noises of the dying man who bleeds, vomits, spits, and tries to speak at the same time, the sounds of a baby choking on its mother's milk, a baby who vomits on the breast, but too of the choked-up lover or the *chanteuse*. This sound, this almost inaudible murmuring is carried not on the breath but on or in the body's fluids and becomes the channel or current for the *gl*, that sticky syllable that makes us laugh even while a protagonist drowns between glugs. The *gl* is the result of a spasm, like laughter maybe, or like that of the body's response to asphyxiation, as in a gas chamber. It is a syllable whose death knell is spasmatic, like the urination of an icy person, perhaps a guard who at one time bothered to piss against the cattle cars as people were hauled out to extermination sites during World War II. The *gl*, a peculiar reminder

---

12. Jacques Derrida, *Glas*, trans. J. P. Leavey, Jr. (Lincoln: University of Nebraska Press, 1986), pp. 120b–121b; translation slightly modified. "Une voix sans voix étouffant un sanglot ou un caillot de lait dans la gorge, le rire chatouillé ou le vomi glaireux d'un bébé glouton, le vol impérial d'un repace qui fond d'un coup sur votre nuque, le nom gluant, glacé, pissant froid d'un impassible philosophe teuton, au bégaiement notoire, tantôt liquide et tantôt gutturo-tetanique, un goître enflé ou roucoulant, tout ce qui cloche dans le conduit ou dans la fosse tympanique, le crachat ou l'emplâtre sur le voile du palais, l'orgasme de la glotte ou de la luette, la glu clitoridienne, le cloaque de l'avortement, le hoquet de sperme, l'hiatus rythmé ... " (Jacques Derrida, *Glas* [Paris: Galilée, 1974], pp. 137b–138b).

or remainder of genocide, haunts *Glas* with inappropriate and yet unrelieved hilarity, as if the sound itself were not simply a curse, intended and executed, but a far more subtle kind of humiliation on the order of a bodily symptom.

It is in terms of this *gl* that we must bear witness to the approach of an apocalyptic tone, a mundane, automatic, inevitable, and often hardly noticed spasm of the ethical, a *hoquet* or hiccup. But can we hear it? Can we sense this death knell, this *gl* directed at our being and which passes beyond our ability to separate mind from body, speech from biology, *eros* from *thanatos*? This knell which, like the cinder, we cannot properly mourn? In both *Glas* and *Three Poems* we ought to hear the spasm of the text and the breaking down of the system, what in both Derrida and Ashbery appear as textual fractures, explosions, catastrophes.

> What I am trying to write—gl—is not just any structure whatever,
> a system of the signifier or the signified, a thesis or a novel, a poem,
> a law, a desire or a machine, but what passes more or less well,
> through the rhythmic stricture of an annulus.[13]

The spasm neutralizes, makes impossible, any text that would accede to be something particular, nullifies the attempt to write within a particular genre or type of writing. It is the corporeality and the premeditated rhythms and outbursts that impede the production of a classical or systematic text, an outburst that produces its own kind of systematic discourse, its own kind of analytic. If we see this in Derrida and Ashbery, we have seen it before: in Milton's *Lycidas* with its curious outbursts or interruptions, or in George Herbert's quiet, muffled, "ejaculations." Derrida's *Glas*, of course, takes the notion of spiritual outburst rather far, but not without good reason. He calls it "the saccadanced spasm of an eructojaculation, the syncopated valve of tongue and lips."[14] Here the tolling of the bell is grafted onto metaphors

13. Ibid., p. 109b. "Ce que je cherche à écrire—gl—ce n'est pas une structure quelconque, un système du signifiant ou du signifié, une thèse ou un roman, une poème, une loi, un désir ou une machine, c'est ce qui passe, plus ou moins bien, par la stricture rythmée d'un anneau" (Derrida, *Glas*, p. 125b).

14. Ibid., p. 121b; "le spasme saccadancé d'une éructojaculation, le clapet syncopé de la langue et des lèvres" (Derrida, *Glas*, p. 138b).

of the body, and here too a curious hybrid is the result. Derrida's term for it is *invagination*. What is relevant for us, however, is not so much this type of condensation or catachresis but the sense of catastrophe, violence, or cataclysm that is aroused in the reader.

Ashbery's poems, of course, have a flat and insouciant tone, something inherited from Frank O'Hara but which owes considerable debt to the weightlessness of American conversational style, what amounts to an evasiveness masked over by a casual "what me worry?" delivery. It is this false neutrality, this mastery of the insincere that Ashbery does not mock so much as exploit to produce a limpid zero-degree of writing, which he calls a "calm world." Yet, in this even-tempered style whose voice does not, perhaps cannot rise, there is an involuntary disquietude or spasmatic outburst like the beginning of a hiccup. It is,

> a jagged kind of mood that comes at the end of the day,
> lifting life into the truth of real pain for a few
> moments before subsiding in the usual irregular way, as
> things do. These were as much there as anything, things
> to be fumbled with, cringed before: dry churrings of no
> timbre, hysterical staccato passages that one cannot
> master or turn away from. These things led into life.
> Now they are gone but it remains, calm, lucid, but
> weightless, drifting above everything and everybody
> like the light in the sky, no more to be surmised, only
> remembered as so many things that remain at equal
> distances from us are remembered. The light drinks the
> dark and sinks down, not on top of us as we had
> expected but far, far from us in some other, unrelated
> sphere. This was not even the life that was going to
> happen to us.[15]

In such passages the remoteness of the effect becomes an index of how extensive and massive is the catastrophe that goes unnamed but into whose ambit we are, as Ashbery says, "slurped up." The jagged mood is not produced so much as sustained, and the real pain subsides and is irregular. It is "as much there as anything." What we must consider

15. Ashbery, *Three Poems*, p. 54.

above all is the distance that allows the voice to say, "This was not even the life that was going to happen to us." As if experience and discourse were somehow incommunicable.

In *La Folie du jour* by Maurice Blanchot, the narrator or voice is at once embodied and disembodied.

> At times I said to myself, "This is death. In spite of everything, it's really worth it, it's impressive." But often I lay dying without saying anything. In the end, I grew convinced that I was face to face with the madness of the day. That was the truth: the light was going mad, the brightness had lost all reason: it assailed me irrationally, without control, without purpose.[16]

Not unlike Ashbery's voices, his "us" that speaks in the passages from the *Three Poems,* the voice in *La Folie du jour* is trying to determine what life might be involved with it; but for the moment there is only the sense of distance and light. If in Ashbery the light drinks the dark and sinks down, and if that light participates in an unrelated sphere, in Blanchot's récit the light is itself the madness of day, an unrelatedness into whose ambience the voice is uncontrollably caught up.

There is not simply a stream of consciousness at work in these texts but spasmatic, or as Ashbery says, irregular movements, words, and expressions which disappear and protrude in a limpidity neither prose nor poetry, voice nor writing. The hysterical staccato passages and direct encounters in Ashbery are muffled in the eerie calm of mind and text, the sedation of words. The outbursts and spasms lead into life only to be dissipated there, leaving in their wake a calm, drifting, and genreless writing that turns into light, distance, difference, otherness. The subject or Cogito is not so much a center where identifications are resolved or counterpointed but a pervasive field or saturation of vocal and attitudinal densities conveyed through a calm or limpid style. One might say that through the tone of the writing the subject is evacuated

16. "Parfois, je me disais: 'C'est la mort; malgré tout, cela en vaut la peine, c'est impressionnant.' Mais souvent je mourais sans rien dire. A la longue, je fus convaincu que je voyais face à face la folie du jour; telle était la vérité: la lumière devenait folle, la clarté avait perdu tout bon sens; elle m'assaillait déraisonnablement, sans règle, sans but" (Maurice Blanchot, *The Madness of the Day* [bilingual edition], trans. Lydia Davis [Barrytown, N.Y.: Station Hill, 1981], pp. 25, 11).

or dissipated, the voice estranged or made remote to itself. In this way the voice achieves a passivity at the same time that it asserts itself most clearly and lucidly in what Blanchot has called the madness of the day, the climate of a scene whose traumatic content he cannot ever specify.

∞

What has happened? The "I" has achieved what Emmanuel Levinas calls a difficult liberty, a break in participation with the life-world as world. We are on the brink of infinitude, since in the negativity of nonparticipation the difference between selfhood and otherness is surrendered and intelligibility gives way to a certain madness or disequilibration. Whatever holds the life-world together is by means of a difficult freedom unhinged and by the subject vertiginously swept into an excessive abyss or catastrophe of relations where no word serves to reobjectify or systematize what has been unloosed. This is the moment that Levinas terms the ethical. It is the silent moment, though words can be uttered there, since the word stops before that which is radically other. It is at this passive moment, this articulated silence, that the ethical manifests itself and gives shelter to meaning. "To have meaning," Levinas writes, "is to be situated relative to an absolute, that is, to come from that alterity that is not absorbed in its being perceived. Such an alterity is possible only as a miraculous abundance, an inexhaustible surplus of attention arising in the ever recommenced effort of language to clarify its own manifestation."[17] It is the voice or tone that addresses the absolute from this liberated aspect, this catastrophic horizon which Derrida calls the apocalyptic. Its tone is part of a plural that cannot be unified or centered or institutionalized, however much postmodernism and deconstruction will operate as recuperative code words to the vulgar for such purposes. Moreover, the apocalyptic tone is irregular, wavering, jagged, spasmatic, like the burst of a *gl* or the beginning of a hiccup.

In "Of an Apocalyptic Tone Recently Adopted in Philosophy," Derrida writes,

17. Emmanuel Levinas, *Totality and Infinity: An Essay on Exteriority* (Pittsburgh: Duquesne University Press, 1969), p. 97.

If, in a very insufficient and only just preliminary way, I draw your attention to the narrative sending, the interlacing of voices and envois in the dictated or addressed writing, I do so because great attention no doubt would have to be given this differential reduction or gearing down of voices and tones that perhaps divides them beyond a distinct and calculable plurality—at least in the hypothesis or the program of an intractable demystification of the apocalyptic tone, in the style of the Lumières or of an *Aufklärung* of the twentieth century, and if we wanted to unmask the ruses, traps, trickeries, seductions, the engines of war and pleasure, in short, all the interests of the apocalyptic tone today. We do not know (for it is no longer of the order of knowing) to whom the apocalyptic dispatch returns; it leaps from one place of emission to the other (and a place is always determined *starting from* the presumed emission;) it goes from one destination, one name, and one tone to the other; it always refers to the name and to the tone of the other that is there but as having been there and before yet coming, no longer being or not yet there in the present of the *récit*. And there is no certainty that man is the exchange (middle) of these telephone lines or the terminal of this computer without end.[18]

The apocalyptic tone comes unannounced, out of nowhere, or, to be more accurate, out of that somewhere unmoored from sender and receiver. It is in this context that the apocalyptic tone can be considered not only to be spasmatic, like the *gl,* but extremely violent, sudden, unassimilable. Hence its difficult liberty, that break in participation with the life-world which concerns Levinas. It is the infinitude or negativity of nonparticipation, that difference between self and other, me and you. It is also, to recall Levinas, the ethical moment precisely because it concerns a violent emission whose dispatch escapes our ability to comprehend it in terms of day-to-day communication in whose speech acts we often invest an uncritical trust.

Ashbery reflects these ideas on tone with admirable effortlessness or at least stylistic relaxation when he writes in *Three Poems,*

18. Jacques Derrida, "D'un ton apocalyptique adopté naguère en philosophie," in *Les Fins de l'homme* (Paris: Galilée, 1981), p. 470. Trans. John Leavey, under the title "Of an Apocalyptic Tone Recently Adopted in Philosophy," *Semeia,* no. 23 (1982): 87.

> Such particulars you mouthed, all leading back into the
> underlying question: was it you? Do these things
> between people partake of themselves, or are they a
> subtler kind of translucent matter carrying each to a
> compromise distance painfully outside the rings of
> authority? For we never knew, never knew what joined
> us together. Perhaps only a congealing of closeness,
> deserving of no special notice.[19]

Certainly there is an indeterminate quality to the relationship between a self and an other, but it is not so much the vagueness of the attachment but the tone of it which is significant. For this tone (the writing's pose, rhetorical staging, manner of informality, precision, and so on) quietly establishes through the iteration of small, almost imperceptible shocks, a difficult liberty, one that articulates the relationship to alterity uncovered in the familiar and the intimate. Here, as in Derrida, the voice disembodies itself, recovers itself as always already disembodied, uninvested in a specific sender or a specific receiver. "Was it you?" Ashbery asks. Did "you" say these "particulars?" And more ambivalently, "Do these things between people partake of themselves?" that is, the people themselves or the things themselves, so hard to tell which. Or are we subjected to something subtler, something "outside the rings of authority," something that establishes a "compromise distance?" "For we never knew, never knew what joined us together." We never can know because the *what* is not recoverable as someone's speech or intention or affection, because the *what* is not recoverable as anything but Ashbery's curious tone, which evades sources and destinations, a tone of what Derrida above calls ruses, traps, trickeries, seductions, the engines of war and pleasure, or "all the interests of the apocalyptic tone today." Like Derrida, Ashbery admits that we cannot know to whom the envoi returns. Rather, it just seems to leap and refers to the tone of the other "that is there but as having been there and before yet coming, no longer being or not yet there in the present of the récit," as Derrida says above. What is of most importance, perhaps, is that in Ashbery, as in Levinas and Derrida, the tone does address apocalypse and within an ethical context. Yet as has been stressed, we are not

19. Ashbery, *Three Poems*, p. 10.

talking about the kind of apocalyptic address that moralizes but the kind of apocalypse we now can see in its Levinasian ethical perspective. "For the ethical relationship which subtends discourse," Levinas writes, "is not a species of consciousness whose ray emanates from the I; it puts the I in question. This putting in question emanates from the other." This discourse, or apocalyptic tone, emanates as language, and "Language," Levinas insists, "is perhaps to be defined as the very power to break the continuity of being or of history."[20] In Levinas, Blanchot, Derrida, and Ashbery this thought is not only considered but is, as I have suggested, also thematized in terms of Holocaust.

In *Three Poems* Ashbery writes,

> There was however, a residue, a kind of fiction that
> developed parallel to the classic truths of daily life
> (as it was in that heroic but commonplace age) as they
> unfolded with the foreseeable majesty of a holocaust,
> an unfrightening one, and went unrecognized, drawing
> force and grandeur from this like the illegitimate
> offspring of a king. It is this "other tradition" which
> we propose to explore. The facts of history have been
> too well rehearsed (I'm speaking needless to say not of
> written history but the oral kind that goes on in you
> without your having to do anything about it) to require
> further elucidation here.

Later, Ashbery adds,

> From the outset it was apparent that someone had played
> a colossal trick on something.[21]

Ashbery speaks of two Holocausts: the foreseeable, recognizable, plain, and political, and the fantastic, imagined, visceral, but also extremely remote and hard to remember. The historical is a kind of inaccessible reality or otherness that we know but cannot conceive outside objectified facts, which like things resist penetration. The "other tradition"

20. Levinas, *Totality and Infinity*, p. 195.
21. Ashbery, *Three Poems*, pp. 55–56.

is what is achieved by a difficult liberty, what goes on inside one without one's having to do anything about it. The latter, not unlike the hiccup, threatens the coherence of the system. Moreover, like the oral tradition or voice in Blanchot's texts, the "other tradition" in Ashbery does not recoil at the foreseeable majesty of a Holocaust: for with the recognition of a difficult freedom an indifferent tone emerges, one that is unfrightened. The catastrophe is neutralized, sopped up, forgotten, muffled, understated. "It was apparent that someone had played a colossal trick on something," the voice says about the vanishing of millions of people.

Both Blanchot and Derrida recognize that the apocalyptic tone exceeds naming, a point Ashbery implicitly shares when he talks about the colossal trick "someone" played on "something." In *L'Écriture du désastre*, Blanchot considers this as follows:

> *The unknown name, beyond nomination: The Holocaust, the* absolute *event of history, which is a date in history—that utter burn-all where all history took fire, where the movement of Meaning was swallowed up, where the gift, which knows nothing of forgiving or of consent, shattered without giving place to anything that can be affirmed, that can be denied—gift of very passivity, gift of what cannot be given. How can it be preserved, even by thought? How can thought be made the keeper of the Holocaust where all was lost, including guardian thought? In the mortal intensity, the fleeing silence of the countless cry.*[22]

To Blanchot, the Holocaust is an absolute event of history, an otherness, an unnameable event, which in itself recognizes its own estrangement by forcing about a denial of the name (genealogy, race, paternity) by means of a reinscription, the tattooing of numbers on arms: *l'écriture*

22. Maurice Blanchot, *The Writing of the Disaster*, trans. Ann Smock, (Lincoln: University of Nebraska Press, 1986), p. 47; translation very slightly changed. "*Le nom inconnu, hors nomination: L'holocauste, événement absolu de l'histoire, historiquement daté, cette toute-brûlure où toute l'histoire s'est embrasée, où le mouvement du Sens s'est abîmé, où le don, sans pardon, sans consentement, s'est ruiné sans donner lieu à rien qui puisse s'affirmer, se nier, don de la passivité même, don de ce qui ne peut se donner. Comment le garder, fût-ce dans la pensée, comment faire de la pensée ce qui garderait l'holocauste où tout s'est perdu, y comprise la pensée gardienne? Dans l'intensité mortelle, le silence fuyant du cri innombrable*" (*L'Écriture du désastre* [Paris: Gallimard, 1980], p. 80).

du désastre. It is this expression, this inscription of otherness, which breaks the continuity of being and history, and it is here that the ethical projects itself as excess, that a curious genealogy of morals reveals itself in the midst of cataclysm. Yet if the ethical intrudes on its own veiling, it maintains its withdrawal in terms of the radicality of a break whose facticity eludes thought, and whose morality is eclipsed by the unnameable, the unspeakable, the unrecuperable, the unrepresentable. Hence "the movement of meaning is swallowed up," even if its trace still makes itself known to us.

But if that is so, isn't the trace a fantasm? And even an originary fantasm of sadistic destruction at that? Derrida himself cannot help such a recovery of the traumatic fantasm as mise-en-scène when he refers to Holocaust as the disaster of writing in *La Carte postale.* "The symbol? a great Holocaustic fire, a burn-everything into which we will throw finally, along with out entire memory, our names, the letters, photos, small objects, keys, fetishes, etc. And if nothing remains . . ."[23] Again, "I have always known that we are lost, and that from this very initial disaster an infinite distance has opened up . . . this catastrophe, right near the beginning, this overturning that I still cannot succeed in thinking was the condition of everything, not so?, ours, of our very condition, the condition for everything that was given us or that we destined, promised, gave, loaned, I no longer know what, to each other . . . we lost each other—one another, understand me?"[24]

For Derrida, as for Blanchot, the fantasm of destruction weighs heavily as the "condition of everything." It is the real as unrepresentable trace in whose audibility the destruction of the past announces itself as something that is waiting in our future.

"Ah shucks," Ashbery might reply. "The great careers are like that: a slow burst that narrows to a final release, pointed but not acute, a life of suffering redeemed and annihilated at the end, and for what? For a casual moment of knowing that is here one minute and gone the next, almost before you were aware of it?"[25] In *Three Poems* the shock of collapse is over. Here Ashbery is most at home with the apocalyptic

23. Derrida, *The Post Card,* p. 40.
24. Ibid., p. 19.
25. Ashbery, *Three Poems,* p. 69.

tone, having domesticated it, or cultivated it in his own back yard among the rutabagas. He too realizes that the end has always already happened. Like any good psychologist or "crazyologist" (an apt bop term) the poet must recognize that the problem with people is that they fear the very thing that has already occurred to them: the collapse is past history, a trivial or banal occurrence that the subject still fears. In *Three Poems* the voice comes from on high, *le très haut*. It is flat and absolute, all-knowing, yet obnoxiously cute and abrasive. It is what Derrida might call synthesized. It is an irregular and sometimes tenuous tone, which admits that "In the end it falls apart, falls to the ground and sinks in."[26] That is, something is swallowed up, imperceptibly, automatically almost. It is in this sense that in "Litany" Ashbery writes a remark touching so apocalyptically on a passivity that, curiously, is not without traces of its own primal fantasy that resists insouciance.

> *Yet somehow it doesn't bode well that*
> *In your sophistication you choose to disregard*
> *What is so heavy with potential tragic consequences*
> *Hanging above you like a storm cloud*
> *And cannot know otherwise, even by diving*
> *Into the shallow stream of your innocence*
> *And wish not to hear news of*
> *What brings the world together and sets fire to it.*[27]

26. Ibid., p. 15.
27. Ashbery, *As We Know*, p. 41b.

9

Durassian Extimacy

My tutor text is a passage from a book which some might consider an unlikely starting place for a study of Marguerite Duras. And yet, when I first opened Alphonso Lingis's *Deathbound Subjectivity,* the following remark struck me as germane to Duras's texts: "The inability to put oneself back at one's beginning, to find oneself once again at the commencement of one's initiatives, to recuperate and re-present again what one had begun, which is the inner diagram of the fatigue in effort, is, across time, the condition of a subject that forms by aging."[1] This passage, though prolix and unidiomatic, reminded me of a comment made by the anonymous woman in *La Maladie de la mort,* "Elle dit: Le jour est venu, tout va commencer, sauf vous. Vous, vous ne commencez jamais."[2] The woman, you may recall, says this while opening her eyes; and she says this to a man (he has paid her to make love) because she does not want him to lie. She speaks, therefore, in the name of a certain truth that he himself is hardly able to grasp. "Tout va commencez, sauf vous." Yet she could have said something like the following: "The inability to put oneself back at one's beginning, to find oneself once again at the commencement of one's initiatives, to

1. Alphonso Lingis, *Deathbound Subjectivity* (Bloomington: Indiana University Press, 1989), p. 154.
2. Marguerite Duras, *La Maladie de la mort* (Paris: Minuit, 1982), pp. 50–51. "It's day, everything is about to begin, except you, you never begin." *The Malady of Death,* trans. Barbara Bray (New York: Grove, 1987), p. 48.

recuperate and re-present again what one had begun, which is the inner diagram of the fatigue in effort, is, across time, the condition of a subject that forms by aging."

But she does not say this. She closes her eyes instead. She sleeps and lets him do to her whatever he wants. And much of the story depends on this capacity she has for release. Of how she lets him explore her body. Of how she submits to his gaze, his penetration, his silencing her. And it is after much of this that she makes her remark, "Tout va commencer, sauf vous," in place of a much longer speech that could have started "the inability to put oneself back at one's beginning."

But what does it mean to say that "everything begins, except you"? Does it mean that the man has merely dropped out of the stream of life? Does it refer to a condition of apathy or ennui? Or does it refer to the man's repetition compulsion, the circular on-goingness of his arduous exploration of her. No doubt all of these meanings are suggested, but perhaps more important, the phrase suggests that the man has lost a beginning without which one can intuit the trajectory of one's desire, a condition the woman calls *la maladie de la mort*. This is why much of the time the man is contemplating what it would be like to murder the woman, an impulse that the woman perceives. For a murder would break the circularity of their relationship and would definitively situate them within a determinate event. But since he is a man who cannot begin, she knows he is incapable of going through with it. And therefore she knows she will be able to slip out of his sight with impunity. Still, if the woman sees through the pretense, this does not mean that his payment for the right to imprison her several nights running is the result of a capricious desire; rather, it is being made for the sake of a *recherche*, for the sake of finding something that has eluded him. And it is this she has intuited quickly enough— that he is in search of lost origins. That he would like to begin, like everything else.

"Elle recommence: Et regarder une femme, vous n'avez jamais regardé une femme? Vous dites que non, jamais."[3] Elsewhere the narrator, who is more intimately positioned toward the male than the

3. *La Maladie de la mort,* p. 35. "She goes on: What about looking, haven't you ever looked at a woman? You say no, never." *The Malady of Death,* p. 31.

female figure, says, "Elle ouvre ses jambes et dans le creux de ses jambes écartées vous voyez enfin la nuit noire. Vous dites: C'était là, la nuit noire, c'est là."[4] Elsewhere the man has remarked that the sea, too, is black. Of course, only a very unpracticed reader would miss the suggestion that the darkness of the sea and the black night that is the woman's sex are not exactly unaligned. They correspond. And yet, this does not make them comprehensible. Even if the man patrols the woman's body watchfully all night long with his eyes, his lips, his fingers, the woman's unclothed body does not become any more comprehensible to the man. It remains inappropriable and other, but perhaps even more significant, it suggests itself as a metaphor for an inner diagram that maps fatigue in effort, a fatigue the woman will disclose when she sleepily asks a question concerning the sea. "Qu'est-ce qu'on entend? Vous dites: La mer. Elle demande: Où est-elle? Vous dites: Là, derrière le mur de la chambre. Elle se rendort."[5] The entirety of *La Maladie de la mort* is from the woman's side little else but an undulation between sleeping and waking, the cyclical alternation of these two states. She hears the sea, and then she drops off into sleep. We don't know whether she merges into the oceanic rhythm or retreats from its roar. But what we can intuit is that something of an originary nature has been considered when the woman asks, "Qu'est-ce qu'on entend?" and the man answers, "la mer." For in his answer we hear a rather obvious pun. And one wonders, is it the mother he is looking for when he inspects the sleeping woman so studiously with his gaze?

We may recall, too, another moment in which the narrator counterpoints the woman's distant awareness of the sea with the man's distant sense of what reveals woman's pleasure.

Peut-être prenez-vous à elle un plaisir jusque-là inconnu de vous, je ne sais pas. Je ne sais pas non plus si vous percevez le grondement sourd et lointain de sa jouissance à travers sa respiration, à travers

---

4. *La Maladie de la mort*, p. 52. "She parts her legs, and in the hollow between you see the dark night at last. You say: It was there, the dark night. It's there." *The Malady of Death*, pp. 50–51.

5. *La Maladie de la mort*, p. 13. "What's that sound? You say: The sea. She asks: Where? You say: there beyond the wall. She goes back to sleep." *The Malady of Death*, pp. 7–8.

ce râle très doux qui va et vient depuis sa bouche jusqu'à l'air du dehors. Je ne le crois pas.

Elle ouvre les yeux, elle dit: Quel bonheur.

Vous mettez la main sur sa bouche pour qu'elle se taise, vous lui dites qu'on ne dit pas ces choses-là.[6]

One can already anticipate a feminist reading that would position Duras as ideologically exposing the silencing or suppression of woman by man, not to say, man's inability to hear the murmur of woman's pleasure. Although *écriture féminine* makes such unheard pleasure audible, we must be prepared to recognize something else here as well, namely that the silencing of the woman is a gesture that makes it possible for one to become aware of what Jacques Lacan called *lalangue*, that which swallows up the space between the feminine definite article and noun and opposes itself to *le langage*, as if to say that *lalangue* represents a feminine proximity that does not allow for linguistic space or distance. The mother tongue, Lacan is suggesting, is too close to us. Therefore, by silencing the woman, the man in *La Maladie* may have managed to bring himself closer to *lalangue*, the murmur of her pleasure, or what Jacques Alain Miller, in explicating Lacan's neologism, calls *la multiplicité inconsistante*, the excess that determines the unity it ruptures.

Lalangue, Miller tells us, is a universal language that is paradoxically not intersubjective; hence, it remains largely incommunicable even though it is the stuff through which *le langage* comes to pass.[7] As such, *lalangue* is the unformed stuff of language which determines us because the unconscious recognition of pleasure is murmured there. *Lalangue* is the sound that mother makes, the sound to which the child returns,

6. *La Maladie de la mort*, p. 15. "Perhaps you get from her a pleasure you've never known before. I don't know. Nor do I know if you hear the low, distant murmur of her pleasure through her breathing, through the faint rattle going back and forth between her mouth and the outside air. I don't think so. She opens her eyes and says: What joy. You put your hand over her mouth to silence her. Tell her one doesn't say such things." *The Malady of Death*, pp. 9–10.

7. Jacques-Alain Miller, "Theorie de lalangue (rudiment)," *Ornicar?* (January 1975): 16–34. "L'inconscient est fait de lalangue, dont les effets vont plus loin que de communiquer, puisqu'ils vont jusqu'à troubler le corps et son âme, comme dans la pensée" (p. 31) ["The unconscious is made up of *lalangue* whose effects go much further than mere communication, since, as in thought, they go so far as to trouble body and soul"].

the murmur given at the beginning of things. The sea, the breath, silence ... these are only some appearances of *lalangue* in *La Maladie de la mort*. Indeed, the dissipation of conversation into sleep and the rhythms of the woman's breathing suggest that the power of this novel is not given in terms of what is spoken, of what is written on the page, and this suggests that most likely an origin or beginning has not been concealed after all, but has always been given.

For the man to be conscious, then, does not mean to be conscious of a lack or absence, but of a sound that has been heard from the beginning of time, an inconsistent multiplicity that is not inherently intersubjective even though it unites or binds consciousness. What are we hearing? a voice asks. And someone responds, the sea. So that suddenly one is urged to listen to what it is that can be heard from the other side of the wall, a sound that for the woman has always been inaudible until now, now that she begins to intuit what it is the man is searching for and where in his order of things *lalangue* is given. Yet, even if she hears it, she hears nothing at all and slips back into deep sleep. And, similarly, of *her* low and distant murmur, he hears nothing.

Yet, even if they are unable to pay the kind of attention to *lalangue* which would allow them to synchronize their desires, the sea, the breath, and the silence have alerted us to something: that it is not unusual or perverse to have an inability to put oneself back to a beginning that can be objectified and mutually comprehended. Indeed, this is an inability that everyone has in common, though it appears the man has gone out of his way to problematize it. For when he hears the sea, he hears something else, too, something inaccessible and elusive, as if he were troubled by what does not give itself in *lalangue*. To put it in Lacanian terms, there are things given in *lalangue* which language doesn't know anything about. So when we hear "la mer," this may not enable us to find ourselves at the commencement of our initiatives, since the sound holds back the origin even as the subject is brought into relation with the archaic. Moreover, as the mother (*la mère*), the sea (*la mer*) holds something back so that the sounds that the man hears disclose a relation to one whose joy can never be made accessible to him, since he can grasp her pleasure only within what must necessarily be a limited or restricted field (that is, the Imaginary). This would mean not only that in *La Maladie de la mort* one is unable to put

oneself at the beginning but that this inability will be a consequence
of not being able to represent or figure *lalangue.*

No doubt the touch or sight of the woman's body is closely related
to this phenomenon, since like *lalangue,* the woman's body is a totality
inconsistent with the sum of its parts. In a passage only distantly reminiscent of a celebrated description in Proust's *La Prisonnière,* we read:

> Ensuite c'est presque l'aube. Ensuite il fait dans la chambre une
> sombre clarté de couleur indécise. Ensuite vous allumez des lampes
> pour la voir. Pour la voir elle. Pour voir ce que vous n'avez jamais
> connu, le sexe enfoui, voir cela qui engouffre et retient sans ap-
> parence de le faire, de le voir ainsi refermé sur son sommeil, dor-
> mant. Pour voir aussi les taches de rousseur répandues sur elle
> depuis la lisière des cheveux jusqu'à la naissance des seins, là ou ils
> cèdent sous leur poids, accrochés aux charnières des bras, jusques
> aussi sur les paupières fermées et sur les lèvres entrouvertes et pâles.
> Vous vous dites: aux endroits du soleil de l'été, aux endroits ouverts,
> offerts à être vus. Elle dort. Vous éteignez les lampes. Il fait presque
> clair.[8]

The physiognomy itself speaks *lalangue,* given that the figure is described in terms of the woman's lips, the hidden sex, and the pale half-
open mouth. The organization of the body's topology around the lips
is not accidental; it occurs again later in a description of the man
touching the woman's body. "Vous regardez la fente des lèvres et ce
qui l'entoure, le corps entier." But what remains constant in both cases
is that the entire body is closed up around the lips in its sleep, as if the
body was itself organized around the archaic. As such the woman's
body is not disclosed in *le langage,* even as it falls within the field of

8. *La Maladie le la mort,* pp. 28–29. "Then it's almost dawn. Then there's a dark
light in the room, of indeterminate hue. Then you switch some lights on, to see her.
Her. See what you've never seen before, the hidden sex, that which swallows up and
holds without seeming to. See it like this, closed up around its own sleep. And also to
see the freckles strewn all over her from the hairline right down to where the breasts
begin, where they give under their own weight, hooked onto the hinges of the arms,
and right up to the closed lids and the pale half open lips. You think: They're in the
places of the summer sun, the open places, the places on view. She sleeps. You switch
the lights off. It's almost light." *The Malady of Death,* pp. 24–25.

lalangue. "Vous regardez la fente des lèvres et ce qui l'entoure, le corps entier. Vous ne voyez rien."[9]

Clearly it is hard for the man to decipher *lalangue,* a difficulty that the woman herself identifies with *la maladie de la mort.* The narrator says, somewhat accusingly, "Vous ne regardez plus. Vous ne regardez plus rien. Vous fermez les yeux pour vous retrouver dans votre différence, dans votre mort."[10] But, of course, by death Duras is not referring to a literal death; rather, she is talking about something that is expressed in Lingis's phrase "the condition of a subject that forms by aging." This, he tells us, is how the inner diagram of fatigue is defined. But one wonders about Lingis's unidiomatic turn of phrase. For an English speaker would commonly say that a subject ages, not that it *forms* by aging, as if it were a mollusk. Indeed, Lingis's turn of phrase first caught my attention when I came across the passage about the inability to situate oneself at the beginning, since in Duras one has to recognize that the subject does not simply age. Rather he or she experiences an inner diagram of a fatigue in effort which marks the inability to begin even though, however inaccessible this beginning, something has, nevertheless, formed over time. A subject has been deposited, as it were, on the shore. And this subject has not simply aged in terms of a self-conscious passage of time in which the subject has permitted itself to become this or that; rather, the Durassian subject has been formed without giving time the permission to affect one's being. In *Le Marin de Gibraltar,* for example, one notices that Anna has embarked on a kind of wide sargasso sea of life in which time has not been given the permission to age her, though, of course, like everyone else, she must grow older. Hence she becomes a subject that is formed by aging rather than a subject who ages.

But the process of aging in Duras is also reminiscent of how pearls develop: a bit of sand or irritant causes something hard and lustrous

9. *La Maladie de la mort,* p. 39. "You look at the opening and what surrounds it, the whole body. You don't see anything." *The Malady of Death,* p. 35.

10. *La Maladie de la mort,* p. 36. "You stop looking. Stop looking at anything. You shut your eyes so as to get back into your difference, your death." *The Malady of Death,* p. 32.

to form through time. The elusive sailor from Gibraltar, the pure phys-
icality of the woman's body in *Maladie,* the poem that the Captain
burns in *Emily L.,* and the white stone that Madeleine recalls in *Savannah Bay* function like unassimilable foreign bodies around which
a lustrous and impenetrable structure forms independently of the subject through time so that, in Lingis's words, the subject forms by aging.
In existential terms this would mean that the subject is not there where
the structure of its form is deposited.

At the end of *La Maladie de la mort* the narrator looks ahead to
this depositing of a form that will obsessively wrap itself around the
woman's absence and the fragmentary recollections of what she has
said. The man will try to tell this story, and he will look for the woman.
But the search will have to be given up. "Even so," the narrator says,
"you have managed to live that love in the only way possible for you.
Losing it before it happened." What initiates the structure that forms
by aging, then, is itself something that can be called a beginning, though
one that is lost even before it has begun. And what will form by aging
is a structure that is given *après coup* around that which has been lost,
that Thing which has refused to show itself since the commencement
of one's initiatives.[11] In *La Maladie de la mort* that "thing" is the
woman herself.

Jacques-Alain Miller might agree that such a thing conforms to yet
another neologism of Lacan's, namely *extimité,* the otherness of that
which is given in *intimité.* After all, as Lacan rightly puts it, the exterior
is always given or present in the interior. And here, of course, one can
quote St. Augustine or other religious figures who tell us that God is
more interior than our own innermost beings. What the subject contains, in short, is the extimacy of the Other. Within the circle of the
subject one discovers that what is the most intimate of its intimacy is
the extimacy of the Other. Miller argues that this is what Lacan means
when he says the unconscious is the discourse of the Other, an Other
who, more intimate than my intimacy, stirs me. The intimate that is
radically Other, Lacan expresses with a single word: extimacy.[12] As

11. On the question of aftereffects in recent French literature and culture there is
the work of Steven Ungar to be considered. I thank him for letting me see his work
still in manuscript on the topic.

12. Jacques-Alain Miller, "Extimité," *Prose Studies* 11 (1988): 121–31. The lecture

the English implies quite well, extimacy can be experienced as ecstasy; however, for the subject this jouissance is experienced as something else (or as Other, alien), as something not entirely compatible with the subject even if it is the most intimate experience the subject can know.

In Duras this extimacy is precisely what comprises the foreign body about which the subject is formed by aging. Moreover, it is the extimacy of the subject which creates a temporality of the *après coup,* which is only somewhat like Freud's concept of *Nachträglichkeit.* Like Freud, Duras emphasizes traumatic shock as unrepresentable and unrecoverable. But her fictional subjects do not, in fact, live *nachträgliche* hysterical existences so much as they live all too calmly on the hitherside of extimacy. In *Hiroshima mon amour,* for example, the woman's love for the German soldier is politically that of an *extimité,* which characterizes so well the relationship between France and Germany. When the woman recalls being let out of the cellar in Nevers, she realizes she will always walk on the *extimité* or wrong side of history, and that what takes place in the aftermath or *après coup* of her affair is a mad passion for the catastrophe itself, for a pleasure or jouissance that is alien to the subject. Such jouissance is a pure negativity or insanity that has no moral redemption and utterly fails to define or circumscribe subjecthood. Speaking to her Japanese lover, she says calmly, "Hiroshima. C'est ton nom." And, in response, he calls her "Nevers," as if to confirm that they both exist outside or in *extimité* where an Other pleasure has come to pass. Yet, as Michèle Montrelay has suggested in another Durassian context, such a mentality cannot work itself back to a moment when the subject, however alive and well, can appear as anything else but the assassinated or the disappeared. They are deposited in the aftermath of extimacy as the residue of an *aphanisis,* a fading of the subject before the presence of an Other's pleasure that is understood only at that moment when it has been lost.

To live *après coup* in Duras means to recollect this *extimité* as a beginning that is experienced as having ended before it was given a

---

was originally delivered in Spanish to the Sixth International Convention of the Champ Freudien (1986). It develops notions developed in a course Miller gave during 1985–86 in the Department of Psychoanalysis, University of Paris. Especially interesting is Miller's remark that with respect to *extimité,* "Jouissance is precisely what grounds the alterity of the Other when there is no Other of the Other," p. 125.

chance to start. To understand Duras's literary handling of this phenomenon, it is helpful to compare *La Maladie de la mort* to its important precursor text, Fyodor Dostoyevsky's "Notes from the
Underground," in which there is a first-person narration by a man who
has, like the man in *La Maladie,* made love to a prostitute whom he
has entirely humiliated, disavowing his love at every turn. Without
doubt, the underground man closely resembles those Durassian male
figures for whom woman is very alien (cf. *Le Vice Consul, Yeux bleus
cheveux noirs*). And toward the end of Dostoyevsky's story we see a
strong parallel in the action with *La Maladie* when the prostitute,
having passionately made love to the man who openly scorns her, runs
into the street, never to be seen by him again. This despite the fact that
he has just a moment too late recovered his balance and run after her
down the stairs. In Duras this scene is reduced to only the following:
"Un jour elle n'est plus là. Vous vous réveillez et elle n'est plus là. Elle
est partie dans la nuit. La trace du corps est encore dans les draps, elle
est froide."[13] Between that trace and the woman's presence only silence
has passed in Duras. But between the final panic state of loss and the
underground man's narrative in the Dostoyevsky story a lifetime may
have already passed. The man has aged, and although his is a love that
has formed him as a subject *après coup,* he can take us back to that
unbearable beginning where all was lost so that he may reenact an
obsessional love. Like the man in *La Maladie* the underground man
has been given the opportunity to avow love, but he has refused. And
for that he is eternally damned—punished by the beloved. Still, the
narrator is in complete self-possession; he is capable of recovering and
symbolizing every detail of the traumatic moment of loss with all of
its pain and moral truth. If the man is wretched, he is not unenlightened,
albeit too late. And he is therefore not incapable of experiencing considerable guilt, of surviving in a way that is not entirely without dignity.
For this reason he is able to stand forth, however wretched, as the
subject who is supposed to know, the one who speaks to us from
experience.

13. *La Maladie de la mort,* p. 53. "One day she isn't there anymore. You wake and
she isn't there. She has gone during the night. The mark [*trace*] of her body is still there
on the sheets. Cold." *The Malady of Death,* p. 51.

But in Duras's fiction such experience counts for little. The woman, for her part, is quite oblivious. After all, it's just her job to submit to the man's wishes. And even if *La Maladie* turns vaguely accusatory at the close, its final sentences suggest that all the man will remember are a few words the woman said in her sleep and that he will not be able to tell the kind of narrative that characterizes Dostoyevsky's story. Rather, Durassian man will live out the aftershock of something that cannot be recollected, and will live through a condition that, to a large extent, forms as if the subject were in absentia. The narrator therefore comments: "Ainsi cependant vous avez pu vivre cet amour de la seule façon qui puisse se faire pour vous, en le perdant avant qu'il soit advenu."[14] Here *extimité* would refer to precisely what the subject has lost a priori, though it only becomes manifest later in the *après coup* of the woman's defection.

Dostoyevsky's underground man is oriented to Liza altogether differently, since for him the beginning of his love has been given a priori; he loved her from even before the time when she entered his life. For he has always been waiting for such a woman to come into his life. What crushes Dostoyevsky's narrator is not his inability to get back to the origin of what he feels for Liza, but his idiotic bungling of the romance. In its aftermath the underground man marks time against an event that was only too tangible and remains endlessly accessible to memory. Whereas in Duras the determining moment of a grand passion is always under erasure or *après coup*, and cannot posit itself as a ground that supports even the imaginary happiness of the subject. In Duras the erasure casts one adrift in an emptiness or indeterminancy that reduces one to an anonymous vigilance or waiting that has no proper object. Whereas time in Dostoyevsky is marked by the irruption of a passion that forces characters to confront their moral integrity, in Duras passion does not require individuals to affirm or deny themselves as subjects; rather, it is lived through as a pure negativity, which is experienced as doldrum, indolence, the inessential, the outside, or *extimité*. And yet, even on the strand of this negativity something is

14. *La Maladie de la mort*, p. 57. "Even so you have managed to live that love in the only way possible for you. Losing it before it happened." *The Malady of Death*, p. 55.

deposited, a subject will be formed by aging as something ancillary or supplementary to itself. Which is to say as an *extimité* exterior to *extimité*, a thing formed on the margins of what Duras calls the Outside, or what I prefer to call the existent.

No doubt, to pursue the notion of the existent, one would do well to explore a number of works, among them the film *Son Nom de Venise dans Calcutta Désert,* the novel *L'Amour,* and the two plays titled *Savannah Bay.* I will limit my remarks, however, to the plays, in which Duras emphatically insists that the role of the character called Madeleine may be played only by an actress who has reached "la splendeur de l'âge." Madeleine's *splendeur,* we recall, is that of not being able to put herself back at her own beginning, of not being able to recuperate what she had begun, and the attempt by Madeleine and her companion, the Young Woman, to reconstruct that past is, once more, the inner diagram of fatigue in effort. Indeed, *Savannah Bay* was conceived and written for the sake of this splendor, this living out of an inner diagram that manifests itself as *ravissement* and *ravagement.* But here the "inner diagram" is extraordinarily complex, given that one has to abandon the expectation that it will be easy to distinguish between what is inside and outside the diagram.

In the 1983 edition of *Savannah Bay,* two versions of the play are published, the first rather longer than the second, though the second is more complex than the first. In both versions the story focuses on a young woman who has fallen in love with a man who commits suicide. The woman has turned sixteen when the affair begins, and we learn that by the time she has turned seventeen, she is pregnant. In both versions of *Savannah Bay* only Madeleine and her young interlocutor are visible on stage. In the earlier version it is suggested that the Young Woman who speaks may well be the daughter of Madeleine. Their discourse, then, would characterize an attempt by the daughter to inscribe her relationship with her mother into the love affair between her mother and father, which exists in a distant and mysterious world apart. In the second version the inaccessibility of this love between the parents, that is, the adolescent woman and her lover of the white rock, is elaborated and explained when Madeleine says, "C'était une affaire entre les amants.... Je dis que c'est un instant comme la pierre est blanche. Sans plus personne. Tout à coup." The Young Woman answers, "seulement la mer autour de la pierre."[15]

The inviolability of this dead space in which love precipitates as "un instant d'infinie douleur" is performatively developed in terms of Madeleine's inability to recollect an affair that takes place everywhere and nowhere, and which violates the distinction between the imaginary and the real. Moreover, this dead space is identified, in addition to Madeleine's personal story, as a play that Madeleine may once have acted in, an unwritten and unproduced drama that she obsessively develops, a film called *Savannah Bay* that she has seen, acted in, or directed, or a dialogue that Madeleine and the Young Woman improvise, each taking on certain roles. In the shorter, 1983 version, the Young Woman who speaks may well be Madeleine's granddaughter who is trying to understand why her father and mother committed suicide. This is a very curious modulation of the story in that if one reads the plays in relation to each other it is clear that Madeleine can occupy multiple subject positions both inside and outside the affair. For example, she is the outsider who relates the story of her daughter's passion for a man who had chosen her "pour aimer et mourir" as well as the insider who herself was the man's lover.[16] In fact, the 1983 version of *Savannah Bay* seems to go out of its way to enact a trading of places between the mother and daughter which creates an intersubjectivity that has completely effaced the borders between them even as each is maintained as radically isolated or other. For her part, the Young Woman on stage is not only perhaps the daughter of Madeleine but also perhaps her granddaughter, an even more distant relative (perhaps a cousin), or simply a stranger who is fascinated by Madeleine. In the stage directions of the 1981 version we are told only that Madeleine treats the young woman as if she were her child, a point that adumbrates the 1983 version in which the Young Woman is, in fact, the granddaughter. The dialogue between the two figures on stage, then, has to traverse a fairly

15. Marguerite Duras, *Savannah Bay* (Paris: Minuit, 1983), pp. 126–27. "It was an affair between lovers. I think it was a moment much as the rock being white. Without anyone. All of a sudden." The Young Woman answers, "Only the sea around the stone."

16. Ibid., p. 125.

diverse field of subject positions that are at once too intimate and too distant.

Binding these figures is an existential deficit: they discover themselves in a futile effort to catch up to what has been demanded, which is the maintenance of a passionate relationship whose expectations are inhumanly sublime. Although the Young Woman would like to project herself imaginatively into this sublimely inhuman if not Promethean space of the white rock in order to establish her identity, she is, nevertheless, foreclosed by this sublimity and finds herself in the curious position of being defined within a relationship that cannot acknowledge her presence as anything other than an aftereffect that may or may not be relevant to her as a being. Not unlike other female figures in Duras's writings, the Young Woman is defined within a relationship that is incapable of sustaining her as a person who can make an authentic claim on the world, since it is precisely her attachment to those who brought her into the world which is so painfully compromised. In other words, it is not enough to say that a person's presence should be acknowledged in and of itself; rather, at stake is one's status as a being who *belongs* to the world, a belonging made representable in a beginning or birth functioning as the structural moment that situates her as a being-in-the-world.

Lacking in *Savannah Bay,* however, is an intelligible, not to say univocal, inscription of the subject into this very important structural position. It is not surprising that the subject is unable to ask a basic Oedipal question such as "Who am I?" since the identity of her father has been obliterated at the same moment it has become the very rock that anchored Madeleine's obsessive passion. Indeed, the plays outline a very unusual variation of the Oedipus triangle in which the father does not symbolically position the daughter's desire, if not her identity, by stepping in between her and the mother—an intercession that, in any case, never entirely holds—but takes his life as if in order to intercede as an absence, which, as Duras's play demonstrates, annihilates any possibility for the daughter to come into her own even as it requires her to stage her desire on the rock of her mother and father's passion, the rock of extimacy. What results is a relation between mother and daughter which is so close that the child can project herself into a world that precedes her birth and in so doing holds herself back from ever coming into being, as if she were always talking from a radically estranged position. Hence the Young Woman speaks as if she has not actually "taken place." The complex slippages of identity which accompany the many retellings of the story of an inviolable love occur in an *après coup* that reminds one of the moment in *La Maladie de la mort* when the woman accuses the man of not being able to begin, except that in *Savannah Bay* it is not the lovers who have this experience so much as their child. Indeed, the 1983 version gives us some important clues to why this is the case. Madeleine asks, "Comment voulez-vous comprendre des gens comme ça, qui ne s'adressent qu'à l'un l'autre face à l'Éternel? Comment?"[17] Elsewhere she explains that what the lovers wanted was an empty world in which they would be left completely alone. In short, theirs was the kind of love that could not survive the intrusion of a child and therefore could not continue beyond the confines of the white slab of stone, which, in one variant, is a very tiny island surrounded and drenched by water. Given the solitude of their love, the child is not afforded a place, but will come to be a kind of unwanted by-product or thing.

In the 1983 version of *Savannah Bay* the child-as-thing is not even given a name; only much later does she she name herself Savannah, after the place of her conception, which, as we recall, is associated with the reeds of an estuary. Yet since her being named follows the Durassian logic of the *après coup,* one is not surprised that the Young Woman's attempt to be born (borne) as a subject involves a narration that forecloses the ability to put herself at the beginning of her history. In other words the name Savannah is an instance when language is undecidably interior and exterior to an originary moment from which subjectivity can get few reliable bearings even as it motivates an inner diagram of fatigue. Although Madeleine's accounts must serve as the most accurate guide, they are themselves liminal, given that Madeleine is living an existence that is excommunicated from what was once her grand passion with the anonymous young man. Hence she lives a "deathbound subjectivity," which Lingis identifies as senescence: "the

17. Ibid., p. 126. "How do you want to understand people in that way who only address each other in the face of the eternal. How?"

process of one's initiatives turning into habitus, into weight, by which time is irreversible."[18]

What is not immediately apparent in *Savannah Bay* is that the Young Woman too has reached "la splendeur de l'âge." For she also manifests a consciousness characterized as senescence in which initiatives succumb to a predisposition for inertia—or a running counter to a participation in being. The subject is not oriented to existence, but to what Lingis calls existents. "An existent as a commencement is not *in* being; it breaks with the beginningless, endless force of being (the "there is") and rises out of it."[19] The condition of the existent exists exterior to a commonplace existential framework of Dasein as being-in-the-world. In *Savannah Bay,* the white rock, the sea, the reeds in the estuary, and the fetus are all existents whose commencement is not in being but in not-being, or what Madeleine reveals as the "forgetting of being."

Senescence, then, would be exemplary of how a deathbound subjectivity characterizes the Cogito as an absence in being that is nevertheless weighed down by its own existence, or, to be more precise, existents *(extimité)*. No doubt, even such a state of mind is not without its pleasure, though from the perspective of the existent, that pleasure is desolate and self-enclosed. Even if the Young Woman takes up Madeleine's narrative in order to comprehend its secret joy, she always manages to miss her appointment with the mother's pleasure. For example, in the following quotation the Young Woman attempts to situate Madeleine's desire into a familial triangle of relations. And were she successful, she would have crossed over into the realm of the existential. But, of course, this does not occur. "Dix-sept ans. Un enfant de lui. Un enfant au-dedans du corps, scellé. Elle nage avec l'enfant au-dessus des profondeurs terribles de l'eau bleue. Lui se tient au bord de cette profondeur de leurs corps sur la plate-forme blanche désertée par la vie et il leur sourit, les bras tendus vers elle comme le premier jour. Il a peur."[20]

18. Lingis, p. 154.
19. Ibid., p. 152.
20. Duras, *Savannah Bay*, p. 50. "Seventeen Years. A child by him. A child, sealed, in the body. She swims with the child beneath the awesome depths of the blue sea. He stays on the margins of these profound bodies on a white platform which life has

In *L'Être et le néant* Jean-Paul Sartre writes, "Ainsi le désir est désir d'appropriation d'un corps en tant que cette appropriation me révèle mon corps comme chair. Mais ce corps que je veux m'approprier, je veux me l'approprier *comme chair*. Or, c'est ce qu'il n'est pas d'abord pour moi: le corps d'Autrui apparaît comme forme synthétique en acte."[21] To the contrary, in *Savannah Bay,* the man and woman have made love without appropriating the body as flesh (that is, pleasure). Rather, the lovers have each endured an exposure to the other without allowing the Other to appear as a synthetic form in action, that is, as a convergence of experiences that situate either as a desiring and desired subject. The play, then, resists the idea that "la caresse fait naître Autrui comme chair pour moi et pour lui-même" or that "la caresse est faite pour faire naître par le plaisir le corps d'Autrui."[22] That is, Duras's play resists the idea that the caress causes the Other's body to be born through pleasure. Rather, *Savannah Bay* performs the negation of such an existential birth. For however ecstatic the touching or kissing of the lovers, such caresses are incapable of causing the Other's body to be born, and, of course, this extends even to the child who may be (Duras leaves it up to us) the consequence of this passion—one born on the *extimité* and in the *après coup* of life. As such the Young Woman has difficulty transcending herself as an existent and therefore lives a death-bound consciousness for whom existence is experienced as a never fully disclosed limit or border, one to which that consciousness is held hostage on a day-to-day basis. "Negatively," Lingis writes, "this condition by which subjectivity exists subjected is described as being inessential, a nonexistent, a non-quiddity, a non-identity, that is, a movement that does not identify itself of itself, a non-existent that does not stand on its own beneath its deeds, in possession of its own existence, a term

deserted, and he smiles at them, his arms stretched toward her as on the first day. He is afraid."

21. Jean-Paul Sartre, *L'Être et le néant* (Paris: Gallimard, 1943), p. 439. "Hence desire is the desire of appropriating a body such that in this appropriation my body is disclosed as flesh. But this body which I want to appropriate, I wish to appropriate *as flesh*. However, the Other's body is not immediately flesh for me; the body of the Other appears as a synthetic form in action."

22. Ibid., p. 440. "The caress allows the Other to be born as flesh both for me and the Other." "The caress occurs in order to give birth through pleasure to the body of the Other."

that discovers itself not in the plenitude of being but in the want of failing and offense, an insubstantiality that does not contain its own resources but knows them only in the exposure to another."[23] To read Duras from the side of what Lingis calls "this condition" would be, at the very least, a means of reorienting ourselves away from those ready-made specular readings in which the writings of Duras are viewed chiefly from the perspective of an Imaginary access to "l'autre scène, celle de l'inconscient."[24] That is to say: at the *extimité* of the text, I would like to suggest that it is precisely the Imaginary that is absent. Therefore, even though the Young Woman and Madeleine are staged in front of a mirror, it is the hole in the real which comes to pass as that which ex-ists as non-identity, the in-essential, the existent. Not the unconscious, *l'autre scène,* but the lack of it is what the text bounds, as if the unconscious were remaindered ... set aside ... or simply dropped. To be mad without the assistance of the unconscious, how might this be thought? Duras's work bears largely on this question.

23. Lingis, p. 155.
24. Marcelle Marini, *Territoires de féminin: Avec Marguerite Duras* (Paris: Minuit, 1977), p. 62. Much criticism written along Marini's lines jumps too quickly to the conclusion that Duras's writings imitate a radically other space, namely "celui du féminin." The problem here is not that the feminine itself is being invoked, but that it is linked to a set of psychological assumptions about writing the unconscious which neglects an analysis of *extimité* and of the *existent.*

IO

"Can You Say Hello?"—
Laurie Anderson's *United States*

And I said: Listen, I've got a vision.
I see myself as part of a long tradition
of American humor. You know—Bugs Bunny,
Daffy Duck, Porky Pig, Elmer Fudd,
Roadrunner, Yosemite Sam.
And they said: 'Well actually, we had
something a little more adult in mind.'
And I said: 'OK! OK! Listen, I can adapt!'

      —Laurie Anderson, *United States*

"Hello. Excuse me. Can you tell me where I am?" A voice unsure about a turn made in a car at night is asking for directions. "Hello. Excuse me," the voice says, aware of its hollowness, its persistence. "Hello ... "

Searching for its whereabouts on a darkened nightclub stage, the voice of Laurie Anderson casts us deep into the precarious loneliness and awkwardness of postmodern space. It is here that saying "hello" sounds life-threatening, that initiating conversation can seem at once natural and mindlessly flippant, while disintegrating into a number of confusing tonalities and gestures bordering on nightmare. A postmodern United States. Which is to say, a postmodern unification and minimalization of experiential states, a voyage into those common experiences within which the reduction of meaning and neutralization of apprehension betray uneasy polyvalences. Call it the exacerbation of dead pan. "In our country, this is the way we say Hello. It is a diagram of movement between two points. It is a sweep on the dial. In our country, this is also the way we say Good bye." Curious that the gestures so close to us conceal a crazy semiotics.

"Say Hello" is a gesture through which bodies become signs. For example, on a spacecraft there are drawings suggested by Carl Sagan in which the outlines of a man and a woman are sketched. They are sixties figures, the woman with a rather awkward though seductive posture, the man a bit more erect. It is the man, interestingly enough, whose right arm is bent up at the elbow in a ninety-degree angle. For it is he who is supposed to make contact first. "Do you think that They will think his arm is permanently attached in this position?" Anderson's blunt question is expressionless, exposing the fatuousness of "big science," the silly presupposition that aliens are going to be able to read our "signs." She suggests that in a postmodern culture scientists are so overspecialized that when it comes to basic questions they are enormously obtuse. No one has noticed that saying "hello" is exactly the same as saying "good-bye," that even if aliens could read our signs, they would be confused. The fallacy of science: "let $x = x$," identity, the "united state."

❦

United States. It is a performance piece of several hours' duration, which is narrated, illustrated, and accompanied by music. A short version has been released in a five-record set by Warner Brothers, and texts with photographs have been published by Harper and Row.[1] "Say Hello" marks the beginning and end of the performance and has iconic force, since it reminds us of a dial or clock marking not only the beginning and end but a sense of gradation or change during the piece. "Say Hello," then, is the analogue to the clocks on Anderson's projected image of the United States relating to time and space, which is to say, in *United States* greeting takes on spatial attributes. Indeed, the whole of *United States* can be read, watched, listened to as an analysis of how communication is determined by the conditions of postmodern space. In this sense, Anderson undertakes an anthropological project that attempts to define postmodern consciousness in terms of how communication is, in fact, subordinated to an artistic frame of reference

1. Laurie Anderson, *United States* (New York: Harper & Row, 1984). All quotations are from this print edition. *United States* was about a decade in the making; in the 1970s Anderson referred to it as "Americans on the Move."

within which the question of how things are situated in space becomes of greatest importance.

Postmodern architecture, of course, is most intriguing because it manifests a subtle articulation of what Robert Venturi (in collaboration with Scott Izenour, Denise Brown, and Scott Brown) has called elite and vernacular cultures.[2] Charles Jencks acknowledges this articulation when he writes in *Architecture Today,* "A postmodern building is doubly coded—part Modern and part something else: vernacular, re-vivalist, local, commercial, metaphorical, or contextual. In several important instances it is also doubly coded in the sense that it seeks to speak on two levels at once: to a concerned minority of architects, an elite who recognizes the subtle distinctions of a fast-changing language, and to the inhabitants, users, or passersby, who want only to understand and enjoy it." Postmodern space, in other words, conflates elitist domination with spontaneous vernacular modes of apprehension. Use of the vernacular, in particular, helps speed up public comprehension and ensures that because the new is somehow always something old and familiar, people will not be required to ask reflective questions, since what they are seeing is self-evident, literal. Jencks speaks for the elite when he says that "the inhabitants, users, or passersby . . . want only to understand and enjoy it." He means, in fact, that passersby are to immediately accept the relation set up between elite and vernacular cultures. That the postmodern building is, in fact, not a unity but a coalition of styles is frankly admitted by postmodern architects. Again, note Jencks's reflection on the postmodern classicism of Michael Graves's work: "It does not try to achieve the integration, consistency, and propriety of a Vitruvian or Palladian language, but rather attempts to reach out to a variety of languages—including the industrial style—in an effort to be more broadly based.[3] Postmodern architecture is, in

2. Robert Venturi, *Learning from Las Vegas* (Cambridge: MIT Press, 1977), pp. 6, 119, 152. "Bauhaus Hawaiian" is a typical expression used in discussing those moments in which high and low, elite and vernacular, come into contact. I should add that whereas Venturi uses the word "vernacular" in order to express the stylistic tendencies of any architectural orientation—for example, "commercial vernacular," "electronic and space vernacular"—he does separate this use of the term from elitist context as in the phrase "classical vocabulary" (p. 106). Venturi's point is that the vernacular is the *general appropriation* of high culture's unacknowledged symbolism.

3. Charles Jencks and William Chaitkin, *Architecture Today* (New York: Henry Abrams, 1982), p. 111.

this sense, cumulative but not integrative, aesthetic but not organic, vernacular but not antiauthoritarian. Postmodern space signifies a medley of architectural rhetorics whose interplay is appreciated on a metastylistic level that cannot be reconciled within a single interpretive glance. The work is composite and made up of stylistic zones, which often break down into time zones, since the work's coherence ultimately depends on our ability to locate, date, and align the discontinuous and fragmentary suggestions of various periods and practices of both high and low culture. The work's coherence is, therefore, accidental, or what we might consider forced in the baroque sense. But, thanks to the work's rhetoricity or semiosis, these stylistic fractures only strike us as playful and consonant revisions of old styles that nostalgically remind us of something at once familiar and fresh. If, as some architects assume, architecture is really to be defined as a "sphere of influence" rather than as a set of pure formal concerns, postmodern architecture's influence is transmitted by heterogeneous styles and piebald bits of fantasy, whose manner is to "invite" the eye or to "say hello." It is in this sense that the play with the vernacular is important, since it functions to make people receptive to space even as its violent interplay of styles keeps that space at a distance, asserts an aesthetic remoteness of space from within what is familiar.

Anderson's *United States,* because it is a "performance piece," begins with the assumption that as landscape the United States is a postmodern work in which elite and vernacular cultures are often so intimate in our society that the difference between them is sometimes undecidable. Yet it is an undecidability that is conveyed through the literal, the use of commonplaces and clichés that delimit what reality is supposed to mean for us. It is as if the vernacular is always saturated with authoritarianism, hence becoming sinister, and as if the authoritarian were always being contaminated by the vernacular in such a way that it seems ridiculous, idiotic, in its oversimplification of complex thoughts. This transference between vernacular and elite is reflected everywhere in postmodern architecture, and in Anderson's *United States,* we hear the rhetoric of that transaction taking place within a particular spatial condition.

This is thematized in "Voices on Tape," in which reference is made to an empty room that after twenty years is being monitored by a microphone and a tape recorder for sound residues. The phrases supposedly captured on the tape recorder as well as the whole "scientific" project are delimited by the question of spatiality, for it is as if space itself were fantasmically speaking. But throughout "Voices on Tape" the collision in this space is that of elitist culture (science) and a vernacular culture (e.g., "Goethe ist ein Diplomat," "So viel Licht hier"). Obviously, the frame of the room as space imitates the empty stage that Anderson herself is occupying, and the collision of elitist and vernacular styles is emphasized through the engagement of ordinary talk with sophisticated electronic equipment whose effect is to emphasize the spectral.

In "Say Hello," as well, one notices how something simple in the vernacular when performed within an authoritarian or elitist space— for example, Carl Sagan's noble experiment to talk to aliens—becomes an embarrassment. Here it is not so much that a class of speakers is resisting high culture but that within the vernacular itself there are spectral resonances that have great potential for making scientists appear idiotic. Conversely, however, in a piece titled "O Superman," authoritarianism saturates vernacular or popular culture in such a way that behind flimsy expressions we intuit something at once maternal and murderous, protective and catastrophic. Indeed, the placid crying of birds in the background of the piece suggests extinction, because in mass culture the sounds of nature have become associated with authoritarian messages about living in a world where life is becoming extinct. Yet it is a message that is communicated by muzak, that is to say, a very unthreatening, even pleasant, experience that conjures up fantasies of public spaces. And it is this "invitation" to consider disaster which constitutes a postmodern receptivity or familiarity with that which is life threatening.

> So hold me Mom, in your long arms . . .
> in your automatic arms,
> your electronic arms,
> in your arms . . .
> So hold me Mom, in your long arms,
> your petrochemical arms,
> your military arms,
> in your electronic arms . . .

Here mom is the united states(s) of a dis-identification that is national, political, and psychological. It is, as Laura Kipnis might point out, the postcolonial state of a decentered culture in which first-world nation-hood still relies on the fantasm of mother-country in order to figure itself as a dominant world force. Kipnis: "In the recent appearance of the category of the 'decentered subject,' lurks the synecdoche of the decline of the great imperial powers of modernity, the traumatic loss of hegemony of the West, which here in the psychic economy of the United States, we have continually reflected back to us in compensatory fantasies like *Rambo, Red Dawn,* and Ronald Reagan."[4] In Anderson's *United States,* however, the focus is not on the return of the Dionysian father, the Rambo type who when humiliated reveals the annihilating power of his identity, but on the incongruous maternal resonances of the defense industry and its suppliers. For, after all, the Superman or Rambo is imagined as part of an environment or space that comes prior to him, namely mother-country, that space which Rambos master and become a part of to the cost of their enemies, as if mother nature were itself the technology of destruction rather than an environment that is being destroyed. At issue, then, are suggestions of staging the death drive on the body of the mother, a staging that does not ground so much as it accompanies numerous unsettling political inferences that are given as part of a cultural vernacular of which we are never fully conscious. As if in a postmodern context a primal fantasy can never be primal.

Even Anderson's map of the United States is conveyed to us as something other than fundamental or primal, for it is but a childlike and inoffensive representation that one might find on TV, its time zones demarcated with the appropriate partitions and clocks. *United States* performs these zones and in doing so develops themes like greetings, love, signs, women, outer space, government, homelessness, catastrophe, science, business, ethnocentrism, objects, and rituals. Like Brecht, Anderson is not rigid about final versions of her work, and *United States* is very much a collage of music, words, and pictures which the performer can change at will without really disturbing the overall scheme too much. Perhaps it is because the tonality of the performance as a whole is so strong that the individual parts of *United States* do

4. Laura Kipnis, "Feminism: The Political Conscience of Postmodernism," in *Universal Abandon?* (New York: Routledge, 1988), p. 158.

not depend on plotting or sequencing so much as they do upon multiple "voicings." And it is in this sense that music is a crucial element, sustaining, as it does, a number of moods that saturate the individual song-pieces. Like a postmodern building, of course, Anderson's work stresses the accidental and the element of surprise, not to mention the fundamental ambivalences about how elite culture affects popular culture and vice versa. That is, *United States* is about space as a "sphere of influence," which is comprised of ambiences of meaning that are, like postmodern buildings, at once self-evidently literal and yet unassimilable because of their blending of subtle harmonies of elitist and vernacular expressions. The four zones of *United States* represent (1) travel, (2) politics, (3) money, and (4) love. As Stephen Melville has observed, the "bits" and "parts" of *United States* have connections "at once tenuous and multiple, over-determined to the point that the whole takes on the simultaneous coherence and arbitrariness of a dream."[5] Each of these temporal/spatial zones is associated with a movement, such as panning, dropping, grabbing, free standing. And these visual "movements" suggest a mode of erotogenetic development which concerns not just body zones but stages of personal growth. Yet if *United States* concerns such notions of growth, it does so only to show how, contrary to an American emphasis on development and getting ahead, America reflects a network of relations that only lead to a postmodern condition of advanced underachievement, a Gesamtwerk of late capitalist underdevelopment. In itself this is already a part of the American postmodern landscape, for what one detects is the collision of vernacular styles signifying a purposeful retardation of critical power, a stunting of conceptual development, opting for instantaneous motifs, nostalgic fixations, cultural leitmotifs. Instead of styles that show a capacity for development and growth, the postmodern displays little

5. Stephen Melville, "Between Art and Criticism: Mapping the Frame in *United States*," in *Theatre Journal* 37, no. 1 (March 1985): 31–44. Melville discusses Anderson's performance piece largely in terms of images and their flatness of presentation: "It could be said to be claiming that [Anderson's] work is properly called 'painting' " (p. 34). I don't agree with Melville concerning the live performances, since the semiotics in performance is transitive, not intransitive. Melville may have developed an important point with respect to something his article does not study, Anderson's video pieces. In these works the semiotics does become intransitive and self-reflexive, and even achieves closure.

more than resonance or the power of evocation, what Fredric Jameson has considered a commodification of the unconscious.[6]

Whereas architects consider questions of form and function or, more recently, the semiotics of architecture, Anderson notices space less as an area in which to be confined than as a surface to be crossed. In "On Modern and Postmodern Space," Alan Colquhoun has written that "modern" architecture involves the

> blowing apart of perceptible urban space, its insistence on high-rise housing, and the precedence it gave to fast automobile circulation. It seems that what started as a utopian critique of nineteenth-century housing conditions turned into nothing more than what was needed for the success of twentieth-century economic centralism, whether in the form of monopoly capitalism or socialist bureaucratic control. This raises the whole problem of the unbridgeable gulf between what the individual can perceive and feel at home in, and the vast, abstract infrastructural network that is necessary for the operation of the modern consumer and media-based society.[7]

Colquhoun is very much aware of modern space as a dimension of mass culture, which is to say, the production of space as a sphere of influence whose purpose is to advance a "media-based" culture. Architecture itself functions like a medium, a network that makes possible the propagation of a utopian but elitist culture that depends on consumption as much as on production. Central to this view, Colquhoun points out, is the fact that at the turn of our century architects and social planners begin to think of space as preexistent and unlimited, as abstract and essentially undifferentiated.

Anderson's *United States* is largely about how a vernacular culture is situated within this modernist notion of space. In a section of part

6. Fredric Jameson, "Architecture and the Critique of Ideology," in *Architecture, Criticism, Ideology,* ed. Joan Ockman (Princeton: Princeton Architectural Press, 1985), p. 67.

7. Alan Colquhoun, "On Modern and Postmodern Space," in *Architecture, Criticism, Ideology,* ed. Ockham, pp. 108–9.

4 of *United States,* "The Stranger," Anderson projects four pictures of suburban houses onto a screen behind her. These houses are typical of any one would find in a current real-estate market booklet, though the styles Anderson has chosen are somewhat similar: two-story homes built in the 1950s or thereabouts. As she projects the photographs, Anderson comments: "It's the one with the pool. . . . It's the one on the corner with the big garage. . . . It's the one with the fir tree in the front yard. . . . Leave the lights on. It's twilight." Anderson intuits that even though the houses are all different, their owners would probably demarcate their homes by vernacular descriptions, such as "It's the one with the pool." Differences are extremely minimal in the vernacular imagination, as if it were impossible to describe where one lived in terms of the architectural style. For vernacular culture has adapted itself to the idea that living space is so abstract that only some very minimal detail can distinguish one place from another. "It's the one with the fir tree in the front yard." Similarly, with respect to a map of the United States, it is only the minimal cue of the time zone which really differentiates one zone from another. For, once more, space is abstract, undifferentiated, monotonous, and, above all, limitless in the eyes of the "developer."

Space, because it is so abstract, is less a place in which to live than a flat surface to traverse. And this traversing occurs, Anderson suggests, in the service of communication, since it is through making and breaking contacts that the postmodern individual comes to be. Most striking is that the subject undergoes a certain reduction as it becomes more and more involved in crossing space for the sake of establishing communication, and Anderson symbolizes this condition in terms of making references in words, pictures, and music to the image of a dog.

> I came home today
> and you were all on fire.
> Your shirt was on fire,
> and your hair was on fire,
> and flames were licking all around your feet.
> And I did not know what to do!
> And then a thousand violins began to play,

> And I really did not know what to do then.
> So I just decided to go out
> and walk the dog.

"Walk the Dog" reads like a poem by Éluard, though its surrealism underscores the mobility which allows one to simply walk out on someone in trouble, that mobility which we have in common with dogs. In "Dog Show," we are told,

> I dreamed I was a dog in a dog show.
> And my father came to the dog show.
> And he said: That's a really good dog.
> I like that dog.

The identification of narrator and dog suggests that the more minimal one becomes the more attractive one becomes. And it suggests that the minimalism of the canine condition is the primary means by which we gain access to others.

> And then all my friends came and I
> was thinking:
> No one has ever looked at me like this
> for so long.

The subject as dog is "safe," for such a subject has the mobility through which to break off relations that demand obligations of the subject and establish relations that make possible a certain necessary popularity.

In a postmodern age, the modern is assimilated rather than rejected, and it is in this sense that *United States* is not so much a celebration of modernism as it is a demonstration of the degree to which we have internalized what previous generations have considered alien and pernicious. That we have acceded to the condition of dogs is less a criticism of our postmodern condition than it is a recognition of what we really are, an acceptance that we succeed best when we take on a dog's minimal appearance, a point echoed, as well, by William Wegman,

whose video art and photographs of dogs—Man Ray and Fay Ray—
simulate even as they merge into our condition of postmodern existence.
The disinterested (and undifferentiated) condition of our dog lives is
what postmodern architects take as endemic to our aesthetic relation
to space: mere traffic, nonconsciousness. Since postmodern space is
meant to be minimally hermeneutic for the casual passerby, these urban
complexes withdraw from intellectual reflection and apprehension, and
not only do these buildings not belong to us—they are, after all, "private
property"—they refuse even to appear as constructions worthy of attention themselves. Yet, as Anderson notices in "Dog Show," it is this
vacuity which elicits an elongated staring whose expansiveness is a
measure of a failure to grasp the object. "No one has ever stared at
me for so long, for such a long time, for so long."

Postmodern space thus becomes fantasmic and dreamy as the gaze
is dissipated in the massive thereness of the inappropriable. One is
reminded here of Cecelia Condit's video piece, "Possibly in Michigan"
(1983), in which the commodity becomes the site of an inappropriability that Condit conflates with bits and pieces of a sadistic sexual
scene whose primal materials have been disarticulated and recollaged.
In "Possibly in Michigan" the dreaminess of the gaze is released into
the inappropriability of everyday life in the shopping mall and the
suburban home. Similarly, in Cindy Sherman's well-known polaroids
the female figure is itself a fantasm made up of cultural appropriations
that do not subordinate themselves to the figure on which they con-
verge, as if to say that Sherman were somehow irrelevant except as a
propping structure or model necessary for setting the tone of the inappropriable. Moreover, in the work of David Salle or Eric Fischl, in
which the female figures are not infrequently pornographically de-
picted, the inappropriability of mass culture mediates the seductive
primal scenes of the human figures, as if it were mass culture that were
more primal (more sexual) than sex.

Anderson's work may be less interested in revising the primal scene
according to the postmodern interpellation of the commodity than in
showing that the resistance of mass culture to appropriation facilitates
a fugitive glance and a trafficking of the self through space which makes
the individual somewhat spectral. Visually, we find ourselves moving
through space rather than in it, a point also made in another work

about America, *Koyaanisqatsi,* a film about postmodern space with music by Philip Glass, which privileges the notion of life as traffic. But whereas *Koyaanisqatsi* is meant to sicken with its prolonged redundancies of futile transit in New York City and Los Angeles, Anderson's *United States* investigates our trafficky relation to postmodern ambience in more nuanced and individualistic terms. For Anderson is more receptive to the fact that our conversations and intimate encounters are patterned on a mode of inhabiting space which has much in common with transitional states of consciousness, with a traveling consciousness. Our conversations are no longer grounded in deep originary psychosexual scenes or in any one place, but are patterned on the model of a superficial placelessness, the expressway where we are always suddenly encountering signs or gestures indicating entrances, exits, continuations, turn offs, detours, mergings, speed signs, and so on. Like a track, talk is made up of cues indicating directionality, facilitating passage, noting locations. This is a space where one never gets too hung up, since one is always circulating. Which is to say, talk is itself embedded within the codes of postmodern space. Notice, for example, "New York Social Life."

> Hi! How are you? Where've you been? Nice to see you. Listen, I'm sorry I missed your thing last week, but we should really get together, you know, maybe next week. I'll call you. I'll see you. Bye bye.

Or,

> Listen, Laurie, uh, if you want to talk before then, uh, I'll leave my answering machine on . . . and just give me a ring . . . anytime.

These excerpts from "New York Social Life" focus less on the outrage of what is evidently an awkward discourse painfully aware of its own compulsion toward insincerity, what is a wavering between sympathy and selfishness, than on the superficiality of conversation as a slick surface of ready-made signs or gestures used to break off or establish contact quickly. It is what in business is called "one minute management." In "New York Social Life" it appears that the persona has been psychologically depressed; yet the conversations surrounding her use a rhetoric of concern to maintain an interpersonal network whose purpose is to map an individual's relationship within a social system. Concern is merely an excuse for finding out "Are you there?" The notion of United States as map, then, so basic to Anderson's work, relates to the true purpose of postmodern talk: to determine where one is on a social grid when en route. To make telephone calls, in this way, is to establish something close to radar contact with other entities, and this is reflected in Anderson's fascination with airplanes, missiles, and spacecraft. We are ourselves but phantom-like vehicles that not only cross spaces but are monitored, and the answering machine in "New York Social Life" is simply a monitoring device that fulfills a primary condition of postmodern communication: to make contact and check in with someone who is always already absent. Conversation itself is superfluous, since no one is really ever "there" for us. Thus in a postmodern world it is through tracking that we affirm our niche in a community always on the move, and our attachments, obligations, and sympathies are only ways of facilitating the kinds of contact needed to perform a map of social relations.

Much like the social function of a dog, feelings, concerns, issues, and information become excuses to open and close conversations. They are merely "switches" in a network of relations where, thanks to communications technology, the social subject makes minimal contact and is rarely there in person as someone who makes a committed bond of what was once known as friendship. Today, Americans commonly establish simulated friendships, which is to say, the illusion of friendship maintained by long-distance communications.

Much of *United States*, then, is a performance of this use of operators through which conversations become less about messages than about the making and breaking of contacts in the Jakobsonian sense.[8] The purpose of communication is to draw people's relations, to map our position, rather than enter into situations as part of day-to-day experience. To "walk the dog" is precisely to negotiate inhabiting a space

---

8. Roman Jakobson's linguistic model is well known. Between addresser and addressee one finds contact, code, message, and context. Anderson's work privileges contact.

on the margin of "situations" such that one can relate without having to be related to. And performance art itself is but the reenactment of this mapping or "drawing" of relations, a reenactment of what can be found writ large in the culture. Perhaps not surprising for the mid 1980s, we find the caption "Fido as Mentor" in the "Working Smart" section of *The Executive Female:* "In a poll of Fortune 500 company chief executives, the Pets are Wonderful Council in Chicago found that 94 percent of 76 respondents have a cat or dog as a 'child.' The executives said pets helped them develop positive character traits. 'My dog taught me about love, devotion and sacrifice,' said one."[9] The subtext of this article is that for people to work smart they should consider loving a dog in place of committing themselves to another human being, since, after all, pets are far less trouble and leave more room for business productivity. The ideal executive relationship strives for minimalization of content, maximization of contact. In Anderson— as in life during the go-go eighties—the minimalization of content and maximization of contact require "undercommittedness," and Anderson exaggerates the weakening of social contact through tautology, the preferred master trope of Reagan and Bush. Undercommitment permits bonds that are strong enough to establish one in a social position without allowing that position to solidify into a situation where one can become bound. The tautology is crucial because it asserts position without defining what occupies this space. This kind of postmodern phantomization relates as well to postmodern architecture, which promotes circulation, immediacy, passage, movement, in short, a passageway of multiple tonalities that depend on weak contacts in order to come across as ambient, unassertive, and undercommitted.

In *United States* Anderson is well aware that she is, herself, a postmodern topos, and writes of herself,

> Well I was trying to think of something to tell you about myself and I came across this brochure they're handing out in the lobby. And it says something I wanted to say—only better.
>   It says: Laurie Anderson, in her epic performance of United States Parts 1 through 4, has been baffling audiences for years with her

9. *Executive Female*, January/February 1985, p. 7.

> special blend of slides ... films ... tapes ... films (did I say films?)
> ... hand gestures and more. Hey hey hey hey hey hey hey! (Much
> more.)

The tautology of saying "I am what this says I am" allows for a re-performance of preestablished relations, mainly those set out in the promotional literature. Anderson and her work are established as a sign (not as person or expression) that involves a stable contact rather than a specific content. The promotional material is not an accurate description of what Anderson does, because its function is not meant to be mimetic; rather, it is supposed to make familiar through the manipulation of easily assimilated signs. The point is to give the performer position or location (space) at the expense of definition. And in this sacrifice of definition, Anderson gains the freedom of ambiguity, which allows her to be many things in many places while through contact always remaining minimally the same. It is in this sense that she "deconstructs" the border between identity and difference, that she appears as something at once determinate and indeterminate.

The tautology establishes Anderson as postmodern motif as well as statue to the extent that she is fixed as minimal cue, as a "really good dog," that is, as the facsimilie of a person. This relates to the business of performance art generally, of course, in that success is everywhere based on such minimalization, since one must be active as a contact in proximity to other contacts on a performance map: other performance artists, entertainers, singers, actors. Anderson becomes like a movie star whose conversations on television talk shows ironize the fact that speaking in person on camera does nothing else than serve to reinforce one's minimal reference position relative to others in the media and society at large. In this sense the performance acts as a complex signifier whose significance is syntactic. This minimalization of the performer as content and maximization of the performer as contact or relay reveals a structuralist view of television that accounts for why this medium is so powerful for entertainers: it activates and maps the reduction of the star to a point that is related or drawn within a mobile array of faces and figures that present themselves synchronically on contiguous stations. That we are not particularly interested in or fascinated with certain figures as agencies of a visual content is compensated for by the fact that these figures are meaningful only in terms of how they are set up in reference to one another. In this sense the communication between figures is intimately connected within a televised space, predicated on the conditions of postmodern, structuralist space. Indeed, it is the figure's vacuousness or minimalism that allows for its powerful mobility as fantasmic cursor within an electronic system of mapped and transistory relations. Hence to have character in this context becomes a measure of one's inability to become present as something determinate. One accedes to becoming "Pac Man," and in large part Anderson's *United States* is a long meditation about how such reductionisms are performed or imitated.

It is in terms of this performance, however, that we see not merely the minimalization of the artist but also the propagation of the minimalization within a media culture, and it is for this reason that Anderson's work becomes strangely allied with mass culture. For she herself accedes to an authoritarian system of cultural production by distributing her work through Warner Brothers and Harper and Row. Therefore, in Anderson's performance art we see the easy alliance of both vernacular and elite culture, the postmodern replication of a hegemonic structure which has caused alarm for some critics of her work. For *hegemony*, as critics such as Dick Hebdige use the term, means, "a situation in which a provisional alliance of certain social groups can exert 'total social authority' over other subordinate groups, not simply by coercion or by the direct imposition of ruling ideas, but by 'winning and shaping consent so that the power of the dominant classes appears both legitimate and natural'."[10] And yet one could argue that this replication of the hegemony is itself but an imitation of something that is occurring in our culture generally, that in performing the hegemony Anderson is also miming it and by doing so is releasing or activating those resonances within the collision of vernacular and elitist cultural expressions that undermine that hegemony's efficacy as a stable equilibrium in which the power of the elite culture appears natural. In *United States* Anderson performs the postmodern hybridization of the elite and vernacular, as established through the transmission and over-

10. Dick Hebdige, *Subculture: The Meaning of Style* (London: Methuen, 1979), pp. 15–16. Hebdige cites Stuart Hall as originator of this definition.

lapping of media whose spatiality is the united state. Thus Anderson "performs" the hegemony's illusory unifications and subtly reveals its dissonances and discrepancies without necessarily enacting a critical stance of her own, which would be recovered merely as another ideological or theoretical formation intended to dominate a field of relationships.

> I had this dream
> and in it I wake up in this small
> house . . . I'm not
> a person in this dream; I'm a
> place. Yeah . . . just a place.

In *United States* woman is herself considered a space or topos of postmodern existence. And as such she is tautologous, minimal. Especially in the last part of *United States,* Anderson explores not merely the position one occupies on a map of social relations, but the existential "moods," as Heidegger might have called it, of postmodern being. This is already well anticipated in "modern" literature, and particularly important in this respect is Marcel Proust's depiction of Albertine in *A la recherche du temps perdu.* Marcel recounts his apprehension of the tomboy at Balbec: "To be quite accurate, I ought to give a different name to each of the selves who subsequently thought about Albertine; I ought still more to give a different name to each of the Albertines who appeared before me, never the same, like those seas—called by me simply and for the sake of convenience 'the sea'—that succeeded one another and against which, a nymph likewise, she was silhouetted."[11] Throughout Marcel's lengthy descriptions of Albertine in *A la recherche* we notice that she is viewed as a refracted, luminous surface. She is approachable but not appropriable. Like the movie star of the silver screen she is a topos of projected light, a minimal being whose

---

11. Marcel Proust, *Remembrance of Things Past* (New York: Random House, 1981), vol. 1, p. 1010.

indistinctness becomes a measure of her power to fulfill her ambitions as a social climber, to become "known." Of all the women Marcel meets, Albertine is the closest to being "nothing." For she says and does nothing to give substance or ballast to the impressions she makes. Even the fact that she is a bicyclist only emphasizes her vacuity and fugitive qualities. She is, finally, more an atmosphere than a character, a minimal finitude that is only traced or drawn from within the hypotheses of a hypochondriac's mercurial wishes and fears. She is, in terms of Marcel's mean-spirited jealousy in *La Prisonnière*, a fantasm of possible liaisons whose constructions are as fictional as they are plausible in the wake of Marcel's careful trackings of Albertine's movements.

There is, admittedly, little of the high seriousness of Proust in the flippant portrayal of postmodern woman in Anderson's *United States*, no sense of judgment in this anything-is-okay world. And yet in the song-piece, "Blue Lagoon," Anderson's persona, "Blue Pacific," has much in common with Proust's Albertine, except that she is even more minimal. Blue Pacific is also a sea surface, an atmosphere of modulating moods. Like Albertine, Blue Pacific is seen as a tourist whose state is an undercommittedness of consciousness, a studied underachievement. Like Albertine, Blue Pacific appears to sleep even while awake, an enigmatic minimal surface basking in the unaccountability of its actions, slipping into habitual and monotonous personal abandonments that are unconsidered and unrecoverable. Like Albertine, Blue Pacific is beyond remembrance of things past, not retrievable.

Blue Pacific's letter is read to an accompaniment of sonorous music: overlays of the new consonance, unfocused, busy, in suspension, the metallic drumming contradicting the pacific references. The heat and lazy acquiescence to dives by the wreck, the nightly swims in the lagoon, and tanning are submerged in waves of aural unfocusings. Anderson's slow and deliberate reading accentuates tonal registers of depression, lassitude, and longing, as well as a remote pleasure and bliss within a space of quiet forgetfulness reminding us of lotus eaters by the beach. As a whole, "Blue Lagoon" does not try to achieve integration or cohesion, but ripples out into a variety of tonal saturations as Blue Pacific modulates attention from the letter to the weather, from her remembering cities and her dreams about perfect places.

> I got your letter. Thanks a lot.
> I've been getting lots of sun
> and lots of rest. It's really hot.
> Days,
> I dive by the wreck.
> Nights,
> I swim in the blue lagoon.
> I always used to wonder who I'd bring
> to a desert island.

As in a postmodern structure there are metatextual allusions; for example, Shakespeare, Melville, T. S Eliot, Adrienne Rich, but also the film *Blue Lagoon,* starring Brooke Shields. These intertexts are not cited but simply merge or float into Blue Pacific's reveries, suggesting, however remotely, a vague yet poignant hostility toward men and paternity (death of the father in Shakespeare, death of Ahab in Melville, the death of parents in *Blue Lagoon,* the rejection of males by Rich, Amfortas in Eliot, and so on). Here the intellectualism of the allusions meets the tonality of burnt-out existence, particularly with the desperate last line in which an S.O.S. can be detected in the aftermath of the subject's disappearance as such. "Love and kisses. Blue Pacific. Signing off."

Although Blue Pacific knows where she is on the social map of leisure, she has, nevertheless, lost self-reference, closure, embodiment. She is at the furthest limit of attenuated contact and as such in the heart of postmodern mass culture, basking in the sun at a high-class resort. Whereas Proust's Albertine is capable of harboring secrets, Blue Pacific is emptied of all interiority. She is herself the island space on which she lies, a sleepy surface suspended in the water, perhaps an image on a video screen embedded in some ad for corn flakes or the Hilton. "Days, I dive by the wreck. Nights, I swim in the blue lagoon." The name Blue Pacific resonates contradictions that defy coherence, while overall a sense of tranquility is communicated, for Blue Pacific suggests "sad ocean" or "sad peacefulness" while also suggesting the play of light on a beautiful sea, azure and calm. Perhaps "Blue Pacific" isn't a name at all (like that of a hotel or swimwear company), but just the topos associated with a flotation of voicings, the dissipation of woman

into landscape. "I'm not a person in this dream; I'm just a place. Yeah
... just a place." And yet, despite this dissolution of voice into space—
the fantasmic space of the archaic mother country—we feel traces or
residues of volition uneasily affirming themselves. For the narration
suggests a question never explicitly formulated but hovering. "But if I
am what everyone desires to be, why don't you want me?" Traces of
willed confrontation make up an underconsciousness of words, a submerged, marginal insistence that pleads from beneath: the "wreck" in
Shakespeare, Melville, Eliot, Rich, *Blue Lagoon*. It is this "wreck," of
course, that the "letter" elides even as it sounds its depths, careful to
avoid intimacy.

Readers will no doubt notice that as "poetry" the lyrics of "Blue
Lagoon" are reminiscent of an American poetry written in a self-
consciously flat and laconic style in which colloquialisms typically introduce pathetic ironies of everyday life. One is reminded not only of
Adrienne Rich, but of Howard Nemerov, or Carolyn Kizer. Anderson's
lyrics, however, are not meant to satirize so much as they re-perform
while carefully abandoning pretensions of the well-craftedness of poetry. For it is in the awkwardness of approximations that Anderson
captures tonalities of an American lingo. Her project is to produce a
mock-up or facsimile, to draw, as it were, from real life a model in the
medium of the things themselves. In this sense performance art is by
nature ephemeral, since the copy offers itself as something almost in-
terchangeable with the object it mimes. That is to say, the performed
work deconstitutes the difference/identity between object and facsimile.
It is, to recall the work of Jacques Derrida, deconstructive. Yet whereas
Derrida's deconstructions always give rise to "saying," Anderson's
trace-work has much more in common with the autistic drift of the
New Realism. Its translation into performance occurs, of course, by
way of figures such as Yvonne Rainer, a dancer associated with the
Judson Dance Theater, who in the mid 1960s drew up a chart outlining
the relation between objects and dance. In this schema she opposes
"illusionism" (objects) to "performance" (dance). She has written,
"The artifice of performance has been reevaluated [in the sense that]
what one does, is more interesting and important than the exhibition
of character and attitude, and that action can best be focused on
through the submerging of the personality; so ideally one is not even

oneself, one is a neutral 'doer.' " Also, "The display of technical virtuosity and the display of the dancer's specialized body no longer make
any sense." Rainer was especially interested in translating objects into
"the indeterminate performance that produces variations ranging from
small details to a total image."[12] And this is precisely what Anderson's
version of the new realism achieves as a performance: the production
of an indeterminacy whose variations are at once extremely nuanced
and unpredictable, yet uncomfortably faithful to the "objects" themselves. It is in this performance that personality is submerged, as Rainer
suggested in 1968, and that technical virtuosity is abandoned. In "Blue
Lagoon" we see the apogee of this type of performance insofar as the
tonalities of a represented object, Blue Pacific, are performed such that
character itself is never quite established, since the performer has successfully "submerged" herself in a neutrality of doing. The performance
of the words, themselves so reminiscent of contemporary American
poetry, accedes to an anonymity through which both the apparatuses
of elite and vernacular culture can be heard in what literary critics
today call a "dialogic relation," that is to say, an interpenetration of
cultural voices.[13] Yet whereas dialogic structures are often considered
to be polyvalent, massive, complex, modernist, in Anderson they are
achieved more economically through a minimalist approach that is
much closer to Yvonne Rainer's notions of minimalist dance than has,
perhaps, been recognized.

❧

In "Postmodernism and Consumer Society," Fredric Jameson talks
about the postmodern production of "blank parody" or "pastiche,"
and he notices it not in performance art but in film.[14] Jameson argues
that postmodern parody has the aim of pointing out the "death of the

12. Yvonne Rainer, "A Quasi Survey of Some 'Minimalist' Tendencies in the Quan-
titatively Minimal Dance Activity Midst the Plethora, or an Analysis of Trio," in *Minimal Art*, ed. Gregory Battcock (New York: Dutton, 1968), pp. 267, 272.

13. M. M. Bakhtin, *The Dialogic Imagination*, ed. Michael Holquist, trans. Caryl
Emerson and Michael Holquist (Austin: University of Texas Press, 1981).

14. Fredric Jameson, "Postmodernism and Consumer Society," in *The Anti-
Aesthetic*, ed. Hal Foster (Port Townsend, Wash.: Bay Press, 1983), pp. 111–25.

social subject"—the end of consciousness—and the total degradation of language. What Jacques Ehrmann addressed in the late sixties as a "death of literature" on the avant-garde horizon has in our time, in Jameson's view, become a generally recognized feature of contemporary life. Hence in place of authentic works we have pastiches: "Pastiche is, like parody, the imitation of a peculiar or unique style, the wearing of a stylistic mask, speech in a dead language: but it is a neutral practice of such mimicry, without parody's ulterior motive, without the satirical impulse, without laughter, without that still latent feeling that there exists something *normal* compared to which what is being imitated is rather comic. Pastiche is blank parody, parody that has lost its sense of humor."[15] With respect to cinema, pastiche marks, in Jameson's opinion, the loss of a historical point of reference, that basis on which satire in previous periods depended. For Jameson, "blank parody" is an indictment of the decadence of consumer culture, a formation of art that is symptomatic of an ahistoricism, an anti-intellectualism. At issue is whether such art is not simply uncritical, but fundamentally anticritical, whether it is, as Susan Sontag noted long ago, "against interpretation." In this sense, works such as "Blue Lagoon" or *United States* maintain their positions between elite and vernacular culture in a manner that replicates something very fundamental to our society: a presentation of a now that is inaccessible to critical consciousness, that elides the very capacity to gain that point of view by means of which contemporary culture can be evaluated, thought, represented.

"Blue Lagoon" uses "blank parody" or "pastiche" not to indict postmodern space, but to perform it. Reminiscent of Yvonne Rainer, Anderson herself has said, "In a performance, though, you don't have to have character. If you want to talk about earthquakes all you have to do is say 'earthquakes.' " And concerning space itself, she has said, "You become aware, because of [the sending of standing] waves, of your placement in the room. It's like being blind, in a sense, because you feel the space behind you; it's a way to prevent falling into an illusion, into film space."[16] Both of these statements address questions

---

15. Ibid., p. 114.
16. Laurie Anderson, "Interview," in *View*, January 1980; reprinted in *American Artists on Art*, ed. Ellen Johnson (New York: Harper & Row, 1982), pp. 241–42.

of how representation or illusions are "framed" in a mimetic sense, concerned not with structuring an uncritical space so much as with producing an ambiguous or undecidable space within which sonorities, textures, or tonalities can be aired such that their incipient judgements, worn and torn through use, make themselves felt. It is here that character or "film space" only gets in the way, that it pre-structures our apprehension of ephemeral nuances that have become so much a part of our our everyday talk. That Blue Pacific is a texture of wornout American vernacular signals a blending of speech: the clichés of vacationers, the institutionalized lyric, ham radio, the talk show, and so on. It is within this surprising harmony or consonance that critical space is filled in and judgments apparently suppressed. And yet within this foreclosure of criticism we still hear the traces of judgment, the residues of attitudes, the underconsciousness of vacuity. Especially in "Blue Lagoon," pastiche is less a celebration of the death of the subject than it is the performance of authoritarian colonization, the takeover by mass culture—that articulation of the vernacular and the elite—of the subject whose very acquiescence is a measure of historical consciousness. This, of course, is what Jameson views as an effect of postmodern art in any case; however, it is an effect not intuited from without by the critic, but always already part of the act of performance itself.

Anderson's work is not part of a historical forgetting but an attempt to describe through pastiche how the articulation of vernacular and elite culture manages to suture the historical subject. It is a suturing that paradoxically elicits experiences of a decentered and detotalized consciousness whose nostalgic, vernacular expressions reveal an uncomfortable alliance between elite and vernacular culture. In "Blue Lagoon" the vacationing woman is at once consonant with elite culture, that of the "island vacation," though she is dependent on ready-made expressions, with vernacular overtones. In fact, her reliance on banalities ensures that she can gain, at the cost of decentering, what is known as coverage, reach, extension. That is, by acquiescing, she accedes to a particular kind of power: "Always wondered who I'd bring to a desert island." Emphasis, then, is not on who one is, but on where one can be.

Rather than searching the wreckage of culture for depleted bits of language, Anderson looks for expressions that resonate in terms of the postmodern relations between vernacular and elite culture. Hence one has to be sensitive to the possible kinds of vernacular bits and pieces that Anderson could successfully appropriate, what we might call the postmodern lexicon of everyday life. To this degree, *United States* is merely a mimetic depiction of our world; it is "realistic." The problem is not so much that art has changed but that our world has changed, for there is certainly something very new about recognizing in phrases strange medleys of tonalities, at once silly, pathetic, vacuous, uncritical, cynical, naive. Indeed, even in such words as "hello" the fate of speaking and being appears to be determined.

If historians such as Michel Foucault have analyzed at length the cultural implications of institutionalized spaces, noting their impact on structuring communication itself, artists such as Laurie Anderson have performed such spaces as a communicative structure, one in which the relationship between elite and vernacular cultures is awkwardly reflected through an accumulation of details that however consonant reveal their suturings. Whereas in societies such as Brazil's one necessarily observes the stratification of discursive practices in terms of pronounced class antagonisms, in American culture one must interrogate the democratization of such practices, the blending of differences whose sharp edges or antagonisms are invaginated, fused, harmonized. In this sense, Anderson's postmodern work resembles an architecture adept at assimilating extremely heterogeneous modes of stylistic expression, a space in which a hegemony of stylistic relations suggest an effacement of the line between dominator and dominated, even as the social subject has been defined in terms of the spatial and communicative relays particular to a postindustrial capitalist society. In Anderson this is often particularly relevant for the condition of woman—in large part, Anderson's social subject—to the extent that like *all* social subjects she must perform in a way that stresses copying, imitating, borrowing, assimilating, appropriating, taking on styles, phrases, attitudes, forms, notions from outside, from a culture that prefers not to express domination in terms of subjecthood, in terms of naked power. Indeed, to exist in this kind of culture one must be prepared to be decentered, assimilated, appropriated, prepared to understand that living requires less and less effort from us, since success depends not on being able to challenge the system and master it but on being able to acquiesce, as Blue Pacific does, to its resonances, its uncritical pathways of thought. Unfortunately, to perform successfully in such a life is to become like a dog in a "dog show," to have people say, "That's a really good dog; I like that dog." Postmodernism is easy, provided one knows how to negotiate relations as a phantom in a world where being there for others isn't necessary anymore as long as one has access to cellular phones and fax machines, so that one can call from time to time and say hello.

"Can you say hello?"

Index

Library of Congress Cataloging-in-Publication Data

Rapaport, Herman, b. 1947
    Between the sign and the gaze / Herman Rapaport.
    p.   cm.
    Includes bibliographical references and index.
    ISBN 0-8014-2898-X (cloth : alk. paper). — ISBN 0-8014-8133-3
(pbk. : alk. paper)
    1. Psychoanalysis and literature.   2. Fantasy.   I. Title.
    PN56.P92R37 1993   93-25324
    801'.92—dc20